Business
Its Legal, Ethical, and Global Enviroment

EIGHTH EDITION

Marianne Moody Jennings
Arizona State University

Prepared by

Kristine M. Tabor

SOUTH-WESTERN
CENGAGE Learning

Australia • Brazil • Japan • Korea • Mexico • Singapore • Spain • United Kingdom • United States

SOUTH-WESTERN
CENGAGE Learning

Business: Its Legal, Ethical and Global Environment, 8e
Marianne M. Jennings

VP/Editorial Director: Jack W. Calhoun

Publisher: Rob Dewey

Acquisition Editor: Steve Silverstein, Esq.

Sr. Developmental Editor: Laura Bofinger

Marketing Manager: Jennifer Garamy

Sr. Content Project Manager: Tamborah Moore

Manager, Editorial Media: John Barans

Associate Technology Project Manager: Rob Ellington

Associate Marketing Communications Manager: Jill Schleibaum

Marketing Coordinator: Gretchen Wildauer

Manufacturing Coordinator: Kevin Kluck

Production House: Newgen, Chennai

Compositor: ICC

Sr. Art Director: Michelle Kunkler

For product information and technology assistance, contact us at
Cengage Learning Academic Resource Center,
1-800-423-0563

For permission to use material from this text or product, submit all requests online at **www.cengage.com/permissions** Further permissions questions can be emailed to **permissionrequest@cengage.com**

ISBN-13: 978-0-324-65540-7
ISBN-10: 0-324-65540-1

South-Western Cengage Learning
5191 Natorp Boulevard
Mason, OH 45040
USA

Cengage Learning products are represented in Canada by Nelson Education, Ltd.

For your course and learning solutions, visit **academic.cengage.com** Purchase any of our products at your local college store or at our preferred online store **www.ichapters.com**

Printed in the United States of America
1 2 3 4 5 6 7 11 10 09 08

PREFACE

Updated for the eighth edition of *Business: Its Legal, Ethical, and Global Environment*, this study guide is designed to help you review, retain, and analyze the material covered in the textbook.

You will find each chapter is outlined with sufficient detail for exam preparation. The main points of the outline will also provide you with a broad overview of the chapter topics and can be used as a means to recall key chapter topics.

Following the chapter outline you will find a list of key terms. A good way to review the chapter material is to be certain you can define each of the listed terms. In the case of statutes listed as key terms, you should be able to describe the purpose, application, and content of the law.

The final segment of each study guide chapter is interactive. Through the matching, completion, and short answer questions you have the opportunity to test your knowledge and retention of the subject matter.

Each chapter in this study guide gives you three opportunities to review the text materials. This three-time review process will help you understand, retain, and apply those materials.

Here are some final suggestions on use of the study guide to help you:

1. Read the text chapter.
2. Review the chapter problems in the text.
3. After a time break, review the outline for the chapter in the study guide.
4. Examine each key term and provide a definition or explanation; make notes beside each term as you need.
5. Do the matching, completion, and short answer questions. For those questions that seem difficult, review the text sections again.
6. Before your exam or quiz, review the outline, the key terms, your notes, and the questions.

Good luck with your studies and course work. If you have questions or suggestions, please call Professor Marianne Jennings at (480) 727-6655 or e-mail her at marianne.jennings@asu.edu.

- Marianne M. Jennings and Kristine M. Tabor

TABLE OF CONTENTS

Chapter 1

INTRODUCTION TO LAW

CHAPTER OUTLINE

I. Definitions of Law

    A. Aristotle - Law Is Reason Unaffected by Desire

    B. Holmes - Law Embodies the Story of a Nation's Development Through Many Centuries

    C. Blackstone - That Rule of Action Which Is Prescribed by Some Superior and Which the Inferior Is Bound to Obey

    D. *Black's Law Dictionary* - A Body of Rules of Action or Conduct Prescribed by the Controlling Authority, and Having Legal Binding Force

    E. Rules Enacted by a Government Authority that Govern Individuals and Relationships in Society

II. Classifications of Law

    A. Public Law or Statutory Law

    B. Private Law - Contracts, Employer Regulations

    C. Criminal Law - Carries Fine And/or Imprisonment, Governmental Enforcement

    D. Civil Law - Individual Enforcement, Liability

    E. Substantive Laws - Gives Rights and Responsibilities

    F. Procedural Laws - Means for Enforcing Substantive Rights

    G. Common Law
       1. Began in England (1066)
       2. Exists today - nonstatutory law
       3. Exists also in court decisions - *stare decisis*, "let the decision stand," or following case precedent

    H. Statutory Law
       1. Passed by some governmental body
       2. Appears in written form

    I. Law Versus Equity
       1. In common law England, remedies were separated into legal and equitable remedies
          a. Legal = money
          b. Equitable = injunctions, specific performance
       2. Separated the remedies so that courts of chancery could give remedies when courts of law could not
       3. Today all courts are authorized to award legal or equitable remedies

III. Purposes of Law

    A. Keeping Order
        1. Examples: Traffic laws, criminal laws, trespass laws, property laws
        2. Safety – USA Patriot Act
           a. Reporting requirements
           b. Search warrants

    B. Influencing Conduct

        Examples: Disclosure statutes for securities, antitrust laws, negligence and standards of normal or liability-free conduct

    C. Honoring Expectations

        Examples: Contracts, landlord/tenant, securities investment, property ownership

    D. Promoting Equality

        Examples: Title VII, Age Discrimination Act, Pregnancy Discrimination Act, bussing, antisegregation statute, Social Security system, antitrust laws

    E. Law as the Great Compromiser

        Examples: Union/management laws and regulations, contract interpretations, divorce property settlements, probate distributions

IV. Characteristics of Law

    A. Flexibility

        Examples: On-line transactions and fax machines have made us revisit when a contract acceptance occurs

    B. Consistency - Allows Businesses to Rely on Law for Planning

    C. Pervasiveness

V. The Theory of Law: Jurisprudence (legal philosophy)

    A. The Common Law (Ideas and Doubts: Oliver Wendell Holmes)

        Law arises because we have to co-exist; I can only do as much as others are willing to tolerate. Peer pressure is responsible for much of law.

    B. My Philosophy of Law: Roscoe Pound
        Law is social control through the use of force.

C. A Primer on Jurisprudence (Legal Philosophy in a Nutshell; Five Minutes of Legal Philosophy)
    1. One: Positive law; law is what is given as law
    2. Two: Law is what benefits the people
    3. Three: Law is justice or treating everyone according to the same standard
    4. Four: That which is unjust cannot be law
    5. Five: Natural law; principles that exist regardless of laws

VI. Sources of Law

A. Constitutional Law
    1. At federal and state level
    2. Establishes government structure
    3. Establishes individual rights

B. Statutory Law at the Federal Level
    1. Enactments of Congress - United States Code
        Cite or citation = U.S.C. (e.g., 15 U.S.C. sec. 77)
        Examples: Sherman Act, National Labor Relations Act, Occupational Health and Safety Act, the USA Patriot Act, and all treaties
    2. Administrative agency regulations - Code of Federal Regulations
        Cite or citation = C.F.R. (e.g., 12 C.F.R. sec. 226)
    3. Executive orders = presidential orders

C. Statutory Law at the State Level
    1. Enactments of state legislatures - state codes
        Uniform laws are part of state codes
        Cite = Nevada Revised Statutes – N.R.S.
        Examples: Uniform Commercial Code, Uniform Partnership Act, Uniform Limited Partnership Act
    2. State administrative agency regulations
        Cite: various

D. Local Laws of Cities, Counties, and Townships
    1. Ordinances - zoning, traffic, curfew
    2. County or city

E. Private Laws
    1. Contracts
    2. Leases
    3. Employer regulations

F. Court Decisions
    1. Language in statute unclear
    2. Court provides interpretation or clarification of the law

VII. Introduction to International Law

    A.   Customs (Country-By-Country Basis)

    B.   Treaties
        1.   Bilateral - between two nations
        2.   Multilateral - among three or more nations
        3.   Geneva Convention - prisoners of war
        4.   Vienna Convention - diplomatic relations
        5.   Warsaw Convention - air travel

    C.   Private Law In International Transactions

    D.   International Organizations (United Nations)

    E.   Act of State Doctrine
        1.   Expropriation
        2.   Confiscation or nationalization
        3.   Taking of private property by a government

    F.   Trade Laws and Policies
        1.   Tariffs
        2.   Treaties, e.g., GATT, NAFTA

    G.   Uniform International Laws
        1.   Contracts for the International Sale of Goods (CISG)
        2.   For uniformity in international contracts

    H.   The European Union (EU)
        1.   Group of 25 countries (other countries are affiliated)
        2.   Aiming for barrier-free trade; uniform laws; ease of transaction negotiation and execution
        3.   Uniformity in currency, job safety, immigration, customs, licensing, and taxation
        4.   Euro introduced in January 1999

KEY TERMS

Act of State Doctrine	Equity	Private Law
Appropriation	European Union (EU)	Procedural Laws
Bilateral Treaties	Executive Orders	Public Law
Brief	Expropriation	*Stare Decisis*
Cite or Citation	General Agreement on Tariffs	State Codes
Civil Law	and Trade (GATT)	Statutory Law
Common Law	Injunctions	Substantive Laws
Confiscation	Jurisprudence	Treaty
Constitution	Multilateral Treaties	Uniform Commercial Code
Contracts for International	Nationalization	(UCC)
Sale of Goods (CISG)	North American Free Trade	Uniform Laws
Courts of Chancery	Agreement (NAFTA)	United States Code (USC)
Criminal Law	Ordinance	Universal Treaties
Custom	Party Autonomy	

MATCHING

a.	Injunction	g.	Treaty
b.	Public Law	h.	Civil Law
c.	Ordinances	i.	United States Code
d.	*Stare Decisis*	j.	Procedural Laws
e.	State Codes	k.	Executive Orders
f.	Criminal Law	l.	Cite or citation

_____ 1. An agreement between two or more nations on international law.

_____ 2. Laws that are enacted by some governmental body, such as zoning laws.

_____ 3. An order prohibiting certain conduct or ordering certain acts.

_____ 4. Contains the laws passed by Congress.

_____ 5. The legal process of basing a decision and case upon principles of law developed in past cases.

_____ 6. Law concerning a wrong against another person and which is remedied through the payment of restitution or damages.

_____ 7. A form of statutory law passed by a local government, such as zoning laws, curfews, and dog licensing.

_____ 8. Laws that contain states' criminal laws, incorporation laws, partnership laws, and contract laws.

_____ 9. Laws concerning a wrong against society that have penalties such as fines and imprisonment.

_____ 10. Laws that provide the means for enforcing substantive rights.

_____ 11. Legal form of shorthand in the U.S.C.

_____ 12. Laws passed by Presidents of the U.S.

FILL-IN-THE-BLANKS

1. The study of legal philosophy and the search for a theory behind the law or the values a legal system should try to encourage is called _____.

2. State and federal constitutions, the federal securities laws, local zoning laws, and state incorporation and partnership procedures, are all examples of _____ law, while contract law and the laws regulating the relationship between a landowner and tenants are examples of _____ law.

3. A person who shoots a weapon towards another person and causes injury, may be guilty of both a _____ law violation, and therefore, become subject to prosecution, and at the same time be liable in _____ law for any injuries caused to the victim.

4. After the Normans invaded England in 1066, they established a system of laws in England which is called _____ law, the guiding principle of which is referred to as _____ or "let the decision stand."

5. _____ is a body of law that attempts to do justice when the law does not provide a remedy, or when the remedy is not adequate, or when the law is unfair.

6. Law of the people that can only be changed by longer and more demanding procedures than those used to change statutes are _____.

7. Proposed codes written by business people, educators, and lawyers to make business between states easier are called _____.

8. The laws governing how a lawsuit is brought and the trial process are _____ laws; the laws regarding subject matter and issues of the litigation are the _____ laws.

9. _____ or _____ is the taking of private property by the government of a foreign country.

10. Treaties between two nations are _____ treaties; treaties among several nations are _____ treaties; and treaties that are recognized by almost all nations are general or _____ treaties.

11. International firms can operate uniformly world-wide if they have _____.

12. Governments are protected from review by other countries' courts by the _____ theory.

SHORT ANSWER

1. What are the three characteristics of law?

    a. _____

    b. _____

    c. _____

2. List the five purposes of law.

    a. _____

    b. _____

    c. _____

    d. _____

    e. _____

3. Name the five sources of law.

    a. _____

    b. _____

    c. _____

    d. _____

    e. _____

4. What are the sources of international law?

    a. _____

    b. _____

    c. _____

    d. _____

    e. _____

    f. _____

    g. _____

    h. _____

5. Explain what these sources of law are and how they are adopted.

    a. United States Code _____

    b. Uniform Commercial Code _____

    c. Court Decisions _____

6. How do each of the following define "law"?

    a. Aristotle _____

    b. Oliver Wendell Holmes _____

    c. Sir William Blackstone _____

    d. Black's Law Dictionary _____

Chapter 2

BUSINESS ETHICS AND SOCIAL RESPONSIBILITY

CHAPTER OUTLINE

I.   What is Ethics?

    A.   Examples
       1.   Randy Cunningham taking bribes from defense contractors
       2.   Jason Blair – *NY Times* reporter who made up stories
       3.   Stock options
       4.   Seeing two movies for the price of one by sneaking in

    B.   The Notion of "It's Just Not Right"

    C.   Ethics Consist of Standards of Behavior Above and Beyond the Law – Common or Normative Standards
       1.   Societal expectations
       2.   E.g., taking cuts in line and not waiting your turn, adultery, cheating on a test

II. What is Business Ethics?

    A.   Three Layers
       1.   Basic values (honest, keeping promises)
       2.   Notions of fairness (how we treat others)
       3.   Issues related to community, environment, neighbors

    B.   Used to Create and Sustain a Level Playing Field

    C.   Application of Standards of Moral Reasoning to Business Dilemmas
       1.   Moral standard is established
       2.   Individual moral standards differ
       3.   Debate over sources of moral standards
       4.   Evaluate moral standards and conflicts as new data appear
           Example: Employee loyalty versus knowledge of employer's wrongdoing

    D.   Sources of Moral Standards
       1.   Actual or positive law
       2.   Natural law (slavery was legal but not moral)
       3.   Moral relativism or situational ethics (theft if you're starving)
       4.   Religious beliefs or divine revelation (Bible, Koran)

III.   What are the Categories of Ethical Dilemmas?

      A.   Taking Things That Don't Belong to You

           Example: Pens to postage to embezzlement; music from the Internet (Napster)

      B.   Saying Things You Know Are Not True

           Example: Blaming others for your slip-ups; sales promises not honored

      C.   Giving or Allowing False Impressions

      D.   Buying Influence or Engaging in Conflict of Interest

           Example: Those who award contracts accept perks from bidders; wife of attorney general making $100,000 in cattle futures

      E.   Hiding or Divulging Information

           Example: In contract negotiations, failure to reveal important/material information; with employees, revealing private information

      F.   Taking Unfair Advantage

           Example: Capitalizing on another's inexperience; credit card companies and 10:00 a.m. cut-off

      G.   Committing Acts of Personal Decadence

           Example: Office parties that result in drunken behavior that harms others

      H.   Perpetrating Interpersonal Abuse

           Example: Harassment

      I.   Permitting Organizational Abuse

           Example: Child labor issues, low wages

      J.   Violating Rules

           Example: Follow procedures for finances because of internal control issues – work to change rules, don't violate them; Stanford and government funds

      K.   Condoning Unethical Actions

           Examples: Disclosing problems and confronting violators

      L.   Balancing Ethical Dilemmas

           Examples: Downsizing – rights of employees vs. shareholder investment, doing business in South Africa or China

IV. Resolution of Business Ethical Dilemmas

    A. Blanchard and Peale
        1. Is it legal?
        2. Is it balanced?
        3. How does it make me feel?

    B. The Front-Page-of-the-Newspaper Test
        1. How would the story be reported?
        2. Use an objective and informed reporter's view
        3. Warren Buffett's warning to employees

    C. Laura Nash and Perspective
        1. How would I view the problem if I sat on the other side of the fence? (Jack-in-the Box)
        2. Am I able to discuss my decision with my family, friends, and those closest to me? (William Aramony and United Way)
        3. What am I trying to accomplish?
        4. Will I feel as comfortable over the long term as I do today?
        5. Forces managers to examine additional perspectives

    D. *The Wall Street Journal* Model
        1. Compliance
        2. Contribution (Herman Miller and Eames Chair)
        3. Consequences

    E. The Categorical Imperative, Golden Rule, Etc.
        1. Are you comfortable in a world that uses your standards?
        2. "The Golden Rule"

V. Why We Fail to Reach Good Ethical Decisions

    A. Rationalization
        1. "Everybody else does it."
        2. "If we don't do it, someone else will."
        Example: Selling O.J. Simpson masks and bloody knives
        3. "That's the way it has always been done."
        Examples: Audit committees, independence, and eventual SEC rules; dot-coms and poor governance
        4. "We'll wait until the lawyers tell us it's wrong." (Napster)
        Example: Derivatives - legality does not determine morality
        5. "It doesn't really hurt anyone."
        Examples: Freeway rubberneckers, health insurance claims and rising premiums
        6. "The system is unfair."
        Example: Cheating does not improve the system
        7. "I was just following orders."
        Example: German border guards - sometimes morality requires disobedience
        8. "You think this is bad, you should have seen…"
        Example: 35-day month was a lot worse than what we're doing now
        9. "It's a gray area."
        Example: HP and the pretexting

VI.   Social Responsibility: Another Layer of Business Ethics

    A.   Conflicts Among Business
        1.   Shareholders - want profits
        2.   Employees - want safe and secure jobs
            Dilemma: Does a company risk short-term profits by shutting down to install safety equipment?
        3.   Community - wants plant's economic base but does not want its environment destroyed
                Dilemma: Should a company shut down to install state-of-the-art scrubbers on its plant?

    B.   Friedman Perspective
        1.   Only answer to shareholders
        2.   Social responsibility takes money from shareholders
        3.   Should only undertake a project if it benefits the business; pollution control for attracting workers is not for the community

    C.   Ethical Postures and Business Practice

        Whose interest does a corporation serve? What is the best way to serve that interest?

    D.   The Inherence School
        1.   Serve shareholders
        2.   Serve shareholders best by only looking out for shareholders
        3.   Friedman view
            Example: School tax issue - would only get involved if it affected the company directly

    E.   The Enlightened Self-Interest School
        1.   Manager is responsible first to shareholders but serves them best by being responsible to larger society
        2.   Business value is enhanced if it is responsive to society's needs
            Examples: Employers resolving child-care issues for employees, employers advocating lifestyle changes to improve health (costs more initially but in the long run cuts down on medical costs and lost work days)

    F.   The Invisible Hand School
        1.   Manager believes larger society should be served but manager does that best by serving shareholders first
        2.   Do not become involved in political or social responsibility issues – allow others to handle issues and they will comply
            Example: Would continue to make company profitable so employees would be paid well and would solve the child-care dilemma themselves; Pepsi and its decision to go into India

    G.   The Social Responsibility School
        1.   Manager should serve larger society
        2.   Become involved in all types of political and social issues
        3.   Encourage managers to be involved

VII. Why Business Ethics?

    A. Business Ethics for Personal Reasons
        1. Not all ethical firms are profitable firms
        2. Not all unethical firms are unprofitable
        3. Really a personal standard of behavior - it is the correct thing to do

    B. Importance of Values in Business Success
        1. Short-term profitability through "ethical shortcuts" can contribute to a firm's demise
        2. Baucus study on correlation between poor financial performance and ethical/legal missteps
        3. Executives feel ethical behavior strengthens a firm's competitive edge
        4. Johnson & Johnson example of Tylenol recall - earned it high respect and higher earnings in spite of cost

    C. Costs of Unethical Behavior
        1. Defense contractors and current reputation
        2. Beech-Nut and the loss in sales from selling "fake" apple juice
        3. Nestlé boycotts over their infant formula marketing programs in Third World nations; inability to sell new formula products because of twenty-year-old incident
        4. Tylenol and the recall of $100 million in inventory
        5. BP
            a. Failure to smart-pig the oil pipelines
            b. Saving money and not realizing safety issues
            c. Production and profits down
            d. Years to recover trust and market capitalization
        6. GM and its Malibu
            a. Failure to take action on memo
            b. Ongoing problems
            c. $1.2 billion in damages

    D. Ethics as a Strategy
        1. Affords opportunity for planning and ability to answer social needs and cultural changes; use Union Carbide and Bhopal example
        2. Creates goodwill between business and the community; absence of goodwill can be costly

    E. The Value of a Good Reputation
        1. Illegal or unfair conduct stays in the public mind
        2. Difficult for firms to recover financially – Salomon's lack of recovery

    F. Leadership's Role in Ethical Choices
        1. Ethical choices are a form of voluntary regulation
        2. Remedying problems before regulation is put into place
        3. Examples of abuses (poor ethical choices) that led to regulation
            a. Credit disclosure
            b. Johns-Manville and asbestos
            c. The Subprime lenders being regulated now
            d. Self-regulation by music industry to avoid censorship of artists
            e. Self-regulation on tamper proof would have helped

VIII.   Creation of an Ethical Atmosphere in Business

    A.   Tone at the Top/Clear Signals Necessary for Good Business Ethics
        1.   Sears and its auto repair issues with pay incentives
        2.   Hotlines for reporting violations
        3.   DuPont and its ethics bulletins
        4.   Sarbanes-Oxley requires these components in an ethics program following collapses of WorldCom, Enron, etc.

    B.   Federal Sentencing Commission Requires
        1.   Code of ethics
        2.   Training
        3.   Anonymous reporting
        4.   Follow-up
        5.   Board action
        6.   Sanctions
        7.   Officer involvement

    C.   Reporting Lines and Hotlines: Have an Ombudsperson

    D.   Developing an Ethics Stance
        1.   Setting parameters for personal and business behavior
        2.   Setting tone of tolerance or intolerance for behavior

    E.   An Ethical Culture: Watch for Dangers of Unethical Environment
        1.   Intense competition/issues of survival
        2.   Managers making poor judgments
        3.   Employees with no personal values
        4.   Avoiding the either/or conundrum
        5.   Be careful about pressure and signals
            a.   Goals
            b.   Quotas
            c.   Signals

IX.   Ethical Issues in International Business

    A.   Cultures, Laws, and Standards Vary
        1.   Issues of bribes, grease payments, and culture-related gifts
        2.   Problems of economic development where bribery is common
            a.   Additional costs
            b.   Lack of trust
            c.   Basic assumptions underlying economic model of capitalism don't exist and make investment more difficult

    B.   Business Must Decide Whether to Operate Under One Uniform Set of Standards

    C.   Delicate Balancing of the Four Legs of Capitalism
        1.   Corruption in any breaks down investment
        2.   All four must be honest for markets to function

KEY TERMS

Business Ethics	Invisible Hand	Positive Law
Code of Ethics	Moral Relativism	Sarbanes-Oxley
Enlightened Self-Interest	Moral Standards	Situational Ethics
Inherence	Natural Law	Social Responsibility

MATCHING

a.	Enlightened Self-Interest	g.	Social Responsibility
b.	Positive Law	h.	Natural Law
c.	Reporting Lines	i.	Ethics Stance
d.	Tone at the Top	j.	Invisible Hand
e.	Inherence	k.	Code of Ethics
f.	Laura Nash Model	l.	Moral Relativism

_____ 1. School of thought philosophy that a corporation should serve the larger society's interests and that the best way to do this is for the corporation to be responsive to the larger society.

_____ 2. School of thought philosophy that a corporation should serve the larger society's interest and the best way to serve this interest is for the corporation to be responsive to shareholders' interests only.

_____ 3. According to this school of thought, a corporation should serve the interests primarily of its shareholders, and the best way to accomplish this is to be responsive to the needs of the larger society.

_____ 4. According to this school of thought, a corporation should serve the needs primarily of its shareholders and that the best way to accomplish this interest is for the corporation to be solely responsible to its shareholders.

_____ 5. Ethical commitment by a company to earn a profit within ethical boundaries.

_____ 6. Theory that our ethical decisions are made simply upon the basis of whether an activity is legal or not.

_____ 7. Theory that our moral standards are derived from a higher source and they are universal.

_____ 8. Theory that our moral decisions are made according to the situation in which the dilemma is faced.

_____ 9. Methods by which employees can anonymously report ethical violations.

_____ 10. Written rules of conduct that state what types of conduct firms would never engage in that will be enforced uniformly.

_____ 11. "Will I feel as comfortable about my decision over time as I do today?"

_____ 12. Officers and executives who "walk the talk."

FILL-IN-THE-BLANKS

1. A business with the _____ philosophy takes the position that managers answer only to shareholders and act solely with the shareholder's interests in mind.

2. A business which adopts the _____ school of thought believes that the purpose of the corporation is to serve the larger society and that such interest is best served if the corporation is responsive primarily to the needs of the larger society.

3. Envisioning your decision described on the front of your local paper is the ethical model known as the _____.

4. Kenneth Blanchard and the late Dr. Norman Vincent Peale developed three questions that managers should ask themselves when resolving ethical dilemmas. These questions are: _____, _____, and _____.

5. Top management must set the _____ when establishing their code of ethics for employees to follow.

6. _____ are ways, such as ombudspersons or hotlines, that employees can anonymously report ethical violations.

7. According to the _____ school of thought, business value is enhanced if business is responsive to the needs of society.

8. The _____ school of thought is the opposite of enlightened self-interest.

9. _____ developed several questions that managers should ask themselves as they face an ethical dilemma. For example, "How would I view the issue if I stood on the other side of the fence?"

10. Compliance, contribution, and consequences are contained in the _____ model for resolution of ethical dilemmas.

11. Milton Friedman's philosophy is an example of the _____ school of thought.

12. Mandating the Federal Sentencing Commission to review the types of things that can be done to improve the ethical culture of a company was brought about by the _____ Act.

SHORT ANSWER

1. Name the key phrases of rationalization employed in ethical dilemmas.

    a. _____

    b. _____

    c. _____

    d. _____

    e. _____

    f. _____

    g. _____

2. List the four schools of thought on ethical behavior in business practice.

    a. _____

    b. _____

    c. _____

    d. _____

3. Name six of the twelve categories of ethical dilemmas developed in *Exchange*, the BYU magazine, and discussed in the book.

    a. _____

    b. _____

    c. _____

    d. _____

    e. _____

    f. _____

4. Give two examples of tests or models you could apply in resolving ethical dilemmas.

    a. _____

    b. _____

5. Give two signs of an atmosphere that is ripe for unethical behavior.

   a. _____

   b. _____

6. List the Federal Sentencing Commission requirements for setting the tone at the top.

   a. _____

   b. _____

   c. _____

   d. _____

   e. _____

   f. _____

   g. _____

Chapter 3

THE JUDICIAL SYSTEM

CHAPTER OUTLINE

I. Types of Courts

    A. Trial Courts
        1. Place where case begins
        2. Jury is here
        3. Single judge

    B. Appellate Courts
        1. Review actions of trial courts
        2. Usually have published opinions of uniformity and consistency
        3. No trials are held

II. How Courts Make Decisions

    A. The Process of Judicial Review
        1. Determine whether error was made
        2. Transcript is reviewed
        3. All other evidence is reviewed
        4. Parties submit written briefs to summarize the evidence and issues
        5. Oral arguments made before panel of judges (generally three judges, but at U.S. Supreme Court   level, it is nine)
        6. Judges vote on whether there is reversible error (error that might have affected the outcome)
        7. Vote on case - can be a dissenting opinion
        8. Possible actions of reviewing court: checking for reversible error
            a. Affirm - no reversible error and decision stands
            b. Reverse - reversible error and decision is reversed
            c. Remand - error that requires further proceedings
        9. Statutory interpretation
            a. Courts at appellate level can review statutory application
            b. Can determine scope of statute

    B. The Doctrine of *Stare Decisis*
        1. Courts will follow previous decisions for consistency: setting precedent
        2. Exceptions (when precedent is not followed)
            a. Cases are factually distinguishable
            b. Precedent is from another jurisdiction
            c. Technology changes
            d. Sociological, moral, or economic changes or needs

    3.   Interpreting precedent
        a.   The rule of law in the case is the precedent
        b.   *Dicta* is not the precedent
        c.   *Dicta* is the discussion of the rule of law
    4.   Changing precedent
        a.   Technology issues
        b.   Economics and nuisance cases
    5.   When precedent is not followed
        a.   Different states/circuits
        b.   Dicta vs. ruling; dissenting opinions
        c.   Distinguishable facts/case
        d.   Moral reason, economics, balance

III. Parties in the Judicial System (Civil Cases)

  A. Plaintiffs
    1.   Initiate the lawsuit
    2.   Called petitioners in some cases

  B. Defendants
    1.   Alleged to have violated some right of the plaintiff
    2.   Party named in the suit for recovery

  C. Lawyers
    1.   Those who act as advocates for plaintiffs and defendants
    2.   Have fiduciary relationship with clients
    3.   Privilege exists with client
        a.   Can keep what client tells them confidential
        b.   Exception is advance notice of crime to be committed
    4.   Sarbanes-Oxley and privilege
        a.   Must notify CEO of financial fraud
        b.   If no action, must notify audit committee
        c.   If no action, must notify board
        d.   If no action, must resign
    5.   Represent client and see that procedures are followed
    6.   Lawyers in other countries
        a.   Canada and Britain – barristers
        b.   Quebec and France – *avocet notaire*
        c.   German – *Rechtsanwalt*
        d.   Japan – *Bengosh Shiho-Soshi*

  D. Judges
    1.   Mediators in the case
    2.   Can be elected or appointed

  E. Name Changes for Parties on Appeal
    1.   Appellant or petitioner - party appealing the lower court's decision
    2.   Appellee or respondent - party who won below and is not appealing
    3.   Some states reverse the name of the case on appeal

IV. The Concept of Jurisdiction

    A.   Authority of a Court to Hear a Case
    B.   Subject Matter Jurisdiction Is Jurisdiction Over the Subject Matter of the Case

    C.   *In Personam* Jurisdiction Is Jurisdiction Over the Parties in a Case

V. Subject Matter Jurisdiction of Courts: The Authority Over Content

    A.   The Federal Court System
        1.   Federal District Court
            a.   General trial court of the federal system
            b.   Subject matter jurisdiction
                (1) when the United States is a party
                      Examples: Criminal prosecutions by federal agencies, contract breach actions by federal agencies
                (2) federal question
                      Examples: Suits by private individuals under securities laws, Sherman Act, etc.
                (3) diversity of citizenship
                      Example: Suit where plaintiff and defendant are from different states and the claim exceeds $75,000
                (4) one issue that arises is what law will be applied to the case; federal courts apply state law, they do not make up a new system of federal common law
            c.   There are ninety-four federal districts
                (1) each state is at least one federal district
                (2) D.C. and Puerto Rico are also federal districts
                (3) number of districts per state is determined by population and case load
             d.   Opinions of federal courts are reported in the *Federal Supplement*
                Cite: F.Supp.
        2.   Specialized courts (courts of limited original jurisdiction)
            a.   Tax court
            b.   Bankruptcy court
            c.   U.S. Claims court
            d.   Judge Advocate General (military courts)
            e.   Courts for other agencies
            f.   U.S. Court of International Trade
        3.   U.S. Court of Appeals – Appellate Level of Federal System
            a.   Formerly known as U.S. Circuit Court of Appeals
            b.   Thirteen federal circuits (14th is proposed via division of the 9th circuit)
            c.   Group federal districts into these thirteen circuits
            d.   Generally a panel of three judges reviews appeals from Federal District Court unless *en banc*
            e.   Opinions found in *Federal Reporter*
                 Cite: F., F.2d or F.3d
        4.   U.S. Supreme Court
            a.   Must decide to review cases
            b.   Issues *writs of certiorari* on those cases they will review
            c.   Has original jurisdiction for
                (1) disputes between and/or among states

(2) charges of espionage or ambassadors and foreign consuls
  d. Nine judges with lifetime appointments
  e. Opinions reported in
    (1) *United States Reports* - official reports
      Cite: U.S.
    (2) *Supreme Court Reporter*
      Cite: S.Ct.
    (3) *Lawyers Edition*
      Cite: L.Ed., L.Ed.2d

 B. The State Court Systems
  1. State Trial Courts
    a. General called superior, circuit, district, or county court
    b. State also have limited, specialized jurisdiction trial courts
      (1) small claims
        (a) lesser damage claims
        (b) no lawyers
      (2) Justice of the Peace courts
        (a) smaller damage claims
        (b) lawyers permitted to appear
      (3) traffic courts - for citations
      (4) probate courts - for wills, guardianships, conservatorships, etc.
  2. State Appellate Courts
    a. Opinions reported in regional reporters
    b. Example: Pacific Reporter, P. or P.2d
  3. State Supreme Courts
    a. Opinions also reported in regional reporters
    b. Example: 45 Wash.App. 442

 C. Judicial Opinions
  1. Reported (published) for precedent
  2. Cases have cross-references for research tools

 D. Venue
  1. Location of court in the system
  2. In some cases the community is so involved in a case that selections of a jury in that community   would seal one's fate

VI. *In Personam* Jurisdiction of Courts: The Authority Over Persons

 A. Ownership of Property Within the State
   Property ownership in the state = *in rem* jurisdiction

 B. Volunteer Jurisdiction - Parties Agree to It

 C. Presence in the State ("minimum contacts")
  1. Residence
  2. Corporations incorporated or doing business in the state
  3. Minimum contacts - constitutional standards of contact with a state
  4. Long Arm Statutes
    a. Procedural statute needed for state court to take jurisdiction
    b. Allows state court to bring in out-of-state defendants if constitutional "minimum contacts" met

VII. The International Courts

    A.   Types and Names of International Courts
        1.   International Court of Justice (ICJ)
            a.   Part of UN
            b.   Jurisdiction is contentious (parties must agree to submit)
        2.   EU Courts
            a.   Court of Justice of European Communities
            b.   European Court of Human Rights
        3.   Inter-American Court of Human Rights
        4.   Opinion Found in *International Law Reports*
        5.   London's Commercial Court - site of many international arbitrations

    B.   Jurisdictional Issues in International Law

    C.   Conflicts of Law in International Disputes
        1.   Court systems vary
        2.   Tort recovery more liberal in U.S. (no contingency fees allowed elsewhere)
        3.   If home country provides adequate forum for relief, plaintiffs can't bring suit in the United States (even if recovery is substantially less)
        4.   Party autonomy controls: parties can agree on forum and applicable law

KEY TERMS

Affirms

Appellate Brief

Appellate Court

Appellant

Appellee

Attorney-Client Privilege

Brief

Concurrent Jurisdiction

Contentious Jurisdiction

County Courts

Court of Justice of European Communities

Defendants

De Novo Appeal

Dicta

Dissenting Opinion

Diversity of Citizenship

European Court of Human Rights

Exclusive Jurisdiction

Federal Circuit Court

Federal District Court

Federal Reporter

Federal Supplement

In Personam Jurisdiction

In Rem Jurisdiction

Inter-American Court of Human Rights

International Court of Justice

Judges

Judicial Review

Jurisdiction

Justice of the Peace Court

Lawyer

Limited Jurisdiction

Long-Arm Statutes

Minimum Contacts

Modify

Oral Argument

Original Jurisdiction

Petitioner

Plaintiffs

Precedent

Regional Reporter

Remand

Respondent

Reverse

Reversible Error

Small Claims Court

Stare Decisis

Subject Matter Jurisdiction

Traffic Courts

Trial Court

Trial *De Novo*

U.S. Supreme Court

Venue

Writ of Certiorari

MATCHING

a. Appellate Brief	g. Reversible Error
b. Bankruptcy Court	h. Jurisdiction
c. Trial Court	i. Appellate Court
d. Venue	j. *Writ of Certiorari*
e. *Stare Decisis*	k. Oral Argument
f. Judge	l. Judicial Review

_____   1.   A court of limited jurisdiction.

_____   2.   Review of a trial court's decisions and verdict to determine whether any reversible error was made.

_____   3.   Timed summary of points made in the party's brief.

_____   4.   The Supreme Court's exercise of its discretion to hear a case.

_____   5.   Refers to the established powers of a court to decide or try a particular case.

_____   6.   Doctrine of reviewing, applying, and/or distinguishing prior case decisions.

_____   7.   Person who controls the proceedings and/or the outcome of a case.

_____   8.   Concept that addresses the issue of location of the court in the system.

_____   9.   Summary of the major points of error alleged to occur during a trial.

_____   10.   An error that may have affected the outcome of the case or have influenced the decision.

_____   11.   Where the facts of a case are presented.

_____   12.   Court that reviews a trial court decision to check the conduct of the judge, trial, lawyers and jury.

FILL-IN-THE-BLANKS

1. The _____ jurisdiction determines which court has jurisdiction over the content of the case, while the _____ jurisdiction is jurisdiction over the people in the case.

2. Federal bankruptcy court, a state's small claims court, and a local traffic court are all examples of courts of _____ jurisdiction.

3. Cases in which the parties are from different states qualify them for _____ status, and _____ courts have the authority to hear these cases.

4. _____ initiate lawsuits, seeking some recovery, while _____ are charged with some violation of law or breach of duty.

5. A resident of California who is injured by a product manufactured by a New Jersey corporation may sue the corporation in California if the shipping of a product to California for sale to a California consumer constitutes sufficient _____ and California has a _____.

6. The appellate court will _____ the lower court's decision if there has not been an error; in some appellate cases, the court will _____ the decision by reversing or modifying a portion of the case.

7. _____ courts review the action of _____ courts to determine whether the latter has made an error in applying the substantive or procedural law involved in a case; these courts do not impanel a jury, take no testimony, and consider no evidence but allow the parties to summarize the case and submit their legal positions by filing a _____ and, in many cases, making a timed _____ at which time the judges may ask questions of the attorneys.

8. If a court decides on appeal that the lower court should have admitted evidence that was excluded and that the admission of this evidence would have affected or influenced the outcome of the case, the court will _____ the lower court's decision and most likely _____ the case, sending it back to the lower court for a new trial.

9. In a case being appealed, the party appealing the case is called the _____ or the _____; while the other party (not appealing) is called the _____ or _____.

10. If a person confesses to a crime or admits breaching a contract to his/her attorney, the _____ assures the client that the attorney will not reveal the information to anyone and will continue to represent the client and make sure that he is given all rights and protections under the law to the best of the attorney's ability.

11. When the appellate judges have a split vote, a _____ is often written by the judge who is in the minority to explain their decision.

12. Reviewing a court's prior decisions to help make a decision on a current case is using case _____ or the doctrine of _____.

SHORT ANSWER

1. List the two types of courts in all U.S. court systems.

    a. _____

    b. _____

2. Name the parties in the judicial system.

    a. _____

    b. _____

    c. _____

    d. _____

3. What are the three types of cases a federal district court can hear?

    a. _____

    b. _____

    c. _____

4. List three types of limited jurisdiction courts.

    a. _____

    b. _____

    c. _____

5. Explain the differences between the roles of an appellate court and a trial court.

    _____

    _____

    _____

6. Explain how the International Court of Justice is comprised and how jurisdiction is determined for international parties.

    _____

    _____

    _____

    _____

Chapter 4

MANAGING DISPUTES: ALTERNATIVE DISPUTE RESOLUTION AND LITIGATION STRATEGIES

CHAPTER OUTLINE

I. What is Alternative Dispute Resolution?

II. Types of Alternative Dispute Resolution

   A. Arbitration - Oldest Form of ADR
       1. Parties submit grievances and evidence to a third-party expert in an informal setting
       2. American Arbitration Association provides many arbitrators
       3. Binding arbitration – can't get court to reverse it
       4. Advantages
           a. Less formality
           b. Moves faster than a trial
           c. Handled privately
           d. Expert handles the cases
       5. Disadvantages
           a. Arbitrator may not have legal training and may not understand the significance of legal points
           b. Rules of evidence don't apply
       6. Federal Arbitration Act
           a. Passed to curb judicial declarations of arbitration clauses invalid
           b. Designed to encourage arbitration except when it is specifically prohibited
           c. Courts rarely interfere with contract arbitration clauses
       7. Process
           a. Parties agree to submit to arbitration
               (1) may be part of their contract
               (2) can agree after the fact
           b. American Arbitration Association (AAA) can handle the proceedings for a fee
           c. Demand for arbitration is filed
           d. Arbitrator is selected
               (1) proposed list sent to parties
               (2) they can object within time limits
           e. Hearing preparation - parties gather evidence
           f. Case is presented in hearing
           g. Arbitrator has thirty days from close of hearing to make a decision
           h. Award is made
           i. Binding arbitration: award is final

   B. Mediation
       1. Parties use a go-between to negotiate and communicate
       2. Used in international transactions
       3. Mediator can offer suggestions for resolution
       4. Not binding

C.   Medarb
1.   Arbitrator tries mediation first
2.   If no success, goes to arbitration

D.   Minitrial
1.   Small-scale trial where parties present case to a judge with experience in the field or to a neutral advisor
2.   Advisor or judge makes decision
3.   Can motivate parties to resolve differences even if the results are not binding

E.   Rent-a-Judge
1.   Trial held in commercial as opposed to a public court
2.   Pay fees for courtroom and judge
3.   Example: "The People's Court" TV show; Judge Judy

F.   Summary Jury Trials
1.   Summary presentation of case to judge and jury
2.   Gives parties an idea about jury's perceptions
3.   Used after discovery is complete

G.   Early Neutral Evaluation
1.   Consultant or volunteer gives parties an assessment of the position
2.   Generally used prior to discovery
3.   Saves expenses if parties settle following the evaluation

H.   Peer Review
1.   Employment dispute method
2.   Company-chosen, employee-chosen and neutral members review employer's actions
3.   High success rate

I.   Impact of ADR
1.   Some states have mandatory ADR for cases below a certain dollar amount ($25,000 - $50,000)
2.   Trends on ADR vary – some lawyers question its benefits because of increasing costs of discovery and hearings

III.   Resolution of International Disputes

A.   International Chamber of Commerce (ICC) Has Used Arbitration Since 1922

B.   Center for Settlement of Investment Disputes (ICSID) is an International Arbitral Organization for Investors; Investment Contracts Can Provide for Arbitration by ICSID

C.   Parties Free to Choose Which Courts Will Hear Their Disputes
1.   Party autonomy
2.   U.S. courts are a popular choice

D.   International Courts (like ICJ) Have No Enforcement Powers
1.   Act as mediators
2.   Provide perspective on dispute

IV. Litigation vs. ADR: The Issues and Costs

    A. Speed and Cost
        1. Arbitration mandatory (non-binding) in 35 states for disputes of lesser dollar amounts ($50,000 is typical)
        2. Hearing is faster/frees up courts for larger disputes

    B. Protection of Privacy
        1. Court records are public documents
        2. Firm's financials, strategies, concerns, and weaknesses are on display for the public

    C. Creative Remedies
        1. Creative resolutions not generally available through courts
        2. More room for give and take of issues and discussion

    D. Judge and Jury Unknowns
        1. Trier of fact presents a variable in outcomes
        2. Problems of hindsight determination

    E. Absence of Technicalities
        1. Evidentiary exclusions limited
        2. More of a search for the truth

V. When You Are In Litigation...

    A. How Does a Lawsuit Start?
        1. People begin civil lawsuits - system does not do it for them
            a. Based on a claim of right
            b. Lawsuits are efforts of individuals to enforce their rights
        2. The Complaint (Petition)
            a. Must be filed within statutory time limits, statutes of limitations
            b. Vary from state to state
            c. Vary for the type of right
                Example: Generally two years for personal injury claims, generally four years for contract   suits
            d. Complaint is general statement of claim
                (1) must describe actions that led to claim of violation
                    (a) could be claim for money damages
                    (b) could be claim for equitable remedies
                        Example: Specific performance, injunctions
                (2) must establish jurisdiction and venue of court in which it is filed
                    Example: For federal district court, must show diversity or that a federal question is invoked
                (3) class actions are often filed against businesses
                    (a) plaintiffs pool together for costs
                    (b) defendant need only try case once
                    (c) possible abuses of class actions

3. The Summons
   a. Complaint or petition and summons is served on defendant
   b. Summons explains to defendant his/her rights
      (1) where to defend
      (2) how long to defend
      (3) the effect of not defending the suit
   c. Delivered by an officer of the court (sheriff or magistrate) or by licensed private process servers
   d. In exceptional circumstances, service is accomplished by publication
   e. Rules on how service is accomplished vary
      (1) statutory agents can accept service for corporations
      (2) leaving with another adult at residence is acceptable
4. The Answer
   a. Second portion of the documents in a case are known as pleadings
   b. Pleadings include:
      (1) complaint (petition)
      (2) answer
      (3) counterclaims
      (4) crossclaims
   c. Failure to file an answer within the statutory time period is a default
      (1) time limits for filing answers are typically twenty to thirty days
      (2) like a forfeit in sports - plaintiff wins because the defendant fails to show up
   d. Answer content
      (1) defendant can admit allegations in complaint are true
          Examples: Can admit court has jurisdiction, can admit incorporation in that state
      (2) defendant can deny allegations in complaint
          Example: Defendant denies that he negligently struck plaintiff
      (3) defendant can counterclaim - effect is the defendant is also suing plaintiff for damages
          Example: Defendant denies contract breach and counterclaims for defamation because of plaintiff's statements about the breach in the business community

B. Seeking Timely Resolution of the Case
   1. Motions for formal requests for a court to take action
   2. Motion for judgment on the pleadings
      a. Even if everything the plaintiff said in the complaint were true, there is no cause for action
         Examples: A suit for defamation where no one heard or saw the remarks (no publication) doesn't give the plaintiff any remedy even though the statements were defamatory, calling a partner dishonest in a closed room where only that partner is present
      b. If court grants motion, the case is over at the trial court level (appeal is possible)
   3. Motion to dismiss
      a. Can be filed any time throughout the case
      b. Can be based on lack of jurisdiction or expiration of the statute of limitations
   4. Motion for summary judgment
      a. Appropriate in cases where there are no factual issues
         Examples: In contract cases, the case often revolves around the interpretation of a statute and not the factual issues in the case
      b. Used to resolve questions of law when the parties agree on the facts
      c. Tort and personal injury cases are inappropriate for summary judgment because of issues of fact

C. How a Lawsuit Progresses: Discovery
   1. Process of gathering evidence for trial - new federal rules and those of most states now mandate timely disclosure of all relevant evidence
   2. Forms of discovery to supplement evidence released
      a. Requests for admissions - request from one party to another for the admission of facts so that proof requested at trial is limited
          Example: Admitting a contract; the contract is signed. The penalty of attorneys' fees is assessed to parties who fail to admit subsequently established facts.
      b. Depositions - statements of parties or witnesses taken under oath in an informal setting
          (1) preserves immediate recollection of witnesses
          (2) helps predict testimony to be given at trial
      c. Limitations on discovery
          (1) evidence must be relevant
          (2) cannot discover work product - the thoughts, strategies, and theories of the attorneys in the case
          (3) applies only to attorneys' work product and not accountants
      d. Requests for production - requests to parties to produce documents relevant to the case
          Examples: Income tax returns (to show lost earnings), memos (internal) on contracts

D. Resolution of a Lawsuit: The Trial
   1. Can be a trial to the court or a jury trial
   2. Jury trial
      a. Required in cases where damages over $20 are claimed
      b. Absolute right to jury trial is only in criminal cases
      c. Jurors selected from voting or drivers' license lists
      d. Process of *voir dire* used to narrow jurors for panel
          (1) ask questions about their knowledge of the case, level of education, background, etc.
          (2) can be challenged for cause - incapable of making an impartial decision when they know parties, when they were involved with the case
          (3) peremptory challenge - limited number of challenges used by attorneys to remove potential jurors with whom they are uncomfortable
      e. Jury selection is an art - lawyers attend seminars to learn tools for selection; consulting firms are available to help with background data and demographics on past juries and attorney success rates
   3. Trial language
      a. Opening statement - gives summary of the case and witnesses and how they fit together to prove necessary elements
      b. Plaintiff's case
          (1) presents witnesses - direct examination
          (2) defendant can cross-examine plaintiff's witnesses
      c. Post-plaintiff's case motion - motion for a directed verdict
          (1) plaintiff must prove all elements - called a prima facie case
          (2) failure to prove all elements entitles defendant to a directed verdict
          (3) made with jury excused
      d. Defendant's case
          (1) presents witnesses - direct examination
          (2) plaintiff can cross-examine defendant's witnesses
      e. Types of evidence
          (1) witnesses' testimony
          (2) documents

            (3) photographs

            (4) tangible items

            (5) hearsay - can be admissible to establish facts other than the issue in the case

            (6) expert testimony – expert must be qualified

    f.   Closing arguments - each side summarizes cases presented

    g.   Jury instructions

            (1) judge explains law to jurors

            (2) law is written in form for jurors to apply

            (3) lawyers have input on instructions

    h.   Jury deliberations

            (1) some states do not require unanimous verdicts in civil cases - a majority

            (2) if jury cannot reach a verdict, hung jury results and there must be a new trial

    i.   Jury verdict

            (1) decisions of jury

            (2) one side can request to have jury polled - occasionally any pressure exerted will come out then

    j.   Post-trial motions

            (1) motion for a judgment NOV (*non obstante veredicto*) - motion for a judgment notwithstanding the verdict; effect is a trial court judge reversing the jury verdict - rarely done

            (2) motion for a new trial - judge orders case retried

VI. Issues in International Litigation

    A.   Which Laws Apply?

    If country of accident has adequate remedies, foreign citizens may not come to U.S. in order to enjoy benefit of our traditionally liberal recovery rules and higher verdicts.

    B.   Differences in U.S. vs. Other Countries

       1.   Tort liability

       2.   Amounts of damages

KEY TERMS

Alternative Dispute Resolution (ADR)	Depositions	Judgment NOV
	Derivative Suit	Jury Deliberations
American Arbitration Association (AAA)	Directed Verdict	Jury Instructions
	Direct Examination	Legal Remedy
Answer	Discovery	Medarb
Arbitration	Early Neutral Evaluation	Mediation
Binding Arbitration	Equitable Remedy	Minitrial
Burden of Proof	Federal Arbitration Act	Motion
Class Action Suits	(FAA)	Motion for Judgment on the
Closing Arguments	Hearsay	Pleadings
Complaint	Hung Jury	Motion for Summary
Counterclaim	Injunctions	Judgment
Cross-Examination	International Chamber of	Motion to Dismiss
Default	Commerce (ICC)	Nonbinding Arbitration

Opening Statement	Redirect Examination	Summons
Peer Review	Rent-a-Judge	Trial
Peremptory Challenge	Request for Admissions	Verdict
Petition	Request for Production	*Voir Dire*
Pleadings	Specific Performance	Work Product
Prima Facie Case	Statute of Limitations	
Process Servers	Summary Jury Trials	

MATCHING

a.	Peer Review	g.	Summons
b.	Hearsay	h.	*Voir dire*
c.	Burden of Proof	i.	Rent-a-Judge
d.	Medarb	j.	Alternative Dispute Resolution
e.	Depositions	k.	Statute of Limitations
f.	Peremptory Challenge	l.	American Arbitration Association

_____ 1. Evidence offered in court by a witness who does not have personal knowledge of the information being given but who has heard it from someone else.

_____ 2. A process by which the attorneys in a case speak with and question prospective jurors to determine whether they are qualified to serve on the jury.

_____ 3. Form of alternative dispute resolution in which the arbitrator attempts to negotiate between two parties and, if not successful, proceeds to take them to arbitration.

_____ 4. Private court system.

_____ 5. Parties' responsibility to prove the facts.

_____ 6. A legal document which tells the defendant that a suit has been filed against him or her and explains his or her rights under the law.

_____ 7. Method of resolving differences outside the courtroom.

_____ 8. The eliciting of oral testimony from the parties' witnesses in a lawsuit, under oath and before trial.

_____ 9. The dismissal or removal of a prospective juror from a case by an attorney which requires that no reason whatsoever be given for the removal.

_____ 10. Review by co-workers of an action taken against an employee by an employer.

_____ 11. The largest ADR provider in the U.S.

_____ 12. Time limit on filing a complaint.

FILL-IN-THE-BLANKS

1. A form of alternative dispute resolution in which both parties meet with a neutral third party who listens to both sides and tries to get the parties to agree to a solution is called _____.

2. In order to give the defendant notice that a lawsuit has been filed against him or her, a _____ must be delivered to the defendant by a _____. The defendant then typically has twenty days (thirty days for out-of-state defendants) to file an _____; a defendant's failure to respond in this manner to the filing of a lawsuit against him or her may result in the court's order of a _____, meaning that the plaintiff wins the case. In some cases, the defendant will also file a _____, alleging a violation of the defendant's rights and requesting damages from the plaintiff.

3. A defendant's answer to a summons may be a _____, wherein the defendant may contend that the court may not hear the case because it lacks jurisdiction.

4. A party will likely file a _____ with the court in those cases where the parties do not dispute the facts of the case but differ on the application or interpretation of the law.

5. In a _____, lawyers present the strongest aspects of their parties' case to officials from both companies in front of a judge with experience in the field.

6. Damages or remedies sought by a plaintiff in a complaint can be either a _____ remedy, such as money, an _____ remedy, such as specific performance requiring a defendant to perform on a contract, or an _____, where the court orders a defendant to stop doing the act in the complaint.

7. At the beginning of the trial, the attorney for each party will likely make an _____ to summarize what that party hopes to prove to the jury.

8. A lawsuit filed by a group of plaintiffs who have the same complaint against one defendant is called a _____.

9. After all the evidence has been presented in the trial, the attorneys for both parties are likely to make a _____ to the jury, in which they will highlight the important points of their case and the weaknesses or defects in the other side's case. Then, the judge will give the jurors _____ in order to explain to them what the law is and how to apply it to the facts presented during the trial.

10. Because of the time, effort, and money, that it takes to conduct successful litigation, many businesses prefer to participate in binding _____, in which an _____ is used to resolve a dispute because of his or her expertise in the subject matter of the contract.

11. When the decision of the arbitrator is final, it is _____ arbitration. If the arbitration is _____, either one of the parties that is not happy with the result of the arbitration can elect to continue on to litigation.

12. A _____ gives both parties the opportunity to see how a jury may perceive their arguments on an issue.

SHORT ANSWER

1. What are the eight types of alternative dispute resolution?

    a. _____

    b. _____

    c. _____

    d. _____

    e. _____

    f. _____

    g. _____

    h. _____

2. List any three types of motions made during litigation and when they are made.

    a. _____

    b. _____

    c. _____

3. List five advantages to arbitration.

    a. _____

    b. _____

    c. _____

    d. _____

    e. _____

4. List the steps/documents in filing (initiating) a lawsuit.

    a. _____

    b. _____

    c. _____

5.   Give three examples of evidence at trial.

      a. _____

      b. _____

      c. _____

6.   Explain how resolutions may be resolved in international disputes.

      _____

      _____

      _____

      _____

Chapter 5

BUSINESS AND THE CONSTITUTION

CHAPTER OUTLINE

I. The U.S. Constitution

    A. An Overview of the U.S. Constitution

    B. Articles I, II, and III - The Framework for Separation of Powers
        1. Article I: Legislative Branch
            a. House of Representatives
            b. Senate
        2. Article II: Executive Branch - President; Election; Powers
        3. Article III: Judicial Branch
            a. Creates U.S. Supreme Court
            b. Authorizes Congress to establish other courts as needed; Congress has established U.S. Court of Appeals and Federal District Court
        4. Creates a system of checks and balances - each branch has some power check over the other to keep any one from becoming too powerful

    C. Other Articles in the Constitution
        1. Article IV: State interrelationships
        2. Article V: Procedures for amendments
        3. Article VI: Supremacy Clause
        4. Article VII: State Ratification of the Constitution

    D. The Bill of Rights
        1. First: Freedom of Speech
        2. Fourth: Privacy
        3. Fifth: Due Process and Self-incrimination
        4. Sixth: Jury trial
        5. Fourteenth Amendment: Equal Protection

II. The Role of Judicial Review and the Constitution

    A. Determination of Rights Afforded by the U.S. Constitution

    B. Determination of Scope of Rights

    C. Checks and Balances - Determines the Appropriateness of the Other Branches' Actions

III. Constitutional Limitations of Economic Regulations

    A. The Commerce Clause: Article I, Section 8
        1. Standards for Federal Regulation of Interstate Commerce

    2. Historical application of Commerce Clause
        a. Initially, Court gave a narrow interpretation
            Examples: Manufacturing was not "interstate commerce," a restaurant in one state was not "interstate commerce"
        b. Resulted in a difficult situation between Roosevelt Administration and the Court as Roosevelt tried to pass the labor regulation scheme
        c. Roosevelt tried the court-packing plan - he wanted to increase the size of the U.S. Supreme Court and load it with his appointees to get the legislation past constitutional challenges
        d. After these political battles, court responded in *NLRB v. Laughlin Steel*:
           (1) affectation doctrine developed
           (2) even though activity is local (e.g., manufacturing; restaurants), if interstate commerce is affected, Congress can regulate
               Examples: interstate travelers at restaurants, interstate suppliers, manufactured goods shipped interstate
    3. Standards for state regulation of interstate commerce
        a. There is an overriding concern about the Supremacy Clause - where Congress has regulated there is a benefit/burden analysis
            Example The mudguards on trucks on Illinois highways when the trucks travel interstate would require change of mudguards – where not enough evidence of safety benefits to require such a burden
        b. Balance police power (state's interest in regulation) with the burden on commerce
        c. State law cannot give in-state businesses an advantage
    4. Congressional authority over foreign commerce if it is international in nature; Congress regulates regardless of where it begins and ends

  B. Constitutional Standards for Taxation of Business
    1. Article I, Section 8 gives Congress the power to regulate
    2. Biggest area of litigation is state taxation of interstate business
    3. Requirements for valid state tax
        a. Tax cannot discriminate against interstate commerce
        b. Tax cannot be an undue burden on interstate commerce
            Example: Requiring out-of-state property to be appraised in state
        c. Must be a "sufficient nexus" between the state and the business being taxed
            Examples: Does business there, holds property titles there, manufactures there, inventory stored there
        d. Must be apportioned fairly
            Example: A corporation doing business in fifty states cannot have all income taxed in all fifty states – must be apportioned according to its revenues in the state

IV. State Versus Federal Regulation of Business - Constitutional Conflicts: Preemption and the Supremacy Clause

  A. Exists to Determine Which Laws Control in the Event Both State and Federal Governments Regulate: Article VI

  B. If State Law Directly Conflicts with Federal Law, State Law Is Unconstitutional

C. Other Areas: State Laws Do Not Directly Conflict

Whether there is preemption is controlled by answering several questions:
1. What does the legislative history indicate?
Examples: Some statutes specifically disallow state regulation: Nuclear Regulatory Commission exclusively regulates nuclear plant construction; other areas of regulation provide for both state and federal participation. Securities laws do allow states to have their own securities registration even if it means two filings.
2. Level of detail for federal regulation - the more detail at federal level, the more likely there is to be federal preemption. Detail and volume are indicative of congressional intent to preempt.
3. Benefits from federal regulation
Example: Trains, planes – interstate transportation is best regulated in a uniform fashion
4. Nature of conflict - can the two laws survive?
Example: State blue laws can require higher disclosure, state credit laws can require higher disclosure than federal disclosure laws

V. Application of the Bill of Rights to Business

A. Commercial Speech and the First Amendment
1. Does provide some protection of commercial speech. Commercial speech - speech used to further the economic interests of the speaker
2. Advertising and commercial speech protection
a. Can regulate advertising
b. Substantial government interest must be furthered
c. Is the regulation the least restrictive means of accomplishing the interest?
Examples: Regulation Z disclosures in ads, requirements of Surgeon General warnings in cigarette ads, requirements of disclosures on odds of winning in prize games, etc.
3. History of commercial speech regulation

B. First Amendment Rights and Profits from Sensationalism

C. Corporate Political Speech - Corporate Participation in Issue Campaigns is Given Full First Amendment Protection

D. Eminent Domain and the Takings Clause
1. Fifth Amendment right of government to take private property for government purposes
2. Requirements
a. Public purpose
Examples: Highways, schools, urban redevelopment, limits on mining, historical preservation, economic development
b. Taking or regulating
Examples: Prohibition on use, elimination of use
c. Just compensation

E. Procedural Due Process
1. Right to notice of hearings
2. Right to be heard
3. Applies to criminal, civil, and administrative proceedings
Example: Summons and complaint provide notice to defendants

F.   Substantive Due Process - State Laws Cannot Substantively Eliminate Rights Without Some Benefit
Example: Sunday blue laws – stores are closed by law – states must be able to show economic, health, social benefits of such closure

G.   Equal Protection Rights for Business - Regulation Must Apply to All Businesses

Example: Many Sunday closing laws have been struck down because they are based on size – small   stores could be open but large stores could not

VI.   The Role of Constitutions in International Law

A.   General Types of Constitutions: United States and England

B.   Code of Law Countries: All Inclusive

C.   Islamic Law: Law is Civil and Religious

KEY TERMS

Balancing Test	Foreign Commerce	Procedural Due Process
Bill of Rights	Fourteenth Amendment	Public Purpose
Checks and Balances	Fourth Amendment	Separation of Powers
Commerce Clause	Interstate Commerce	Sixth Amendment
Commercial Speech	Judicial Branch	Substantive Due Process
Corporate Political Speech	Judicial Review	Substantive Law
Disparate Treatment	Just Compensation	Supremacy Clause
Eminent Domain	Legislative Branch	Taking
Equal Protection	Nexus	U.S. Constitution
Executive Branch	Police Power	
Fifth Amendment	Preemption	

MATCHING

a.	Substantive Law	g.	Substantive Due Process
b.	Disparate Treatment	h.	Sixth Amendment
c.	Procedural Due Process	i.	Preemption
d.	Judicial Branch	j.	Commerce Clause
e.	Separation of Powers	k.	Supremacy Clause
f.	Corporate Political Speech	l.	Just Compensation

_____   1.   Designed to prevent the concentration of too much power in any branch of the three branches of federal government.

_____   2.   Provides that when a state law conflicts with federal statutes, the federal law is superior to the state law.

_____ 3. Provides Congress with the power to regulate commerce with foreign nations and among several states.

_____ 4. A doctrine that might prevent the state from regulating a certain business activity even though the federal government has not enacted a statute or regulation in direct conflict with the state regulation.

_____ 5. Differences in legislation or regulation of businesses that are justified by some rational basis.

_____ 6. Requirement of the government to pay a private landowner when it takes the landowner's property pursuant to its power of eminent domain.

_____ 7. Political speech protected by the First Amendment.

_____ 8. Includes a right that requires notice and the right to be heard and to present evidence.

_____ 9. The right to have laws that do not deprive businesses of property or other rights without justification and reason.

_____ 10. Created by Article III of the U.S. Constitution; establishes the U.S. Supreme Court and its jurisdiction.

_____ 11. Rights, obligations, and behavior standards.

_____ 12. Establishes the right to a jury trial.

FILL-IN-THE-BLANKS

1. The _____ of the U.S. Constitution, contained in the _____, requires that persons similarly situated be treated in a similar manner by the government.

2. The power of the president to veto legislation passed by Congress is an example of the system of _____.

3. The _____ clause is the federal constitutional provision dealing with any business that affects commerce between the states.

4. Advertising is a form of _____, which is communication that is used to further the economic interests of the speaker.

5. The _____ protects individual freedom against governmental intrusion and control.

6. A state law requiring that all trucks using the state's roads be equipped with contour mud guards to promote the public safety is an example of the state's exercise of its _____.

7. A court would employ a _____ to determine if a law would unduly burden interstate commerce, rendering it unconstitutional.

8. The power of _____ allows a governmental body to take title to private property; in order for the government to exercise this power, however, it must be shown that there is a legitimate _____, a _____ as opposed to mere regulation of the property, and _____.

9. Before an administrative agency of either the federal or state government can impose a fine upon a business for violation of the agency's rules and regulations, _____ requires that the business be given an adequate opportunity to present its side of the controversy.

10. If a state law treats one class of businesses differently from another class of businesses, the law could violate the _____ of the U.S. Constitution.

11. Article I of the U.S. Constitution establishes the _____ branch of the federal government, Article II, the _____ branch, and Article III, the _____ branch.

12. Declaring a building a historic landmark is an example of _____ for a _____.

SHORT ANSWER

1. List the three branches of the federal government created by the first three articles of the U.S. Constitution.

    a. _____

    b. _____

    c. _____

2. Name the three factors that must be present for a government entity to exercise eminent domain.

    a. _____

    b. _____

    c. _____

3. What are the standards imposed on the taxation of interstate businesses?

    a. _____

    b. _____

    c. _____

    d. _____

4. What are the questions considered in a preemption issue?

    a. _____

    b. _____

    c. _____

    d. _____

5. List two amendments to the U.S. Constitution and the protections they afford businesses.

    a. _____

    _____

    b. _____

    _____

6. Name the three generalized ways in which corporate political speech takes form.

    a. _____

    b. _____

    c. _____

7. What two factors do the courts consider to determine if a state can regulate without interfering in Congress's domain of interstate commerce?

    _____

    _____

    _____

    _____

Chapter 6

ADMINISTRATIVE LAW

CHAPTER OUTLINE

I. What are Administrative Agencies?

    A. Nonlegislative, Nonjudicial Body
        1. Exist at every level of government
        2. They make, interpret, and enforce regulations
        3. Federal administrative agencies
        4. State administrative agencies
            a. Public Utility Commission
            b. Real Estate Department
            c. Registrar of Contractors
            d. Workers' Compensation
            e. Welfare Department
        5. Structure of agencies
        6. Carry out details needed from legislative enactments
        7. Legislatures pass enabling acts
            a. Sets up basic law, purpose, penalties
            b. Sets up administrative agencies to handle the enforcement

II. Roles of Administrative Agencies

    A. Specialization - Needed to Deal With Complexities of Legislation

        Examples: Environmental, occupational safety, nuclear, securities – regulation in these areas requires special expertise

    B. Protection for Small Business

        Examples: Corrective advertising, consumer complaints

    C. Provide for More Rapid Enforcement: Faster Relief
        1. Don't have to use court system for enforcement
        2. Licensing and permits can also be done quickly

    D. Due Process
        1. Hear benefits cases
        2. *Goldberg v. Kelly* case established precedent

    E. Social Goals
        1. Agency set up to achieve societal goals
        2. Environmental Protection Agency; HUD; Resolution Trust Corporation

III. Laws Governing Administrative Agencies

    A. Administrative Procedures Act (APA)
        1. First passed in 1946
        2. Established uniform procedures for agencies to follow in promulgating rules
        3. Other acts have separate names but are amendments to the APA

    B. Freedom of Information Act (FOIA)
        1. APA amendment passed in 1966
        2. Purpose was to allow public access to agency records
        3. Types of information required to be published
            a. Location of offices
            b. Names of responsible individuals
            c. Rules and regulations
            d. Reports
            e. Policy statements
        4. Types of information not published
            a. Hearing orders
            b. Nonpublished interpretations
            c. Personnel policies and procedures
        5. Unpublished information can be obtained through an FOIA request
            a. Must be written
            b. Must describe the information and/or documents sought
            c. Agency can charge for time and copy costs
        6. Wrongful refusal to supply information allows requester to bring suit and obtain court order for release as well as recovering cost
        7. Exemptions from disclosure
            a. National defense or foreign policy matters
            b. Internal personnel rules of the agency
            c. Statutorily protected information
            d. Trade secrets (includes financial or commercial information which is privileged or confidential)
            e. Inter- and intra-agency memos
            f. Personnel and medical files
            g. Records of investigations
            h. Banking audits
            i. Geological information on well sites

    C. Federal Privacy Act
        1. Passed in 1974 as APA amendment
        2. Intended to cut down on the pervasive and casual exchange of information about individuals between and among agencies
        3. Agencies cannot obtain individual's records from other agencies without the consent of that person
        4. Covers all records including medical and employment histories
        5. Exemptions
            a. Exchanges for law enforcement purposes
            b. Routine exchanges
                Examples: SEC information on stock trade, banking information to Federal Reserve Board

D. Government in the Sunshine Act
1. 1976 Amendment to APA
2. Also known as an open meeting law
3. Applies to meetings of agencies whose heads are appointed by the president
4. Applies only when agency heads are meeting
Example: Staff members can meet without notice
5. Exceptions - meetings covering
a. National defense
b. Foreign policy
c. Personnel issues
d. Law enforcement issues
Example: SEC commissioners meeting to discuss insider trading

E. Federal Register Act
1. Not part of APA
2. Publications act
3. Creates the Federal Register System - system of publication for federal agency information
4. Three publications
a. *U.S. Government Manual*: gives all agencies and their office locations, gives organizational charts, statistics on number of employees, etc.
b. *Code of Federal Regulations*: reports agency regulations; reprinted in paperback each year
c. *Federal Register*: published every working day; an update for CFR of changes in regulations, published notices of meetings, FOIA requests, proposed rules, etc.

IV. The Functions of Administrative Agencies and Business Interaction

A. Providing Input on Regulations During Agency's Promulgation
1. Formal rulemaking
a. Congress passes Enabling Act
b. Agency researches a problem
(1) can be done by agency staff
(2) can hire consultants to do it
(3) cost study involved
(4) also examine risks
c. Proposed regulations
(1) draft is reviewed by staff members and legal counsel – economists, scientists, etc.; review for content
(2) notice of proposed rule must be made public
(3) notice must include
(a) name of agency
(b) statutory authority of agency – enabling act
(c) language of proposed rule or description of proposed rule
(4) some agencies provide background information in their proposals
(5) published
(a) in Federal Register
(b) also in trade publications because Regulatory Flexibility Act has required such additional publication since not many people read the Federal Register

      d. Public comment period
- (1) must be at least thirty days (unless there is an emergency)
- (2) allows anyone to make comments on the proposed rules
- (3) in formal rulemaking procedures, public hearings are also held; may be held regionally; nationally

      e. Difference between legislation and rulemaking
- (1) Executive Branch involved
- (2) cannot use PAC/monetary influence

      f. Action on rules is taken: deciding what to do with the proposed regulation
- (1) rules are adopted
- (2) rules are modified and second public comment period held
- (3) rule is withdrawn
  - (a) adverse reaction
  - (b) congressional pressure
  - (c) further refinement is necessary
  - (d) industry is self-regulating

      g. Challenges to adopted agency rules
- (1) made through the courts
- (2) theory one - arbitrary, capricious, or abuse of discretion
  - (a) agency must show there is some evidence to support the rule
  - (b) study must offer some reason for the rule
- (3) theory two - substantial evidence
  - (a) rule proposed is unsupported by substantial evidence
  - (b) more convincing evidence exists in support of the regulation than evidence against it
- (4) challenges can be based on failure to follow procedures
  - (a) failure to give notice
  - (b) failure to allow comment
- (5) challenges based on constitutionality; FCC and First Amendment challenges
- (6) *ultra vires* challenge; agency went beyond authority given in enabling act

B. Proactive Business Strategies in Regulation
1. Sunset laws - agency created for a limited time; must justify its existence within that time
2. Zero-based budgeting - ongoing budget for agency is not assumed; must justify its budget each year
3. Informal rulemaking
   a. Process is the same
   b. No formal public hearing

V. Enforcing and Adjudicating Rules - Business Rights in Agency Enforcement Action

A. Licensing and Inspections
1. State level - construction permits and progress inspections
2. Federal level - EPA permits for discharge
3. OSHA inspections for safety
   a. Unannounced is okay
   b. Company can refuse without a warrant

B. Prosecution of Businesses
1. Complaint is filed
2. Injunction can be obtained for this period
3. Negotiation is possible - helps in business relationships with agency
4. Consent decree
   a. Like a plea bargain in a criminal case
   b. Like a nolo contendere plea in a criminal case
5. Penalties
   a. Fines
   b. Injunctions
   c. Repayment to buyers
   d. Corrective advertising
6. Can go to hearing without an agreement
   a. Administrative law judge (ALJ) hears the case (can be called hearing examiner or hearing officer)
   b. ALJ is like a judge at trial; makes decisions on evidence; prohibited from one-sided or *ex parte* contacts
   c. Intervenors - interested parties can appear in the case
      Example: insurers, auto manufacturers
   d. Rules of evidence are relaxed
   e. Must allow for due process
      (1) notice of charges
      (2) notice of hearing
      (3) right to present evidence
      (4) right to use attorney
      (5) right to impartial judge
   f. Appeals of decisions go to agency heads, exhausting administrative remedies (unless it would be futile)
7. Go to Court of Appeals

VI. The Role of Administrative Agencies in the International Market - U.S. Is Heavily Regulated

KEY TERMS

Administrative Agency
Administrative Law Judge
    (ALJ)
Administrative Procedures Act
    (APA)
Arbitrary
Capricious
Code of Federal Regulations
Complaint
Congressional Enabling Act
Consent Decree
Enabling Act
Exhausting Administrative
    Remedies
Ex Parte Contacts

Federal Privacy Act (FPA)
Federal Register
Federal Register Act (FRA)
Federal Register System
FOIA Request
Formal Rulemaking
Freedom of Information Act
    (FOIA)
Government in the Sunshine Act
Hearing Examiner
Hearing Officer
Hybrid Rulemaking
Informal Rulemaking
Injunction
Inspections

Intervenors
Licensing
Nolo Contendere
Open Meeting Law
Promulgation
Public Comment Period
Regulatory Flexibility Act
    (RFA)
Rulemaking
Substantial Evidence
Substantial Evidence Test
Sunset Law
Ultra Vires
U.S. Government Manual
Zero-Based Budgeting

MATCHING

a.	Federal Register System	g.	*Ultra Vires*
b.	Sunset Law	h.	Administrative Procedures Act
c.	Code of Federal Regulations	i.	Government in the Sunshine Act
d.	Administrative Agency	j.	Exhausting Administrative Remedies
e.	Federal Privacy Act	k.	Enabling Act
f.	Regulatory Flexibility Act	l.	Promulgation

_____ 1. A law creating an administrative agency and giving it the power to deal with the issues and problems the act addresses.

_____ 2. Requires agencies to follow certain uniform procedures in making rules and resolving disputes.

_____ 3. A U.S. government publication containing all of the regulations of all the federal agencies.

_____ 4. A law requiring that notice of an agency's proposed rules be published in trade and industry journals as well as in the *Federal Register*.

_____ 5. Prohibits agencies from exchanging information about an individual with another agency or person without the consent of the affected individual.

_____ 6. Requires prior public notice of meetings of the agencies with heads appointed by the president.

_____ 7. Statutory creation within the executive branch with the ability to make, interpret, and enforce laws.

_____ 8. Creation of an agency by Congress for a limited period of time during which the agency must establish its benefits and justify its continuation.

_____ 9. The requirement that a dissatisfied party in an administrative prosecution must go through all the required lines of authority within the agency itself before an appeal can be taken to court.

_____ 10. Approval of proposed rules by agency heads.

_____ 11. Overseas publication of federal agency information.

_____ 12. "Beyond its powers."

FILL-IN-THE-BLANK

1. The _____ requires that agencies publicly disclose their procedures and decisions.

2. To determine whether your employer has violated a regulation of OSHA, you could find its rules published in the _____. If a rule has been violated and you want to file a complaint with OSHA, you can find the address of the regional office closest to you by looking in the _____. Your employer could keep current on all proposed regulations of OSHA by subscribing to the _____.

3. To ensure that the public has an opportunity to provide input on proposed agency rules, the agency must allow a _____ of at least thirty days, during which private citizens, industry representatives and business persons send in their public comments.

4. Even though it is constitutional, an agency rule can be successfully challenged if it is _____, meaning that it has exceeded the authority granted to it by the legislature.

5. Some agencies are controlled through _____, which requires agencies to justify its need for funds each year.

6. Parties (other than the agency and the party charged with a violation) with an interest in an administrative hearing is called an _____ and can file motions any time before the start of a hearing.

7. If a complaint has been filed against a business charging it with violating an administrative rule, the business may choose not to contest the complaint but to negotiate a settlement with the agency in a document called a _____, which is comparable to a _____ plea in the criminal system.

8. The judge in a federal administrative proceeding is called a _____; at the state level, the judge is often referred to as a _____ or a _____.

9. Agency rulemaking that is a cross between _____ and _____ rulemaking is called hybrid rulemaking.

10. The _____ test requires that more convincing evidence exist in support of an agency's regulation than against it when an agency's regulation is challenged.

11. All government agencies with the word _____ in their names have agency heads appointed by the president.

12. The Environmental Protection Agency is an example of an agency created for a _____.

SHORT ANSWER

1. What are the roles of administrative agencies?

    a. _____

    b. _____

    c. _____

    d. _____

    e. _____

2. What are the steps in formal rulemaking by administrative agencies?

    a. _____

    b. _____

    c. _____

    d. _____

    e. _____

    f. _____

    g. _____

    h. _____

    i. _____

3. List the laws governing administrative agencies.

    a. _____

    b. _____

    c. _____

    d. _____

    e. _____

4. Name three of the grounds under which an administrative rule can be challenged.

   a. _____

   b. _____

   c. _____

5. Explain the following terms.

   a. arbitrary and capricious _____

   b. public comment period _____

   c. consent decree _____

   d. exhaustion of administrative remedies _____

   e. sunshine/open meeting laws _____

6. List the steps involved in agency enforcement and adjudication.

   a. _____

   b. _____

   c. _____

   d. _____

   e. _____

   f. _____

Chapter 7

INTERNATIONAL LAW

CHAPTER OUTLINE

I.   Sources of International Law

   A.   Types of International Law Systems
      1.   Common law systems
         a.   England
         b.   United States
      2.   Civil or code law
         a.   Statutes or codes are very detailed; little reliance on precedent
         b.   France, Germany, Spain
      3.   Islamic law
         a.   Religious tenets integrated
         b.   Combination of Islamic law and colonizers' laws
      4.   Communism (prior to collapse)
         a.   Non-precedential
         b.   Non-religious

   B.   Nonstatutory Sources of International Law
      1.   LESCANT factors
      2.   Language - some areas require certain language
      3.   Environment and technology
         a.   How good are phone wires?
         b.   Means of communication
         c.   Reliability of communication
      4.   Social organization
         a.   Woman working on deals
         b.   Customs and habits
      5.   Contexting
         a.   Low-context cultures (words matter, not context) - U.S., Canada, Switzerland, Germany, Scandanavian countries
         b.   Mid-level cultures - France, England, Italy
         c.   High-context cultures - Latin America, Islamic nations, Asian countries
      6.   Authority: role of lawyers and negotiators
      7.   Nonverbal behavior
         a.   Silence and its role
         b.   Gestures
      8.   Time concept
         a.   Monochronic nations: time is everything (U.S., Great Britain)
         b.   Polychronic - rest of the world

   C.   Contracts for the International Sale of Goods (CISG)
      1.   1980 Vienna Convention is another name
      2.   Adopted by 60 countries
      3.   Designed to provide an international UCC and its convenience
      4.   Voluntary use by parties to a contract, even in adopting countries

D. Treaties, Trade Organizations, and Controls on International Trade
1. Unilateral
2. Bilateral
3. Multilateral
4. The WTO and GATT
    a. 150 member nations
    b. Trying to work through this approved concept of free trade
    c. Establishes World Trade Organization (WTO)
        (1) has Dispute Settlement Body (DSB) - arbitration
        (2) most-favored nation (MFN) status gets more favorable trade treatment
        (3) can impose fines
5. EU treaty - specifics are pending for free trade
    a. 15 member group and correspondent members
    b. One currency in 1999 (Euro)/Single European Act
    c. Created by the Maastricht Treaty
    d. Aiming toward uniformity in law
    e. Established European Parliament and European Court of Justice (ECJ)
    f. 300 directives in place for governance
6. NAFTA
    a. Has approval
    b. Implemented over 15-year period
    c. Canada, U.S., and Mexico: seamless trade
7. Prohibitions on trade
    a. International tensions politically spill over into trade, e.g., U.S. and Iraq
    b. Primary trade sanctions: can't do business with countries
        (1) can be limited in scope; e.g., during war
        (2) can be limited to items; e.g., all but food and medications
    c. MFN, or "most favored nation", has no trade restrictions
    d. Secondary boycott
        (1) original country is boycotted
        (2) U.S. will not do business with any company that works with government of that nation; e.g., military contractors can't use U.S. banks or get federal contracts
        (3) generally not retroactive
        (4) applies prospectively to new business
8. IMF - International Monetary Fund and World Bank
    a. Currency stability - created at Bretton Woods with this goal
    b. Special drawing rights - using line of credit to stabilize a country's currency
    c. Issues of buying currency
9. Kyoto Treaty
    a. The Kyoto Protocol or global-warming treaty
    b. Designated to reduce the greenhouse gas effect
    c. All countries must reduce emissions to 5% below 1990 levels
    d. U.S. is required to do 7% reduction
    e. Excluded from reductions: China, India and Mexico
    f. EU - agreed to 8% reduction jointly
        Note: Treaty is basically dead; U.S. will not approve; other countries have doubts
10. OPEC
    a. Organization of Petroleum Exporting Countries
    b. Cartel that controls supplies, production, prices and taxes

  E. Trust, Corruption, Trade, and Economics
    1. Focus in Last Five Years on Reducing Bribes and Corruption
    2. Foreign Corrupt Practices Act (FCPA)
      a. Applies to businesses with principal offices in the United States
      b. Requires establishment of internal accounting controls so that bribes are not permitted to flow through easily
      c. Prohibits making, authorizing, or promising a gift to a foreign official with the intent to corrupt; has five elements:
        (1) instrumentality of interstate commerce must have been used
          Example: Phones or mail
        (2) payment or something of value must have been given
        (3) money or item of value is given to foreign official with discretionary authority - a political candidate or political party
        (4) purpose of the payment was to get official to act or to keep from acting
        (5) payment was made with the idea of assisting the giver's business
      d. "Grease payments," or facilitation payments, are payments to get officials to do their jobs, not to influence outcome, and are not prohibited
      e. Criminal violations of FCPA carry penalties of up to $25,000 and five years imprisonment for individuals; corporate fines are up to $2,000,000 per violation
      f. Civil fines under Alternatives Fines Act (not FCPA) are tied to benefits received
      g. International business and the FCPA
        (1) sometimes use grease payments
        (2) U.S. trade has actually increased
        (3) carefully train and remind employees
        (4) amended in December 1998 to bring U.S. laws in compliance with OECD's antibribery provisions
        (5) applies to all U.S. citizens acting outside U.S. and all non-citizens acting within U.S.
        (6) expanded to include IMF and Olympic Committee
        (7) U.S. basically met standards before
        (8) OECD continuing to expand its efforts

II. Resolution of International Disputes

III. Principles of International Law

  A. Sovereign Immunity
    1. Each nation is sovereign
    2. Other nations do not take jurisdiction over a country's internal operations, laws, and people
    3. Does not apply to contractual relations

  B. Expropriation: Act of State Doctrine
    1. Country seizes private property by order of attachment
    2. Leaves these decisions to executive and legislative branches and keeps them away from judiciary

  C. Protections for U.S. Property and Investment Abroad
    1. Hickenlooper Amendment to Foreign Assistance Act of 1962
    2. Allows president to sanction countries that take property of U.S. companies
    3. Treaties afford protections
    4. OPIC is federal agency that provides insurance for U.S. businesses against expropriation (in poor countries)

D. Repatriation
    1. Limits on removal of profits from country where they are earned
    2. Considered acts of state; cannot be litigated
    3. Check limits before deciding to do business

E. *Forum Non Conveniens*, or "You Have the Wrong Court"
    1. Dismiss cases brought in wrong court
    2. Example: Union Carbide and Bhopal, India; proper forum was India

F. Conflicts of Law
    1. No two countries have the exact same commercial laws
    2. Some countries have no commercial codes
    3. Uniform Commercial Code is widely used
    4. Party autonomy controls
    5. If parties have not agreed, law of country where the contract is performed will apply

IV. Protections in International Competition

A. Antitrust Laws in the International Marketplace
    1. All firms doing business here subject to antitrust jurisdiction
    2. All U.S. firms are also subject to EU antitrust laws, which have tended to be more stringent than U.S. antitrust laws currently
    3. Export Trading Company Act
        a. Allows joint ventures among competitors
        b. For business in other countries
    4. Tariffs

B. Protections for Intellectual Property

C. Criminal Law Protections
    1. All those present in a country are subject to that country's criminal law
    2. Subject to all regulations as well

KEY TERMS

Act of State Doctrine
Authority
Civil Law
Code Law
Common Law
Contract for the International Sale of Goods (CISG)
Dispute Settlement Body (DSB)
European Commission
European Court of Justice (ECJ)
European Economic Community (EEC)
European Union (EU)

Export Trading Company Act
Expropriation
Foreign Assistance Act
Foreign Corrupt Practices Act (FCPA)
Foreign Sovereign Immunities Act
Forum Non Conveniens
General Agreement on Tariffs and Trade (GATT)
Global-Warming Treaty
Grease Payments
Hickenlooper Amendment
International Monetary Fund

(IMF)
Iran and Libya Sanctions Act
Islamic Law
Kyoto Protocol
Kyoto Treaty
LESCANT Factors
Maastricht Treaty
Most Favored Nation (MFN)
Multilateral Treaty
Nongovernmental Organization (NGO)
North American Free Trade Agreement (NAFTA)

North Atlantic Treaty
Organization (NATO)
Organization for Economic
Cooperation and
Development (OECD)
Organization of Petroleum
Exporting Countries
(OPEC)

Overseas P`rivate Investment
Corporation (OPIC)
Primary Trade Sanctions
Repatriation
Secondary Boycott
Single European Act
Sovereign Immunities Act
Sovereign Immunity

Special Drawing Rights
(SDR)
Tariffs
World Bank
World Trade Organization
(WTO)

MATCHING

a. Repatriation
b. Overseas Private Investment Corporation (OPIC)
c. Dispute Settlement Body
d. Act of State Doctrine
e. Grease Payments
f. OPEC

g. *Forum Non Conveniens*
h. General Agreement on Tariffs and Trade
i. International Monetary Fund
j. Sovereign Immunity
k. Kyoto Treaty
l. Single European Act

_____ 1. International arbitration body created to resolve trade disputes between countries.

_____ 2. Dismissing cases that are brought to the wrong court.

_____ 3. Payments made to any foreign official for "facilitation."

_____ 4. Bringing back to your own country profits earned on investments in another country.

_____ 5. The concept that each country is an equal with other countries, with exclusive jurisdiction over its operations, laws, and people and that no country is subject to the jurisdiction of another country.

_____ 6. Cartel that works together to control oil supplies and production, prices, and taxes.

_____ 7. A federal insurer for U.S. investments abroad in countries where per capita income is $250 or less.

_____ 8. Primary objectives are trade without discrimination and protection through tariffs.

_____ 9. Created the World Bank.

_____ 10. Protects the government of a country from having its actions reviewed by courts in another country.

_____ 11. Eliminated internal barriers to trade as passed by the EU.

_____ 12. Focuses on reduction of greenhouse gas emissions.

FILL-IN-THE-BLANKS

1. The _____ is charged with administering and achieving the General Agreement on Tariffs and Trade's objectives.

2. The _____ eliminated nearly all of the tariffs on U.S. industrial and agricultural exports to Mexico and Canada.

3. The _____ is a court of voluntary jurisdiction for disputes between nations that was established by the United Nations.

4. The purpose of _____ is to assure monetary stability in countries, thereby enhancing and encouraging international trade.

5. The U.S. and England have a _____ system where our laws are built on tradition and precedent; France and Germany have a _____ or _____ system where they rely on statutes or codes that cover all types of circumstances and there is little need for interpretation; and some other countries have a _____ system where their laws are based on religion and governs all aspects of life.

6. The _____ allows joint ventures among competitors for business in other countries.

7. The _____ Act is meant to curb the use of bribery in foreign operations of companies.

8. The United Nations developed the _____ in order to create more uniformity in international contract formation and performance.

9. The judicial body created to handle disputes and violations of regulations of the EU treaty is called the _____.

10. The _____ allows nations to have _____ or the ability to draw on a line of credit in order to maintain their currency's stability.

11. A country with _____ status has no restrictions on the types of goods and services they can import or export.

12. Taxes on goods as they move in and out of countries are referred to as _____.

SHORT ANSWER

1. Explain the two types of trade sanctions countries can impose.

    a. _____

    b. _____

2. What are the rules on conflicts of law in international transactions?

    a. _____

    b. _____

3. Name the seven LESCANT factors that should be researched before companies attempt negotiations or business in another country.

    a. _____

    b. _____

    c. _____

    d. _____

    e. _____

    f. _____

    g. _____

4. Explain repatriation. _____

    _____

    _____

5. What is the doctrine of sovereign immunity?

    _____

    _____

    _____

    _____

6. Name the ten requirements imposed by the OECD under its Convention on Combating Bribery of Foreign   Public Officials in International Business Transactions.

a. _____

b. _____

c. _____

d. _____

e. _____

f. _____

g. _____

h. _____

i. _____

j. _____

Chapter 8

BUSINESS CRIME

CHAPTER OUTLINE

I. What Is Business Crime? The Crimes Within A Corporation

    A. Cooking the Books

    B. Embezzlement

    C. Computer Hackers

    D. Pilferage and Shrinkage

    E. White-Collar Crimes

II. What Is Business Crime? The Crimes Against A Corporation

    A. Stealing From Competitors

    B. Acting Illegally to Gain a Competitive Advantage - Antitrust

    C. Electronic Eavesdropping

    D. Federal Violations - Securities, Campaign Laws, Antitrust

III. Who is Liable for Business Crime?

    A. Corporation Is Liable

    B. Officers and Directors Are Liable If:
        1. They authorized the conduct
        2. They knew about the conduct and did nothing
        3. White-Collar Kingpin Act - federal law imposes minimum federal mandatory sentences on corporate officers

    C. Federal Laws Targeting Officers and Directors
        1. 1990 – White-Collar "King Pin" laws (S & L crisis)
        2. 2002 – White-Collar Criminal Penalty Enhancement Act of 2002 or Sarbanes-Oxley
            a. Increases penalties
            b. Creates new crimes for certification of false financial statements
            c. Increased penalties for obstruction, mail, and wire fraud
            d. Scrushy first CEO tried, but not convicted

IV.   The Penalties for Business Crime
    A.   Given for Each Crime

    B.   Reforming Criminal Penalties
        1.   Concern is that they are directed at "natural" persons and not "artificial☐ corporate persons
            Examples: Fines are small; imprisonment
        2.   Placing penalties as a percentage of company profits is an alternative
        3.   Prison sentences for officers and directors
        4.   Indictment for criminal offenses (common law type)
            Examples: Murder for product liability death, conversion or theft for fraud
        5.   Federal commission on sentencing put through the Corporate Sentencing Guidelines, which include fines that are a percentage of profit, and are used by all federal courts in determining sentences
        6.   Increased fines for corporations to make them feel the pinch of money
        7.   Use traditional criminal statutes; e.g., trying companies with product liability deaths for murder
        8.   Increased use of shame punishment: public disclosure of wrongdoing

    C.   Corporate Sentencing Guidelines: An Ounce of Prevention Means a Reduced Sentence
        1.   Developed by U.S. Sentencing Commission
        2.   Sentences for officers increase if the following crime prevention methods are not in place at the corporation
            a.   Written crime prevention program
            b.   Officer-level employees assigned responsibility for enforcement
            c.   Screen employees
            d.   Training programs and written materials
            e.   Prevention and detection of crime processes
        3.   Formula of corporate sentencing guidelines
            a.   Uses a culpability multiplier
            b.   Begin with a score of "5" and add or subtract based on factors such as
               (1)   code of conduct
               (2)   ombudsmen
               (3)   hot line
               (4)   mandatory training
        4.   Guidelines reformed by Sarbanes-Oxley mandate
        5.   Corporate boards could be held liable if the board fails to institute and monitor internal controls

V.   Elements of Business Crimes

    A.   Criminal Intent - Scienter or *Mens Rea*
        1.   State of mind required to commit a crime
        2.   For corporations - prove intention on behalf of directors
            a.   Must also show individual intent to prosecute them
            b.   Can establish by showing their knowledge of actions and failure to object

    B.   *Actus Reus* - The Act of the Crime
        1.   Intent alone is not a crime - the act must be committed
            Example: The desire to trade on inside information is not a crime until you actually trade on it
        2.   Each crime has the required conduct described

VI. Examples of Business Crimes

    A. Theft and Embezzlement
       1. Intent to take property
       2. Actual taking of property for permanent use
       3. No authorization to take the property

    B. Obstruction of Justice
       1. Intent to impede, obstruct, or influence investigation or administration of justice
       2. Auditors must retain work papers for five years
       3. Felony – 10 years
       4. Frank Quattrone and Andersen convicted

    C. Computer Crime
       1. Categories of computer crime
           a. Unauthorized use of computers or computer-related equipment
           b. Alteration or destruction of computers, files, programs, or data
           c. Entering fraudulent records or data
           d. Use of computers to convert ownership of funds, financial instruments, property, services, or data
       2. Computer crimes that involve the computer as a victim
           a. Theft of hardware (crime of theft)
           b. Theft of software (larceny, infringement or specialized statutes)
           c. Intentional damage
               (1) physical destruction
               (2) intentionally planting a bug or virus
               (3) often covered by state statutes on viruses or bugs
       3. Computer crimes that involve unauthorized use
           a. Obtaining data
           b. Destroying files
           c. No physical or program destruction
       4. Computer crimes that involve raiding
           a. Print-outs
           b. Scavenging
           c. Computer trespass
       5. Computer crimes that divert delivery
           a. Shipping goods elsewhere
           b. Update on old crime of taking shipping orders and changing them
           c. Can also involve transferring money (embezzlement)
       6. Using computers to commit economic espionage
           a. Covered by Economic Espionage Act (EEA)
           b. Employees take files from old employer to new employer
           c. Felony to copy, duplicate, sketch, download, communicate such information
           d. $500,000 and up to 15 years
       7. Using computers to commit EFT crimes
           a. Covered by Electronic Fund Transfer Act (EFTA)
           b. Covers counterfeit, stolen or fraudulently obtained credit or ATM card
           c. Crime to ship such cards

8.   Using computers to circumvent copyright protection devices
   a.   Digital Millennium Copyright Act (DMCA)
   b.   Can't circumvent to copy songs, movies
   c.   Russian programmer prosecuted with plea deal for his assistance
9.   Using computers for spamming
   a.   CAN-SPAM – Controlling the Assault of Non-Solicited Pornography and Marketing
   b.   FTC has "Do-Not-Call" list, but spam list is in progress
   c.   Industry groups are working on it – Anti-Spam Technical Alliance Register of Known Spam Operations (ROKSO)
10.   International conventions on computer crime
   a.   Berne and Paris conventions allow copyright protections for computer programs and software
   b.   Fifty-nine countries are members of one or more of the conventions
11.   Federal statutes covering computer crimes
   a.   Copyright Act provides protections for computer programs
   b.   Fair Credit Reporting Act
      (1)   limits access to individuals' financial and credit histories
      (2)   no unauthorized access or use
   c.   Counterfeit Access Device and Computer Fraud and Abuse Act (CADCFA)
      (1)   applies only to computers and not typewriters or hand-held computers
      (2)   makes it a crime to use or access federal computers without authorization
      (3)   covers military and foreign policy information - 10-year penalty; 20-year penalty for repeat offenses
      (4)   covers financial records - banks, savings and loan; includes consumer credit records as well as institutional records
      (5)   covers all federal computers; applies to uses without authorization
            Example: *U.S. v. Sawyer* - use by federal employee in excess of job was a violation
   d.   Federal Computer Fraud and Abuse Act
      (1)   unauthorized access to a government computer is a felony
      (2)   trespass into a government computer is a misdemeanor
      (3)   intentional damage to a government computer is also a felony
   e.   No Electronic Theft Act
      (1)   criminal offense to willfully infringe copyrighted material worth over $1,000 using the Internet
      (2)   need not be a transaction for profit
   f.   Economic Espionage Act (EEA) (see earlier)
      (1)   criminal offense to steal trade secrets using downloading, access, etc.
      (2)   passed as a result of the Volkswagen case in which a former GM executive took GM's European supply chain management system to his new job at Volkswagen

D.   Criminal Fraud
   1.   Obtaining money, goods, services, or property through false statements and misleading the other party
   2.   Requires intent to defraud

E.   Commercial Bribery
   1.   Prohibited in most states
   2.   Incentives for those who report corrupt purchasing agents

F. Racketeer Influenced and Corrupt Organization Act (RICO)
1. Complex statute designed to curb organized crime activity
2. Elements
   a. Acquiring an interest in any enterprise with income derived from racketeering
   b. Conducting affairs of company involved in racketeering activity
   c. Conspiring to do any of the above
3. Pattern of racketeering activity
   a. Commission of two racketeering acts in a ten-year period
   b. Racketeering acts include: Murder, kidnapping, gambling, arson, robbery, bribery, extortion, dealing in pornography or narcotics, counterfeiting, pension, union, or welfare funds embezzlement, mail or wire fraud, obstruction of justice or criminal investigation, securities fraud, white slavery, transportation of stolen goods, violations of Currency Reporting Act
4. Carries civil and criminal penalties with civil recovery including treble damages
5. Most RICO suits are based on fraud
6. Prosecutors can freeze a business's assets under a RICO charge
7. Many states have their own RICO statutes
8. Ongoing proposals in Congress for reform of RICO; although definition of racketeering may change, the treble damages rights will remain

G. Business Crimes and the USA Patriot Act
1. Money Laundering Control Act was predecessor
2. Expands controls on money laundering from banks to escrow companies, brokerage firm, travel agents, etc.
3. "Know they customer"
4. Requires reports on $10,000 cash and above transactions
5. Another provision makes it a federal crime for individuals or companies to pay funds to terrorist groups; goal is to prevent funds from flowing into terrorist activities

H. Federal Crimes
1. Violations of federal securities statutes
2. Violations of the Sherman Act
3. Violations of the Internal Revenue Act
4. Violations of the Pure Food and Drug Act
5. Violations of OSHA
6. Violations of Consumer Product Safety laws

I. State Crimes
1. Cover criminal fraud
2. Bribes and kickbacks prohibited

VII. Procedural Rights for Business Criminals

A. Fourth Amendment Rights for Businesses
1. Privacy amendment
2. Search warrant procedures controlled by Fourth Amendment
   a. Must be based on probable cause; i.e., good reason to believe that instruments or evidence of a crime are present at the business location sought to be searched
   b. Must be issued by a disinterested magistrate
   c. If searches done improperly, evidence is inadmissible at trial

3. Warrants and ISPs
    a. ISPs can be subpoenaed to reveal identity of account holder
    b. Some ISPs have disclosure forms
4. Warrants and exceptions
    a. Records are being destroyed - burning warehouse exception
    b. "Plain view" exception - can seize items because privacy was not protected □ allowed the world access to the items
5. Records in possession of a third party
    a. Can recover them
    b. Third party cannot assert Fourth Amendment rights - must be record owners

B. Fifth Amendment Rights for Businesses
1. Protection against self-incrimination – "taking the Fifth"
2. Given to natural persons - not to corporations
3. Corporate officers can assert it to protect themselves but not corporate records
4. *Miranda* warnings
    a. Given when individual is in "custody"
    b. "Custody" means inability to leave - not necessarily jail
    c. Right to attorney; right to silence - notice of evidentiary use of statements
5. Due process protections of Fifth Amendment
    a. Warrant or warrantless arrest begins process: Warrant - you have committed crime and they look for you; warrantless - you are arrested at the scene
    b. Initial appearance
        (1) required within short period (twenty-four hours)
        (2) charges explained
        (3) bail terms set; amount; or released on own recognizance
    c. Preliminary hearing or grand jury
        (1) hearing - information issued; defendant is present and can cross examine
        (2) grand jury - indictment; secret proceedings
    d. Arraignment
        (1) plea is entered
        (2) trial date is set
    e. Discovery - mandatory disclosure of witnesses and evidence
    f. Pretrial conference - try to settle some issues if possible
    g. Omnibus hearing - challenge evidence admissibility
    h. Trial

KEY TERMS

Actus Reus
Arraignment
Arrest
Bank Secrecy Act
Clean Air Act
Clean Water Act
Computer Crime
Computer Fraud and Abuse Act (CFAA)
Conscious Avoidance

Consumer Product Safety Act
Controlling the Assault of Non-Solicited Pornography and Marketing Act (CAN-SPAM)
Corporate Sentencing Guidelines
Counterfeit Access Device and Computer Fraud and

Abuse Act (CADCFA)
Crime
Criminal Fraud
Culpability Multiplier

Digital Millennium Copyright Act (DMCA)
Discovery
Due Process

Economic Espionage Act
   (EEA)
Electronic Fund Transfers
   Act (EFTA)
Elements
Embezzlement
Fifth Amendment
Fourth Amendment
Grand Jury
Indictment
Information
Initial Appearance
Internal Revenue Code
Mens Rea
Miranda Warnings
Money Laundering Control
   Act

1933 Securities Act
No Electronic Theft Act
Nolo Contendere
Obstruction of Justice

Occupational Health Safety
   Act
Omnibus Hearing
Plea Bargain
Preliminary Hearing
Racketeer Influenced and
   Corrupt Organization Act
   (RICO)
Sarbanes-Oxley (SOX)
Scienter
Search Warrant
Securities and Exchange Act

Self-incrimination

Shame Punishment
Sherman Act
Sixth Amendment
Spamming
Theft
Trial
USA Patriot Act
U.S. Sentencing Commission
Warrant
White-Collar Crime
White-Collar Criminal
   Penalty Enhancement
   Act of 2002

MATCHING

a. EFTA
b. Initial Appearance
c. White-Collar Crime
d. Criminal Fraud
e. Shame Punishment
f. CAN-SPAM

g. Discovery
h. Arraignment
i. Digital Millennium Copyright Act
j. RICO
k. Computer Fraud and Abuse Act
l. Sarbanes-Oxley

_____ 1. Required public disclosure of an offense.

_____ 2. Proceeding where the defendant enters a plea.

_____ 3. An appearance before a judge to be informed of defendant's charges, rights, and so on.

_____ 4. Ordered the FTC to create a national do-not-e-mail list for e-mail marketers.

_____ 5. Makes it a crime to use any counterfeit, stolen, or fraudulently obtained card, code or other device to obtain money or goods.

_____ 6. Makes it a felony to cause more than $1000 damage to a computer with a virus program.

_____ 7. A federal statute designed to curb organized crime activity, which is frequently used even in cases where organized crime is not actually involved.

_____ 8. Intentionally lying to another about an issue material to a sales transaction in order to induce the other to enter into a contract for sale.

_____ 9. Period in which each side turns over certain types of information to the other side.

_____ 10. Prohibits destruction of documents when civil or criminal investigations are pending.

_____ 11. Crimes committed for/against a business.

_____ 12. Prohibits tampering with encryption devices that companies use to prevent unauthorized copying.

FILL-IN-THE-BLANKS

1. The _____ Amendment is the basis for requiring warrants to search private property in order to protect individual's privacy.

2. In criminal law, there are two distinct proceedings to determine whether there is sufficient evidence to prosecute a defendant, a(n) _____, which is conducted in secret and a(n) _____, which is a public proceeding. If sufficient evidence to warrant a prosecution is found, a(n) _____ or a(n) _____ will be issued against the defendant, depending on which type of proceeding occurred.

3. The _____ doctrine, designed to protect rights guaranteed by the _____ Amendment to the Constitution, requires that an individual must be told of certain rights once he/she has been subjected to custodial interrogation. This same amendment also contains the _____ Clause, which guarantees certain procedural protections as the case is investigated, charged, and tried.

4. Penalties for mail and wire fraud increased from a maximum of five years to twenty years in prison under the _____ Act.

5. To determine the extent of a sentence for a company (as well as officers, managers and employees) involved in illegal activities, the federal sentencing guidelines provide a score to the company called a _____.

6. The _____ is where all of the challenges are presented to the judge for ruling on the admissibility of evidence.

7. The term scienter, or _____, refers to the intentional element of a crime while _____ refers to the criminal act itself.

8. The _____ Act makes it a criminal offense to steal trade secrets from an employer.

9. The _____ Act prohibits access to U.S. military information without authorization.

10. According to the _____, it is a criminal offense to infringe copyrighted material worth over $1,000 using the Internet.

11. Bribery, arson, counterfeiting, extortion and kidnapping are all examples of _____ acts.

12. The _____ requires financial institutions to disclose and report transactions involving cash transactions of more than $10,000.

SHORT ANSWER

1.   What are the elements necessary for a theft?

    a. _____

    b. _____

    c. _____

2.   List the steps in a criminal proceeding from the time of arrest.

    a. _____

    b. _____

    c. _____

    d. _____

    e. _____

    f. _____

    g. _____

3.   What are the exceptions to the warrant requirements of the Fourth Amendment?

    a. _____

    b. _____

4.   List four of the ten factors that will help reduce the sentence of a corporation under the U.S. Sentencing Commission.

    a. _____

    b. _____

    c. _____

    d. _____

5. Who in a corporation is liable for crimes committed in the course of the corporation's business?

_____

_____

6. Explain the new obstruction section under the Sarbanes-Oxley Act.

_____

_____

_____

Chapter 9

BUSINESS TORTS

CHAPTER OUTLINE

I.   What Is a Tort?

    A.   Latin Word *Tortus*; Means "Crooked, Dubious, Twisted"

    B.   Civil Wrong That Is an Interference with Someone's Person or Property Such That Injury Results

    C.   Tort Versus Crime
        1.   Tort is a private wrong
            a.   Injured party seeks remedy
            b.   Recovers damages from the one who commits the tort
        2.   Crime is a public wrong
            a.   Wrongdoer is prosecuted
            b.   Pays fine to government or is jailed to pay debt to society

    D.   Types of Torts
        1.   Intentional torts
            a.   Done by parties committing intentional acts
            b.   More than an accidental wrong
               Example: Striking someone with your fist when you intend to is an intentional tort; striking someone with your first in exercise class when you are working your arms is not
        2.   Tort of negligence
            a.   Accidental harms that result from the failure to think through the consequences
            b.   Still have liability but there are defenses
               Example: Running a red light is not an act undertaken with the intent of hurting someone but if someone is injured you are negligent for your failure to think things through
        3.   Strict tort liability
            a.   Absolute standard of liability
            b.   Used in product liability cases
         4.   Property torts
            a.   Cause injury to someone's property
            b.   Trespassing
         5.   Personal torts
            a.   Cause injury to your person
            b.   Defamation, battery
         6.   Negligence can cause personal and property damage

II. The Intentional Torts

    A.   Defamation
        1.   Slander is oral or spoken defamation
        2.   Libel is written and, in some states, broadcast defamation

3. Elements
   a. Statement about a business' or person's reputation or honesty that is untrue
   b. Statement is directed at business and made with malice and intent to injure
   c. Publication - someone heard and understood the statement
   d. Damages - economic losses such as damage to reputation
4. Malice required to be established for media
5. Defenses to defamation
   a. Truth is a complete defense
   b. Opinion and analysis: the courts give commentators leeway in their analysis of situations and use of various derogatory terms
   c. Privileged speech
      (1) absolute privilege in Congress and judicial proceedings
      (2) qualified privilege for media – so long as information is not published with malice or reckless disregard for whether it is true or false, it enjoys this privilege
      (3) opinion vs. fact/analysis vs. reporting

B. Contract Interference
   1. Valid contract
   2. Third party interfered by making performance difficult
   3. Third party knew of contract
   4. Third party intended to interfere
   5. Plaintiff is injured

C. False Imprisonment
   1. Shopkeeper's tort
   2. Custody of someone else for any period of time against their will
   3. Need not establish physical damages; just the fact that they are detained establishes sufficient damages
   4. Defense of shopkeeper's privilege
      a. Can detain for reasonable time
      b. Must have basis for detaining the individual
   5. Forty-three states allow civil fines for shoplifting

D. Intentional Infliction of Emotional Distress
   1. Liability for conduct that exceeds all bounds of decency
   2. Difficult for plaintiff to establish emotional distress
   3. Has been used by debtors against collectors

E. Invasion of Privacy
   1. Intrusion into plaintiff's private affairs
   2. Public disclosure of private facts
   3. Appropriation of another's name, likeness, or image for commercial advantage

F. Statutory Privacy Issue: Health Insurance Portability and Accountability Act of 1996 (HIPAA)
   1. Federal law that imposes requirements on medical care facilities and providers who transfer/store medical records electronically
   2. Criminal penalties up to $250,000/10 years
   3. Requires patient permission to discuss records, case, send records, etc.
   4. Restrictions on postcards, calls, and discussions
   5. Complaint system for patients

III. Competition Torts

    A. Appropriation

    B. Unauthorized Use of Someone's Name, Voice, Image, or Likeness for Commercial Advantage

    C. Even If Manner of Use Is Accurate, it Is a Tort Because of the Use Without Authorization

IV. Negligence

    A. Element One: The Duty
       1. All persons are expected to behave as ordinary and reasonably prudent persons do
       2. Standard of the law is not always used
          Example: The speed limit of 35 is not appropriate in ice and snow
       3. References and defamation
          a. Managers must use caution when speaking of former or current employees to potential new employers; the tort of defamation can be established if false statements are made
          b. Most employers have adopted a policy of only confirming that the employee worked at their company and the dates of employment
          c. States now have qualified privileges for reference letters and defamation

    B. Element Two: Breach of Duty
       1. Failure to comply with established standard of conduct
       2. Often connected with element one as courts struggle to determine whether a duty even exists

    C. Element Three: Causation
       1. Breach of duty caused the plaintiff's injuries
       2. "But/for" causation test
       3. Restricted by the zone of danger rule

    D. Element Four: Proximate Cause

    E. Element Five: Damages
       1. Medical bills
       2. Lost wages
       3. Pain and suffering
       4. Loss of consortium (as between spouses)

    F. Defenses to Negligence
       1. Contributory negligence - plaintiff is also negligent
          Example: You cause an accident that could have been avoided had you not been drinking
       2. Comparative negligence
          a. Compare acts of plaintiff and defendant and assess blame for accident
          b. Reduces plaintiff's recovery by amount of fault
       3. Some states have been passing legislation to limit jury verdicts, and there have been court challenges
       4   Assumption of risk - plaintiff knew of risk and went forward anyway
          Example: Assume risks inherent in skydiving, skiing, roller skating, etc.

V. Tort Reform
    A. State Movement to Limit Verdicts

    B. Proposed Reforms on Recovery Only to Deter Future Wrong Behavior, Not Pure Accidents

    C. Judicial Activism on Reductions

    D. New Verdicts on Tort Reform

VI. Strict Liability

    A. Absolute Liability

    B. A Theory for Recovery When Product is Defective

    C. Public Policy is to Encourage Safety

KEY TERMS

Absolute Privilege
Appropriation
Assumption of Risk
Breach of Duty
But For Test
Causation
Comparative Negligence
Contract Interference
Contributory Negligence
Damages
Defamation
Duty
False Imprisonment

Health Insurance Portability
    and Accountability Act
    (HIPAA)
Intentional Infliction of
    Emotional Distress
Intentional Torts
Interference
Invasion of Privacy
Libel
Malice
Negligence
Ordinary and Reasonably
    Prudent Person
Privilege

Product Disparagement
Proximate Cause
Publication
Qualified Privilege
Shopkeeper's Privilege
Slander
Strict Liability
Strict Tort Liability
Tort
Tortious Interference with
    Contracts
Tort Reform
Unauthorized Appropriation

MATCHING

a. Product Disparagement
b. Defamation
c. Negligence
d. Qualified Privilege
e. Invasion of Privacy
f. Assumption of Risk

g. Intentional Tort
h. Contract Interference
i. Unauthorized Appropriation
j. Tort
k. Shopkeeper's Privilege
l. Causation

_____ 1. Interference with a person or property that results in injury to a person or their property.

_____ 2. The media's freedom to print inaccurate or untrue information without being liable for defamation, so long as they do not print the information maliciously or with reckless disregard for the truth.

_____ 3. Untrue statement by one party to another about a third party.

_____ 4. Careless acts done without thinking about the consequences.

_____ 5. Defense to false imprisonment shopkeepers can use while they investigate a shoplifting incident.

_____ 6. Occurs when parties are not allowed the freedom to contract without interference from third parties.

_____ 7. Using someone's name, likeness, or voice for advantage without his/her permission.

_____ 8. Tort actually composed of three different torts: (1) intrusion into the plaintiff's private affairs, (2) the public disclosure of private facts, and (3) the appropriation of another's name for commercial advantage.

_____ 9. A defense in a negligence action, in which a defendant shows that a plaintiff voluntarily undertook a risk of harm.

_____ 10. An element of the tort of negligence, normally using the "but for" test.

_____ 11. Involves deliberate actions.

_____ 12. Defamation of a product.

FILL-IN-THE-BLANKS

1. Unlike a crime, a _____ gives a party injured by wrongful conduct the right to collect damages to compensate for their injuries.

2. _____ is oral or spoken defamation; _____ is written or broadcast defamation.

3. To successfully recover in a defamation action, a plaintiff must show that the untrue statements were _____, or communicated to a third party.

4. Everyone has a duty to act like an _____, which is not always what everyone else does or what the law provides.

5. When there is a strong public interest in protecting the speech regardless of whether it is true, the speakers can enjoy an _____ when they are speaking.

6. The tort of _____ requires showing that defendant knew that a contract existed and intended to prevent its performance or to make performance difficult.

7. The detention of a person for any length of time against their will, with or without physical harm, is called _____.

8. The tort of _____ is used quite frequently by people harassed by creditors and/or collection agencies who are attempting to collect funds.

9. Negligence by the plaintiff that is part of the cause of an accident gives the defendant the opportunity to use the defense of _____.

10. _____ is a negligence defense that assigns liability and damages on a percentage basis based on the contribution to the cause of the accident.

11. A company still has _____ regardless of precautions taken to prevent harm when using risky substances such as dynamite.

12. _____ requires doctors to get patient's permission before releasing any of their medical information to a third party.

SHORT ANSWER

1. What are the elements for defamation?

    a. _____

    b. _____

    c. _____

    d. _____

    e. _____

2. Name the defenses to defamation.

    a. _____

    b. _____

    c. _____

3. List the elements of negligence.

    a. _____

    b. _____

    c. _____

    d. _____

    e. _____

4. List the defenses to negligence.

a. _____

b. _____

c. _____

5. Explain what is meant by the shopkeeper's tort. What are defenses to it?

_____

_____

_____

6. Explain the difference between a tort and a crime.

_____

_____

_____

Chapter 10

PRODUCT ADVERTISING AND LIABILITY

CHAPTER OUTLINE

I. Development of Product Liability

    A. Initially Courts Followed a Theory of *Caveat Emptor* (Let the Buyer Beware) - No Liability for the Seller

    B. *Henningsen v. Bloomfield Motors - Caveat Emptor* Removed

II. Advertising as a Contract Basis for Product Liability

    A. UCC Article II (Sales) Governs

    B. Express Warranties (2-313)
        1. Description of goods and abilities
        2. Promise of performance
        3. Seller need not intend to create warranty or use the terms "promise," "warrant," or "guarantee"
            Example: Preshrunk fabric – will not shrink; 50/50 poly-cotton; nontoxic

    C. Federal Regulation of Warranties and Advertising
        1. Federal Trade Commission given broad authority
        2. Federal Trade Commission Act authorizes FTC as enforcement agency
            a. Passed in 1914
            b. Requires regulation of "unfair and deceptive trade practices"
        3. Broadened by Wheeler-Lea Act of 1938
            a. "Is public deceived?" standard
            b. Not limited to adverse impact on competition
        4. FTC Improvements Act of 1980 - put some restrictions on FTC regulation
        5. Federal regulations of Internet advertising
            a. Ad-blocking software is evolving
            b. Property rights and speed
        6. Types of FTC Regulation
            a. Content control and accuracy: "no aspirin," "aspirin free," all dairy products, and so on (like express warranties)
            b. Performance claims
                (1) like express warranties too - promise of performance
                (2) FTC has required corrective advertising when unsubstantiated claims have been made
            c. Celebrity endorsements
                (1) celebrity must have used the product
                (2) if celebrity has not used the product, source of claims must be given
            d. Bait and switch - prohibits advertising of cheaper product and then getting customers to buy the more expensive product

   e. Product comparisons
    (1) FTC took a laissez-faire approach during the 1980s
    (2) encouraged comparisons
    (3) Congress amended trademark law in 1989 to allow competitors to bring suit for deceptive statements about products in competitor's ads
   f. FTC remedies
    (1) consent decree
    (2) elimination of ads
    (3) damages
   g. Ad regulation by FDA - as more prescription meds are advertised directly, FDA is regulating more
   h. State regulation of advertising
    (1) professional ads (lawyers, accountants)
    (2) similar to FTC, generally through state attorneys general

III. Contract Product Liability Theories: Implied Warranties

 A. The Implied Warranty of Merchantability
  1. Given in every sale of goods by a merchant
  2. Goods are fit for ordinary purposes
  3. Average quality with adequate packaging

 B. The Implied Warranty of Fitness for a Particular Purpose
  1. Arises when seller promises buyer goods are appropriate for a particular purpose
  2. Requirements
   a. Seller has particular skill or judgment
   b. Buyer is relying on that skill or judgment
   c. Seller knows or has reason to know of reliance
   d. Seller makes recommendation to buyer

 C. Eliminating Warranty Liability by Disclaimers
  1. Use "with all faults", "as they stand", "as is" - disclaims both implied warranties
  2. Can also disclaim by using the names of both warranties

 D. Privity Standards for UCC Recovery (§2-318)
  1. Can recover from manufacturer
  2. Privity at buyer level - three code alternatives
   a. Alternative A - buyer, members of household, and guests
   b. Alternative B - any natural person expected to use goods
   c. Alternative C - extends to any person expected to use the goods
  3. Restaurant owner is liable for food defects

IV. Strict Tort Liability: Product Liability Under Section 402A

 A. Strict Tort Liability - § 402A
  1. Defendant had duty to manufacture a reasonably safe product/was in the business of selling or manufacturing product
  2. That duty was breached
  3. Breach of duty caused plaintiff's injury (product reached plaintiff in same condition)
  4. Foreseeable that defect will cause injury
  5. Plaintiff has property or physical damages

      B.   Unreasonably Dangerous Defective Condition
           1.   Design defect
           2.   Improper warnings or insufficient instructions/failure to warn
           3.   Negligent packaging, manufacturing, or handling
                 Example: Drug tampering/food tampering cases

      C.   Reaching the Buyer in the Same Condition
           1.   No substantial change in product design that caused malfunction or injury
           2.   Product not tampered with during distribution

      D.   The Requirement of a Seller Engaged in a Business
           1.   Need not be a merchant
           2.   Need not be "in the business" of selling that product
                 Example: Peanuts sold at games by a baseball club
           3.   Recovery allowed in some cases against defendants who did not manufacture the plaintiff's particular product, but manufacture the product

V.   Negligence: A Second Tort for Product Liability

Same elements as strict tort liability plus prior knowledge of defective condition; punitive damages if plaintiff can show manufacturer/seller knew of defect

VI.   Privity Issues in Tort Theories of Product Liability

      A.   Don't Need Privity

      B.   Was Injury to That Party Foreseeable?

      C.   Should Anticipate Household Use, Presence of Children, and So On

VII. Defenses to Product Liability Torts

      A.   Misuse or Abnormal Use of a Product

           Examples: Exceeding weight limitations, using around flames

      B.   Contributory Negligence
           1.   Is a complete defense
           2.   Overlaps with misuse
           3.   Some states have comparative negligence; reduces the amount of recovery instead of being a complete defense

      C.   Assumption of Risk
           1.   Plaintiff aware of danger
           2.   Does it anyway
           3.   Is a defense to liability

VIII. Product Liability Reform

    A.   Verdicts and Costs Affect International Competitiveness

    B.   Congress Has Made Efforts to Make Laws Uniform

    C.   Restatement (3rd) is Proposed

    D.   Businesses Need to Focus on Prevention

IX. Federal Standards for Product Liability

    A.   Consumer Product Safety Commission
        1.   Federal penalties of $2,000 per Violation
        2.   Up to $500,000 maximum (willful violations carry $50,000 and/or 1 year imprisonment)

    B.   Uniform Product Liability Act

X. International Issues in Product Liability

    A.   EU Trying to Gain Uniformity

    B.   "State-of-the-Art" Defense (product as good as it can be upon release)

    C.   International Standards Organization's 9000 Guidelines for Quality Assurance

    D.   CISG Limits Product Liability

KEY TERMS

Assumption of Risk
Bait and Switch
Caveat Emptor
Celebrity Endorsements
Comparative Negligence
Consent Decree
Consumer Product Safety
    Commission (CPSC)
Contributory Negligence
Corrective Advertising
Design Defects
Disclaimers

Express Warranty
Federal Trade Commission
    (FTC)
Federal Trade Commission
    Act
FTC Improvements Act of
    1980
Implied Warranty of Fitness
    for a Particular Purpose
Implied Warranty of
    Merchantability
Misuse

Negligence
Privity
Punitive Damages
Record
Strict Liability
Title
Unconscionable Disclaimers
Unreasonably Defective
    Condition
Warranty
Wheeler-Lea Act

MATCHING

a. Disclaimer	g. Express Warranty
b. Misuse	h. Corrective Advertising
c. Consumer Product Safety Commission	i. Strict Tort Liability
d. Federal Trade Commission	j. Bait and Switch
e. Contributory Negligence	k. Privity
f. Assumption of Risk	l. Implied Warranty of Merchantability

_____ 1. Seller's act of eliminating warranty protection.

_____ 2. Prevents unfair and deceptive trade practices.

_____ 3. Promise by seller expressing the quality, ability, or performance of a product.

_____ 4. Requires the seller to correct the unsubstantiated claims made in prior ads.

_____ 5. Complete defense to a product liability suit in negligence.

_____ 6. Theory of recovery which holds a seller of a product liable, if the product was sold in defective condition unreasonably dangerous to the consumer, if the seller is engaged in the business of selling such a product, and it is expected to and does reach the buyer without substantial change in the condition in which it is sold.

_____ 7. Sales tactic where a cheaper product than the one in stock is advertised to get the customers into a store.

_____ 8. Plaintiff is aware of a danger in the product but uses it anyway.

_____ 9. Established to protect the public against unreasonable risk of injury from consumer products.

_____ 10. Use of a product in a manner that the defendant could not have anticipated and warned against.

_____ 11. Requires that goods are of fair or average quality and are fit for ordinary purposes.

_____ 12. Direct contractual relationship between parties.

FILL-IN-THE-BLANKS

1. The doctrine of _____ holds that sellers were not liable for defects in products they manufactured and that it was the buyer's responsibility to be alert for defects and take precautions.

2. A _____, which is the equivalent of a no-contest plea, is a negotiated settlement between the FTC and the advertiser.

3. If a seller shows a sample to a buyer or provides the buyer with a description of the goods, he or she has made a(n) _____ to the buyer that the goods will conform to the sample, model, or description.

4. The implied warranty of _____ is a promise given to a buyer by a seller that the goods are fit for their ordinary purpose.

5. A(n) implied warranty of _____ arises when the buyer relies on a seller's skill or judgment to choose suitable goods and the seller knows that the buyer is so relying.

6. The phrases "as they stand," "as is," and "with all faults," constitute _____ of implied warranties.

7. The _____ gave the FTC the power to regulate unfair and deceptive practices when the public is being deceived regardless of any effects on competition.

8. A products liability case based on the _____ theory requires that the plaintiff show that the defendant owed a duty which was breached.

9. Misuse, _____, and _____, are three defenses to a _____ action.

10. Under a _____ defense, the negligence of the plaintiff reduces the amount they are entitled to recover.

11. The _____ has authority to recall products and order their repair.

12. If your car is recalled for repair and you fail to have the repair done, you have _____ the risk of driving your car.

SHORT ANSWER

1. List the requirements for the implied warranty of fitness for a particular purpose.

    a. _____

    b. _____

    c. _____

    d. _____

2. What are the defenses to a product liability suit?

    a. _____

    b. _____

    c. _____

3. What are the responsibilities given to the Consumer Product Safety Commission?

    a. _____

    b. _____

    c. _____

    d. _____

4. What are the three most common types of product liability cases?

    a. _____

    b. _____

    c. _____

5. Explain what is meant by bait and switch. _____

    _____

6. List the three requirements by the FTC in celebrity endorsement ads.

    a. _____

    b. _____

    c. _____

Chapter 11

ENVIRONMENTAL REGULATION

CHAPTER OUTLINE

I.   Common-Law Remedies and the Environment

   A.   Nuisance
      1.   Interference with use and enjoyment
      2.   Damages and injunction possible

   B.   Balancing Test Employed

   C.   EMF and Nuisances
      1.   Electromagnetic fields affect property values, possible health effects, interfere with electronics
      2.   Limitation on hours of operations for data centers

   D.   NIMBYs and Nuisances
      1.   Not In My Back Yard
      2.   BANANAs – Build Absolutely Nothing Anywhere Near Anything
      3.   Businesses must learn to work with them and their objections

II. Statutory Environmental Laws

   A.   Air Pollution Regulation
      1.   Air Pollution Control Act - 1955
         a.   Study by Surgeon General
         b.   Responsibility of states
      2.   Clean Air Act of 1963
         a.   HEW given authority to conduct conferences
         b.   Recommend settlements for interstate pollution problems
      3.   Air Quality Act of 1967
         a.   States to adopt plans
         b.   HEW to approve
         c.   No state came up with a plan
      4.   Clean Air Act Amendments of 1970
         a.   EPA authorized to establish standards
         b.   States required to adopt implementation plans (SIPs)
         c.   EPA approval required for plans
         d.   Economic and technological issues - legislation intended to force compliance
      5.   Clean Air Act Amendments of 1977
         a.   Regulation of business growth
         b.   Nonattainment areas
         c.   Emissions offset - Economic Approach
            (1)   bubble concept followed
            (2)   for new plant to begin operations, its pollution had to be offset by reduction in the area
         d.   Prevention of significant deterioration
            (1)   EPA has right to review proposed plant construction
            (2)   plant has to show that there will not be significant deterioration

6.   1990 Amendments to Clean Air Act
    a.   First comprehensive amendments since 1977
    b.   Focuses on smog, alternative fuels, toxic emissions, and acid rain
    c.   Ozone goals for 101 cities
    d.   3-4 percent per year reduction in smog
    e.   Regulations on tailpipe emissions/warranties on card
    f.   Special nozzles to reduce gasoline fumes at the pumps
    g.   Targeted industries include coal, chemical, printing, and electric
    h.   Plants must use maximum achievable control technology (MACT)
    i.   Acid rain covered
       (1)   sulfur dioxide pollution from factories and coal-fired generating plants
       (2)   proposed controls are not before Congress
    j.   Affected small businesses such as dry cleaners, paint shops, and bakeries
7.   New forms of control
    a.   EPA decided to rely on markets and economics to mold behaviors
    b.   Clean air is now a bought and sold commodity

B.   Water Pollution Regulations
1.   Water Quality Act of 1965
    a.   Created Federal Water Pollution Control Administration (FWPCA)
    b.   States required to establish water quality standards
    c.   No enforcement procedures - states did little
2.   Rivers and Harbors Act of 1899
    a.   Prohibited discharges into navigable waters
    b.   Used for enforcement since other laws had no teeth
    c.   Most industries got around it quickly by obtaining the permits required under the act
3.   Federal Water Pollution Control Act of 1972
    a.   Federal government responsible for standards and control
    b.   Emissions controlled by industrial groups
    c.   Ranges for groups referred to as effluent guidelines
    d.   Permit required to discharge into waters: National Pollution Discharge Elimination Permit (NPDES)
       (1)   required for direct discharges - point source
       (2)   permit requires EPA and state approval
       (3)   releases controlled according to their conventional, nonconventional, or toxic standards
       (4)   pretreatment required under permit with best conventional treatment (BCT) or best available treatment (BAT)
    e.   Renamed in 1977 to Clean Water Act
4.   Safe Drinking Water Act
    a.   Passed in 1986
    b.   States responsible for enforcement but must have minimum federal standards for drinking water systems
5.   Oil Pollution Act of 1990
    a.   Passed in response to huge spills like Exxon *Valdez*
    b.   Companies must either clean up spill or pay federal government its costs for the clean-up
    c.   Applies to all navigable waters up to 200 miles off shore
    d.   Penalties of $25,000/day or $1,000/barrel
       (1)   failure to report spill - $250,000/five years
       (2) $500,000 penalty for corporation

C. Solid Waste Disposal Regulation
  1. Controls garbage or dumping
  2. Toxic Substances Control Act of 1976
     a. Response to chemical dumping
     b. EPA controls manufacture and disposal of toxic substances
  3. Resource Conservation and Recovery Act of 1976
     a. Regulates methods of disposal through a permit system
     b. Discourages dumping
  4. Comprehensive Environmental Response, Compensation, and Liability Act (CERCLA)
     a. "Superfund"
     b. President authorized to issue funds for clean-up of dumping areas
     c. Suit can be brought to recover funds expended from company responsible for the dumping
     d. 1986 amendments to act by Superfund Amendment and Reauthorization Act
     e. EPA can now sue to recover cleanup funds from those who are responsible
     f. 700 hazardous substances are now covered
     g. Lender liability issues
        (1) originally the *Fleet Factors* case imposed liability
        (2) Congress passed the Asset Conservation, Lender Liability and Deposit Insurance Act of 1996
        (3) lenders are excluded so long as their role is as a holder of a security interest
           (a) cannot participate in running the business
           (b) can monitor and enforce mortgage
           (c) can foreclose and sell
           (d) can lease
           (e) activities limited if they wish to avoid CERCLA liability
     h. CERCLA - four classes of liability
        (1) owners
        (2) operators
        (3) transporters
        (4) those who arrange for transportation
     i. Parent corporations can be held liable for actions of subsidiary if they have knowledge
     j. CERCLA and buying land – role of due diligence
        (1) Phase One - check to see if designated as a site
        (2) Phase Two - soil testing
        (3) Phase Three - clean-up
        (4) As of late 2007, EPA is following what legal counsel are calling the "AAI" standard or "all appropriate inquiries made" prior to purchasing the land or building to be codified at 40 C.F.R. § 312.10
     k. Insurance coverage
     l. New developments under CERCLA
        (1) causation
        (2) danger - is it real?
        (3) arbitrary and capricious challenges
     m. Self-audits
        (1) companies can self-report
        (2) reduced fines for doing so
        (3) helps in accurate financial reports disclosure

        n.   CERCLA and brownfields
           (1) so many sites with many unused
           (2) Small Business Liability Relief and Brownfields Revitalization Act provides funding for proposals to clean up and use land without full liability

  D. Environmental Quality Regulation
      1. National Environmental Policy Act of 1969
          a. Requires federal agencies to file environmental impact statements for their major actions (EISs)
          b. Content of EIS:
             (1) environmental impact
             (2) adverse effects
             (3) alternatives
             (4) new effect - short-term versus long-term
             (5) irreversible effects
          c. Can delay real estate developments where government serves as guarantor
          d. A June 1993 federal court ruling found that the NAFTA treaty could not be implemented without an EIS. The U.S. Trade Representative appealed the order and NAFTA was permitted to take effect without an EIS.

  E. Other Federal Environmental Regulations
      1. Surface mining
      2. Noise control
      3. Pesticide Control Act
          a. Must register with EPA to ship
          c. Must label all pesticides
      4. OSHA regulations
      5. Asbestos Hazard Emergency Response Act (AHERA)
          a. Schools must inspect for asbestos and take action
          b. Asbestos is a toxic pollutant and community right-to-know substance
          c. Duty to disclose presence of asbestos
      6. Endangered Species Act
          a. Powerful tool for environmentalists
          b. Habitats cannot be disturbed
          c. Spotted owl and logging

III. State Environmental Laws

  A. State EPA

  B. Carpooling

IV. Enforcement of Environmental Laws

  A. Parties Responsible for Enforcement
      1. Environmental Protection Agency - EPA
      2. Council on Environmental Quality - CEQ
          a. Part of executive branch
          b. Sets national policies and makes recommendations

    3.   Other agencies
        a.   Atomic Energy Commission
        b.   Federal Power Commission
        c.   HUD
        d.   Department of Interior
        e.   Forest Service
        f.   Bureau of Land Management
        g.   Department of Commerce

B.   Criminal Sanctions for Violations

C.   Group Suits: The Effect of Environmentalists
    1.   For authority to bring suit
    2.   Injunctive relief
        a.   Can be sought by EPA
        b.   Can be sought by private citizens
    3.   Environmental groups can bring suits
        a.   Sierra Club
        b.   Environmental Defense Fund
        c.   League of Conservation Voters

V.   International Environmental Issues

A.   The EU and Environmentalism
    1.   Has 200 regulations
    2.   Clearinghouse for information
    3.   Eco-Audit Stickers   Show company's level of
    4.   Eco-Labels   environmental commitment
    5.   Germany's Blue Angel   on its products

B.   ISO 14000
    1.   International Organization for Standardization
    2.   Companies become ISO certified
    3.   Emphasizes self-audits and self-correction

C.   Kyoto Protocol
    1.   Emissions controls by nation
    2.   Opposition is strong
    3.   U.S. is not a party

D.   The Precautionary Principle
    1.   New governance theory (EU origins)
    2.   Must take precautions even before harm is clear
    3.   Burden of proof is on those who oppose regulations to show no harm, not on regulators to show harm

KEY TERMS

Air Pollution Control Act
Air Quality Act
Asbestos Hazard Emergency
    Response Act (AHERA)
Asset Conservation, Lender
    Liability, and Deposit
    Insurance Protection Act
    of 1996
BANANAs
Best Available Treatment
    (BAT)
Best Conventional Treatment
    (BCT)
Brownfields
Bubble Concept
Clean Air Act
Clean Air Act Amendments of
    1990
Clean Water Act
Community Right-to-Know
    Substance
Comprehensive
    Environmental
    Response,
    Compensation, and
    Liability Act (CERCLA)
Conventional Pollutants
Council on Environmental
    Quality (CEQ)
Department of Health,
    Education and Welfare
    (HEW)

Effluent Guidelines
Electromagnetic Fields (EMF)
Emissions Offset Policy
Endangered Species Act
    (ESA)
Environmental Impact Statement
Environmental Protection
    Agency (EPA)
Federal Environmental Pesticide
    Control Act
Federal Water Pollution Control
    Act of 1972
Federal Water Pollution Control
    Administration (FWPCA)
Hazardous Substance Response
    Trust Fund
Injunctions
International Organization
    for Standardization
    (ISO)
Kyoto Protocol
Maximum Achievable
    Control Technology
    (MACT)
National Environmental
    Policy Act of 1969 (NEPA)
National Pollution Discharge
    Elimination System
    (NPDES)
NIMBYs
Noise Control Act of 1972
Nonattainment Area

Nonconventional Pollutants
Nuisance
Occupational Safety and
    Health Administration
    (OSHA)
Oil Pollution Act (OPA)
Point Sources
Precautionary Principle
Prevention of Significant
    Deterioration Areas
Resource Conservation and
    Recovery Act of 1976
Rivers and Harbors Act of
    1899
Safe Drinking Water Act
State Implementation Plans
    (SIPS)
Superfund
Superfund Amendment and
    Reauthorization Act
Surface Mining and
    Reclamation Act of
    1977
Toxic Pollutants
Toxic Substances Control
    Act (TOSCA)
United Nations Framework
    Convention for Climate
    Change (UNFCCC)
Water Quality Act

MATCHING

a. Nuisance
b. State Implementation Plan
c. OSHA
d. Electromagnetic Fields
e. Toxic Pollutant
f. Nonattainment Area

g. NIMBYs
h. Maximum Achievable Control Technology
i. Environmental Impact Statement
j. Council on Environmental Quality
k Superfund
l. Conventional Pollutant

_____   1. Best available methods for limiting emissions, regardless of cost.

_____   2. A federal executive branch agency charged with the setting of environmental policy and
               making recommendations to Congress concerning environmental issues.

_____ 3. EPA can require discharger to pretreat substances with the best conventional treatment for this pollutant.

_____ 4. EPA can require the best available treatment, which is the highest standard imposed, for this pollutant.

_____ 5. Document required of all federal agencies proposing action that will have an effect on the environment.

_____ 6. Responsible for workers' environments.

_____ 7. Established by the Comprehensive Environmental Response, Compensation, and Liability Act for the clean-up of areas that were hazardous waste disposal sites.

_____ 8. Mandatory implementation plans required of states to achieve the federally developed standards for achieving air quality.

_____ 9. The use of one's property in such a manner that it interferes with another's use and enjoyment of his or her property.

_____ 10. Has existing, significant air quality problems.

_____ 11. The cause of litigation against electric utilities for their use of overhead wires, transformers, and power plants.

_____ 12. Challenges the placement of power plants, cell phone towers, or refineries.

FILL-IN-THE-BLANK

1. Under the Clean Air Act, the EPA classified two types of areas in which business growth could be contained: a _____ (or dirty) area and a _____ (or clean) area.

2. In carrying out their emissions offset policy, the EPA follows a _____ concept, which means that it examines all air pollutants within the area as if they came from a single source.

3. Under the Clean Water Act, the EPA has established ranges of discharges permitted for various industrial groups under its _____ guidelines.

4. Under the Clean Water Act, the EPA requires a _____ permit for a plant to discharge waste into watersways.

5. The EPA has developed three categories of water pollutants: conventional, nonconventional, and toxic, which determine whether a company must treat the pollutant with a _____ or a _____ treatment, the highest standard imposed.

6. Asbestos is a _____, which means its presence must be disclosed to potential buyers, tenants, and employees.

7. _____ authorized the president to issue funds for cleanup of areas that were once disposal sites for hazardous wastes. These funds are often called the _____.

8. The _____ Act authorizes the EPA to control the manufacture, use, and disposal of toxic substances.

9. The Water Quality Act established the _____, which required states to establish quality levels for the waters within their boundaries.

10. The _____ provides for the EPA to establish national standards for contaminant levels in drinking water.

11. The court can issue a(n) _____ against someone who is harming the land or the environment.

12. Groups that deal with issues of urban sprawl and urban development are called _____.

SHORT ANSWER

1. The EPA's emissions offset policy requires three elements before a new facility can begin operation in a nonattainment area. What are they?

    a. _____

    b. _____

    c. _____

2. What is the required information in an environmental impact statement (EIS)?

    a. _____

    b. _____

    c. _____

    d. _____

    e. _____

3. What are the EPA's three categories of water pollutants?

    a. _____

    b. _____

    c. _____

4.   What are the four classes of parties that can be held liable under CERCLA?

   a.   _____

   b.   _____

   c.   _____

   d.   _____

5.   Name four things a lender can do and still not be subject to environmental liability.

   a.   _____

   b.   _____

   c.   _____

   d.   _____

6.   Explain what a "brownfield" is as defined by the EPA.

   _____

   _____

   _____

   _____

Chapter 12

CONTRACTS AND SALES: INTRODUCTION AND FORMATION

CHAPTER OUTLINE

I. What Is a Contract?

    A. Definition
        1. Set of promises for breach of which the law gives a remedy
        2. Defined in *Restatement of Contracts* - American Law Institute (ALI)

    B. Helps Businesses with Planning

II. Sources of Contract Law

    A. Common Law
        1. English common law
        2. Summarized in *Restatement (Second) of Contracts*
            a. Developed by American Law Institute
            b. Followed in most states
        3. Applies to contracts with subject matters of land or services

    B. The Uniform Commercial Code (UCC)
        1. Common law is not uniform from state to state
        2. ALI and National Conference of Commissioners on Uniform State Laws drafted it
        3. First appeared in 1940s
        4. Adopted in part or whole in all states
        5. Article II governs contracts for the sale of goods
        6. More liberal than common law
        7. Reformed/revised again in 2003

    C. UCC Versus Common Law - Case Determinations Often Required

    D. Article IIA Leases
        1. New addendum to UCC
        2. Covers leases of goods (long-term leases such as car leases)
        3. Adopted in most states

    E. Evolving E-Commerce Contract Laws
        1. Uniform Electronic Transactions Act (UETA)
            a. Law in 48 states (Dec. 2007) plus District of Columbia
            b. Governs contracts formed over the Internet
        2. Electronic Signatures in Global and National Commerce act of 2000 (E-sign)
            a. Federal law
            b. Mandates recognition of electronic signatures
            c. States cannot deny legal effect to e-signatures
        3. Uniform Computer Information Transaction Act (UCITA)
            a. Not widely adopted yet (Virginia and Maryland)
            b. Governs transactions in software
            c. Governs shrink-wrap and click-wrap contracts

III. Types of Contracts

    A. Bilateral Versus Unilateral Contracts
        1. Bilateral: Both parties promise something in exchange for the other party's promise
        2. Unilateral: One party promises something in exchange for performance

    B. Express Versus Implied Contracts (Quasi Contracts)
        1. Express contracts are written or oral agreements
        2. Implied contracts are nonspoken, nonwritten understandings
        3. Law implies a contract where one does not exist to prevent unjust enrichment
        4. Minors' contracts for necessaries are enforced in quasi contract since they are voidable

    C. Void and Voidable Contracts
        1. Void contract is one to do something illegal or against public policy - neither side can enforce
        2. Voidable contracts are contracts in which one party has the right to end the contract
           Example: Contracts of minors are voidable

    D. Unenforceable Contracts
        1. Procedural problem precludes enforcement
        2. Statute of frauds

    E. Executed Versus Executory Contracts
        1. Executed contract is one in which the promises under the contract have been performed
        2. Executory contract is one that has been entered into but not yet performed; can be partially executory/executed if one side has performed

IV. Formation of Contracts

    A. Offer
        1. Parties
           a. Person who makes offer = offeror
           b. Person who receives offer = offeree
        2. Must have language that indicates intent to contract vs. negotiation
           a. Not just inquiry
           b. More than negotiation
           c. Courts use an objective, not a subjective, standard
              (1) examine language
              (2) examine circumstances
              (3) examine the actions of the parties
        3. Certain and definite terms
           a. Common law - parties, subject matter, price, payment terms, performance times
           b. UCC - subject matter, quantity, parties
           c. Under the UCC, court can consider industry custom and course of dealing in determining whether terms are sufficient
        4. Communication to offeree
           a. Offeree cannot accept offer that never arrives
           b. Ads are invitations for offers - not offers

5. Termination of offers
   a. Can be revoked any time prior to acceptance
      (1) exception is option
      (2) offeror is paid to hold offer open
      (3) it is a separate contract for time
      (4) second exception is UCC merchant's firm offer - offer by merchant signed in writing states it will be kept open (irrevocable) for period stated (maximum of three months)
   b. Termination by rejection
      (1) offeree indicates "no"
      (2) rejection by changes in terms - counteroffer
   c. Termination by counteroffer - UCC
      (1) section 2-207
      (2) changes to UCC (adoption in process) change the impact of 2-207 and battle of forms
      (3) Old UCC: nonmerchants - addition of terms in acceptance does not equal a counteroffer; acceptance results, but additional terms aren't part of contract
      Example: A: I will sell you my white Ford Torino for $450. B: I accept. Throw in new seat covers. Contract for Torino without seat covers results.
      (4) Old UCC: merchants - battle of the forms; invoices and purchase orders sent back and forth - no matching terms
         (a) acceptance with additional terms = contract
         (b) additional terms are part of contract unless:
            i. material - price, warranties (immaterials = shipment or payment terms)
            ii. offer limited - "this offer is limited to these terms"
            iii. objection to new terms
      (5) UCC changes to 2-207
         (a) what contract terms were became very confusing
         (b) new rule is applicable to merchants and non-merchants and is the "terms later" section – if the parties agree on subject matter, the terms can come later
   d. Termination of offer expiration
      (1) time for offer expires
      (2) every offer expires (lapses) after a reasonable time

B. Acceptance: The Offeree's Response
   1. Offeree's favorable response - must be communicated to offeror
   2. If means of acceptance stipulated:
      a. Use means stipulated, then mailbox rule applies
      b. Don't use means stipulated, then counteroffer and rejection
      c. Timing
         (1) mailbox rule if same means or stipulated means used
         (2) arrival if different (slower) method used
         (3) if nonstipulated means used, it is a counteroffer and a rejection
   3. Acceptance with no stipulated means
      a. Can use any method of communication
      b. Same or reasonable method of communication gets you the mailbox rule

C. E-Commerce and Contract Formation
   1. Same requirements
   2. Methodology varies
   3. Acceptance is by point and click
   4. Must show an understanding that there is a contract

    D.   Consideration
        1.   Distinguishes gifts from contracts
        2.   What each party is willing to give up for the other
        3.   The bargained-for exchange
        4.   Unique consideration issues
            a.   Charitable subscriptions are enforceable even though detriment is one-sided
            b.   Reliance (promissory estoppel) provides element of detriment for contracts not yet begun

    E.   Contract Form: When Record is Required
        1.   Statute of frauds controls what must be evidenced by a record
        2.   Types of contracts for a record
            a.   Real property
            b.   Contracts that can't be performed in one year
            c.   Contracts to pay the debt of another
            d.   UCC - contracts for sale of goods for $5,000 or more (new UCC)
        3.   Exceptions
            a.   Performance
            b.   Parties finish contract
         4.   Type of record required
            a.   Need not be one formal document - can be pieced together and can be electronic
            b.   Merchant's confirmation memorandum
               (1)   one side verifies contract
               (2)   summarizes oral agreement
               (3)   signed by one side - enforceable against both (unless there is objection after it is mailed)
        5.   Electronic contracts
            a.   Allows for the identification of electronically transferred documents using encryption technology
            b.   Digital signatures help authenticate users
            c.   E-SIGN and UETA
        6.   Parol evidence
            a.   Once a contract is reduced to final form and it has no ambiguities, cannot introduce evidence to contradict it
            b.   Exceptions are fraud, other defenses
            c.   Modifications are not included

V.   Issues in Formation of International Contracts

    A.   UN's Convention on Contracts for the International Sale of Goods (CISG)
        1.   Adopted in 1980
        2.   United States has adopted

    B.   Party Autonomy Still Controlling in International Contracts

    C.   Must Provide for Additional Risks
        1.   Terrorism
        2.   Bill of lading for payment

KEY TERMS

Acceptance
Article 2A Leases
Bargained-For Exchange
Battle of the Forms
Bilateral Contract
Bill of Lading
Charitable Subscriptions
Common Law
Consideration
Contract
Counteroffers
Digital Signature
Electronic Signatures in
　　Global and National
　　Commerce Act of
　　2000 (E-Sign)
Executed Contracts
Executory Contracts

Express Contract
Force Majeure
Implied Contract
Implied-in-Fact Contract
Implied-in-Law Contract
Mailbox Rule
Merchants' Confirmation Memoranda
Merchant's Firm Offer
Offer
Offeree
Offeror
Officious Meddler
Options
Parol Evidence
Promissory Estoppel
Quasi Contract
Restatement (Second) of Contracts
Revocation

Statute of Frauds
Stipulated Means
Unenforceable Contract
Uniform Commercial Code
　　(UCC)
Uniform Computer
　　Information Transaction
　　Act (UCITA)
Uniform Electronic
　　Transactions Act
　　(UETA)
Unilateral Contract
United Nations Convention
　　on Contracts for the
　　International Sale of
　　Goods (CISG)
Voidable Contract
Void Contract

MATCHING

a. Promissory Estoppel
b. Mailbox Rule
c. Void Contract
d. Electronic Signatures in Global and
　　National Commerce Act
e. Express Contract
f. Acceptance

g. Battle of the Forms
h. Bargained-For Exchange
i. Merchant's Firm Offer
j. Statute of Frauds
k. Voidable Contract
l. Options

_____　1. A contract in which the offeree pays the offeror for the time needed to consider the offer.

_____　2. Positive response by an offeree to a proposed contract.

_____　3. A contract that the courts will not enforce because it is illegal or against public policy.

_____　4. A contract that one of the parties may choose to rescind.

_____　5. Used as a substitute for consideration when someone acts in reliance on a promise that is not supported by consideration.

_____　6. An offer in which a merchant promises to keep a contract or offer open for a stated period of time after the offer is made, put in writing, and signed by a merchant.

_____　7. Involves conflicting terms in purchase orders and confirmations or invoices.

_____　8. Governs the effectiveness of an acceptance when the offeree has used a stipulated means.

_____   9. Requires that certain contracts be evidenced by a record in order to be enforceable.

_____   10. Contract that is evidenced by a record or written or orally agreed to.

_____   11. Federal law that mandates the recognition of electronic signatures for the formation of contracts.

_____   12. What each party gives up under a contract.

FILL-IN-THE-BLANKS

1. The first part of the contract is the _____; the _____ is the person who makes the offer; and the _____ is the person to whom the offer is made.

2. A _____ is a rejection in the form of a new offer from the offeree to the offeror which changes some of the terms and conditions in the original offer.

3. A _____ contract is one in which both parties promise to perform certain things. A _____ contract is one in which one party issues a promise and the other party simply performs.

4. An _____ contract or a _____ contract is enforced by the courts if one party has conferred a benefit on another, both are aware of the benefit, and the benefit would be an enrichment to one party at the expense of the other.

5. A contract that arises from circumstances and not from the express agreement of the parties is called a(n) _____ contract.

6. An _____ contract is a contract that cannot be enforced because of some procedural problem.

7. Contracts are _____ contracts when the parties have performed according to their promises or required actions; contracts are _____ contracts when the promise to perform is made but the actual performance has not been done.

8. _____ occurs when the offeror notifies the offeree that the offer is no longer good.

9. _____ is what distinguishes gifts from contracts.

10. The court will enforce _____ agreements despite their lack of consideration because nonprofit organizations rely on those pledges.

11. _____ is not admissible to dispute an integrated unambiguous contract.

12. A(n) _____ contract is a contract that arises from factual or professional circumstances.

SHORT ANSWER

1. Name all the elements and terms necessary to make a valid contract.

    a. _____

    b. _____

    c. _____

    d. _____

    e. _____

    f. _____

2. Define a contract. _____

    _____

    _____

3. List some of the types of contracts that must be evidenced by a record to be enforceable.

    a. _____

    b. _____

    c. _____

    d. _____

4. Name three ways an offer can be terminated.

    a. _____

    b. _____

    c. _____

5. What is the mailbox rule, when does it apply, and what is it used to determine?

    _____

    _____

    _____

6.   List differences between the CISG and the UCC.

_____

_____

_____

_____

Chapter 13

CONTRACTS AND SALES: PERFORMANCE AND REMEDIES

CHAPTER OUTLINE

I.   Defenses in Contract Formation

    A.   Defense Makes Otherwise Valid Contract Invalid

    B.   Capacity
        1.   Age capacity - most states = age eighteen
        2.   Before that, party is an infant or minor
        3.   Contracts are voidable - minor can get out at his/her option
            a.   Liable in quasi contract for necessaries
            b.   Some exceptions - student loans; military service
        4.   Mental capacity
            a.   Understands contracts are enforceable
            b.   Understands legal documents have significance
            c.   Understands contracts involve costs and litigation
            d.   Contracts are voidable
            e.   If declared legally incompetent - contracts are void

    C.   Misrepresentation
        1.   Remedy can be rescission - contract is set aside
        2.   Must have been material
        3.   Cannot be sales puffing (opinion)

    D.   Fraud
        1.   Knowing and intentional use of false information
        2.   Knowing and intentional failure to disclose
        3.   Many states have statutes exempting the disclosure of a murder or AIDS victims as previous owners or residents - however, if there is an inquiry by the potential buyer, the information cannot be withheld
        4.   The failure to disclose material information can be fraud or misrepresentation

    E.   Duress
        1.   Physical force or threats or economic force
        2.   Party is deprived of a meaningful choice
        3.   Has right of rescission
        4.   Voidable

    F.   Undue Influence
        1.   Must have confidential relationship
            a.   Attorneys/clients
            b.   Elderly parents
        2.   Voidable

G. Illegality and Public Policy
   1. Illegal subject matter
   2. Contract is void
   3. Contracts in violation of criminal statutes
      Examples: Contract to have someone killed, contract to pay for a vote
   4. Contracts in violation of licensing statutes must be competency-based as opposed to revenue-raising for contracts to be void
   5. Contracts in violation of usury laws charging interest in excess of statutory maximum
   6. Contracts in violation of public policy
      a. Exculpatory clauses - full liability elimination is generally invalid
      b. Covenants not to compete must be reasonable in time and geographic scope
      c. Disparity in bargaining power
   7. Unconscionable contracts
      a. No firm definition
      b. Grossly unfair
      c. Lack of bargaining power

II. Contract Performance

A. When Performance is Due
   1. When all conditions are performed
   2. Conditions must be done
   3. Condition precedent required for performance
      Examples: Obtaining financing to buy a car or house, obtaining clear title for land sale

B. Standards for Performance
   1. Either done or not done in most cases
   2. Substantial performance allowed in contract cases
      a. Is it a nonintentional breach?
      b. Is it for practical purposes just as good?
         Example: Construction contracts and materials substitutions

C. E-Commerce: Payments Have Changed
   1. Credit Cards
   2. Digital cash
   3. Person-to-person payment (or PayPal)

D. When Performance is Excused
   1. Impossibility - contract cannot be performed
      Example: Can't build house if the land is washed away
   2. Commercial impracticability - UCC-2-615
      a. Basic assumptions parties made are no longer true
         Example: Embargoes and so forth arise
      b. Can protect themselves by putting in *force majeure* clause - covers problems such as wars, embargoes, depressions
   3. Substitute performance
      a. Novation - two original parties agree, along with third party, to substitute one party for another
      b. Accord and satisfaction - agreement reached to discharge a disputed obligation

III. Contract Remedies

    A. Compensatory - Put Party in Same Position They Would Have Been in Without the Breach

        Example: Sales – buyers has to buy car for $7,000 as opposed to original $6,000 – gets $1,000 in damages

    B. Incidental Damages - Cost of Finding Another Car; Attorney's Fees

    C. Liquidated Damages - Parties Agree on Damage Amount in Advance

    D. Consequential Damages – Damages Experienced in Relation to Third Parties; Late Fees or Loss of Income for Delays

IV. Third-Party Rights in Contracts

    A. Assignments
       1. Original party to contract assigns his/her benefits under the contract to another
          Example: Credit company sells credit contract for present value to another who undertakes its collection
       2. Assignee has same rights as original party

    B. Third-Party Beneficiary
       1. Originally named in the contract to benefit from the contract
       2. Insurance beneficiaries are third-party beneficiaries

VI. International Issues in Contract Performance

    A. Assuring Payment
       1. Use a bill of lading - title to goods controlled
       2. Use in connection with letter of credit or draft

    B. Assuring Performance: International Peculiarities
       1. Need *force majeure* clause
       2. Stability of currencies

KEY TERMS

Accord and Satisfaction	Covenants Not to Compete	Misrepresentation
Age Capacity	Delegation	Novation
Assignment	Duress	Obligation of Good Faith
Bill of Lading	Exculpatory Clauses	Performance
Capacity	*Force Majeure*	Public Policy
Commercial Impracticability	Fraud	Puffing
Compensatory Damages	Impossibility	Rescission
Conditions	Incidental Damages	*Scienter*
Conditions Concurrent	Infant	Substantial Performance
Conditions Contemporaneous	Letter of Credit	Unconscionable
Conditions Precedent	Liquidated Damages	Undue Influence
Confidential Relationship	Material Fact	Voidable Contract
Consequential Damages	Mental Capacity	Void Contract
Contract Defense	Minor	

MATCHING

a.	Unconscionable	g.	Material Fact
b.	Conditions Precedent	h.	Rescission
c.	Fraud	i.	Delegation
d.	Novation	j.	Bill of Lading
e.	Misrepresentation	k.	Exculpatory Clause
f.	Puffing	l.	Confidential Relationship

_____ 1. A contract defense where one party has been misled as to a material fact that was justifiably relied upon.

_____ 2. A contract which is one-sided and gives all of the benefits to one party and all of the burdens on the other.

_____ 3. The type of information that would affect someone's decision to enter into the contract.

_____ 4. Knowing and intentional disclosure of false information or the failure to disclose relevant information.

_____ 5. An event that must occur before there is an obligation to perform under a contract.

_____ 6. Parties agree to substitute someone else for the obligation in an agreement.

_____ 7. Receipt for shipment of goods issued by the carrier to the seller and evidence of who has title to the goods.

_____ 8. The transfer of contractual duties and obligation.

_____ 9. An opinion about a product that does not constitute misrepresentation.

_____ 10. Setting aside a contract and relieving the parties of any obligation to perform it.

_____ 11. Trust and reliance that exists in an undue influence case.

_____ 12. Makes a contract in violation of public policy.

FILL-IN-THE-BLANKS

1. A _____ contract is not honored by the courts and neither party is obligated to perform the contract.

2. When a party is physically forced into entering into a contract, they are said to be under _____.

3. The contract defense of _____ is present if an attorney abuses his attorney/client privilege in order to induce his client to enter into a contract which is particularly favorable to the attorney.

4. The UCC recognizes _____ as a valid excuse to avoid a contract when some basic assumption by the parties when they entered into the contract have been significantly changed.

5. The parties are excused from performance if performance is an _____ because the contract cannot be performed by the parties or anyone else.

6. An example of an _____ clause is a clause put in contracts by a company that says they are to be held completely blameless for any accidents occurring on their premises.

7. In a breach of contract case, the court tries to put the nonbreaching party in the same position they would have been in if the contract had been fully performed by awarding _____; and _____ are damages that result because of the breach and generally involve damages such as lost business, lost profit, or late penalties.

8. If the parties anticipate damages in the event of a breach of contract, they can place a clause in their contract providing for _____ damages, which the court will enforce as long as they are not completely out of line with actual losses.

9. _____ means that the parties must have reached the age of majority; _____ refers to the ability to grasp the importance and ramifications of entering into a binding contract.

10. _____ is a situation, term, or event that makes an otherwise valid contract invalid.

11. Knowledge that information given is false is the element of _____ in a fraud case.

12. When "A" must supply materials to "B" in order for "B" to complete his part of the contract, "A" and "B" have _____ in their contract.

SHORT ANSWER

1. What are the exceptions to the minors' contracts rules?

    _____

    _____

2.   Name the defenses in contract formation.

    a.   _____

    b.   _____

    c.   _____

    d.   _____

    e.   _____

    f.   _____

3.   What are the four types of damages under contract law?

    a.   _____

    b.   _____

    c.   _____

    d.   _____

4.   What are the elements required for misrepresentation?

    a.   _____

    b.   _____

    c.   _____

5.   Define *force majeure*.

    _____

    _____

6.   International contracts for the sales of goods can be difficult because of extensive shipping requirements. What can a company do to protect themselves in these situations?

    _____

    _____

    _____

Chapter 14

FINANCING OF SALES AND LEASES: CREDIT AND DISCLOSURE REQUIREMENTS

CHAPTER OUTLINE

I.   Establishing A Credit Contract

    A.   Credit Contracts Need the Usual Elements of a Contract, Including Offer, Acceptance, and Consideration

    B.   Contracts Must Also Include:
        1.   How much the buyer/debtor is actually carrying on credit or financing
        2.   The rate of interest the buyer/debtor will pay
        3.   How many payments will be made, when they will be made, and for how long
        4.   Penalties and actions for late payments
        5.   Whether the creditor will have collateral
        6.   The necessary statutory disclosures on credit transactions

II. Statutory Requirements for Credit Contracts

    A.   State Usury Laws
        1.   Set maximum rates for interest charges
        2.   Charging in excess can result in:
            a.   Forfeiture of interest and principal
            b.   Forfeiture of interest
            c.   Penalties

    B.   The Subprime Lending Market (a.k.a. Predatory Lending)
        1.   High interest rates
        2.   High debt/equity
        3.   High foreclosure rates
        4.   Regulation pending

    C.   The Equal Credit Opportunity Act
        1.   Passed to be certain credit was denied or awarded on applicant's merits and not on extraneous factors such as age, sex, race, color, national origin or religion
        2.   Cannot consider:
            a.   Marital status
            b.   Receipt of public assistance income
            c.   Receipt of alimony or child support
            d.   Plans for children
        3.   Spouses have rights to individual credit applications
        4.   Penalties
            a.   Actual damage plus punitive damages of up to $10,000
            b.   Class action - punitive damages of up to $500,000 or 1 percent of creditor's net worth (whichever is less)

D. The Truth-in-Lending Act (TILA)
1. Part of Consumer Credit Protection Act
    a. Purpose was full disclosure
    b. Elaboration and forms are found in Regulation Z
2. Application
    a. Consumer credit transactions
    b. Open-end transactions (credit cards and lines of credit)
    c. Closed-end transactions (loans; financing)
3. Open-end disclosure requirements
    a. Interest (finance charges)
    b. Billing dates
    c. Security interest
    d. Bills must have:
        (1) balance from last statement
        (2) payments and credits
        (3) new charges
        (4) finance charges
        (5) billing period dates
        (6) free-ride period (avoid finance charges by paying)
        (7) information for billing errors
    e. Under the 1988 amendments, credit card solicitations must include the following:
        (1) fees for issuing the card
        (2) APR (annual percentage rate) for the card
        (3) minimum or fixed finance charges
        (4) transactions charges
        (5) grace periods (if any)
        (6) how average daily balance is computed
        (7) when payments are due
        (8) if there is a late payment fee
        (9) any charges for going over credit limit
4. Credit card (open-end) solicitation disclosures
    a. Fair Credit and Charge Card Disclosure Act of 1988
    b. Governs solicitations
    c. Disclosure of following required:
        (1) fees for issuing the card
        (2) APR
        (3) minimum or fixed finance charges
        (4) transaction charges
        (5) grace period (if any)
        (6) computation of average daily balance
        (7) payments due
        (8) late payment fees (if any)
        (9) charges for going over limit
5. Credit cards and privacy
    a. Must disclose use of customer information/lists
    b. Must give customer chance to opt out
    c. 2001 warnings

6. Closed-end transactions
   a. Amount being financed
   b. Finance charges
   c. APR (annual percentage rate)
   d. Number of payments and when due
   e. Total cost of financing (price of goods plus all interest)
   f. Penalties for prepayment or late payment
   g. Security interest or lien
   h. Credit insurance
7. Special disclosures and protections for armed services members
   a. Limits on interest
   b. Limits on foreclosures
   c. Limits on delinquencies
   d. Apply during active service
8. Advertising regulation
   a. If parts of credit terms disclosed, must disclose the whole thing
   b. If payments disclosed, must disclose all
9. Credit card solicitation
   a. No unsolicited credit cards can be sent
   b. Limitations on liability
   c. Applies to electronic credit card transactions
10. Credit card liabilities
    a. Creditor cannot send an unsolicited card
    b. No debtor liability for theft of an unsolicited card
    c. Maximum of $50 liability for loss or theft of valid card so long as there is notification
11. Canceling credit contracts: Regulation Z protections
    a. Regulation Z gives three-day cooling-off period
    b. Applies where security interest in home is given or there is a home-solicitation sale
       (1) recent changes govern credit transactions where the home is security
       (2) must disclose consequences of default – home could be lost in a foreclosure
    c. Home Equity Loan Consumer Protection Act of 1988
       (1) three-day rescission period
       (2) additional disclosures on possibility of losing home
12. Penalties under TILA
    a. Two times the amount of finance charges
    b. Minimum of $100 and maximum of $1,000
    c. Class action = $500,000 or 1 percent of creditors' net worth (the lesser of)

E. Fair Credit Billing Act
   1. Requires monthly statement on open-end transactions
   2. Bill must have address to write for errors
   3. Debtors must write bill objections to get damages
      a. Must send within sixty days of bill's receipt
      b. Creditor has thirty days to acknowledge
      c. Creditor has ninety days to take action
   4. Debtor need not pay protested amount or finance charges during protest period
      a. Once resolved, must pay
      b. If creditor does not comply with time limits, debtor need not pay (even if creditor is correct)

F. Fair Credit Reporting Act
    1. Applies to consumer reporting agencies - third parties (not creditors)
    2. Limitations on disclosure
        a. Can disclose to debtor his/her own report
        b. Can disclose to creditor with signed credit application
        c. Can disclose to potential employer
        d. Can disclose for court subpoena
    3. Limitations on content
        a. No bankruptcies longer than ten years ago
        b. No lawsuits finalized more than seven years ago
        c. No disclosures of criminal convictions finalized more than seven years ago UNLESS applying for $50,000 in credit or $20,000/year job
    4. Debtor's right of correction
        a. Notify agency
        b. If no correction, debtor can write 100-word statement of clarification

G. Consumer Leasing Act
    1. Full disclosure in leases
    2. What it costs at beginning and end
    3. Article 2A added to UCC to govern lease contracts - adopted in ten states

III. Enforcement of Credit Transactions

A. The Use of Collateral: The Security Interest
    1. Take Article IX security interest
    2. Is a lien on personal property
    3. Written agreement required
    4. Gives creditor the right of repossession in the event the debtor defaults

B. Collection Rights of the Creditor
    1. Regulated by the Fair Debt Collections Practices Act (FDCPA) if it is a consumer debt
    2. Application
        a. Third-party collection agencies
        b. Attorneys
        c. Does not apply to:
            (1) banks
            (2) IRS
            (3) original creditors
            (4) commercial accounts
    3. Collectors' obligations
        a. Must provide written verification of debt if debtor asks or within five days after contact with debtor
        b. Must include
            (1) amount of debt
            (2) name of creditor
            (3) debtor's right to disputed debt

  4. Collectors' restrictions
    a. Debtor contact
      (1) not before 8 AM or after 9 PM
      (2) home contact OK
      (3) no contact at club, church, or school meetings
      (4) no contact at employment if employer objects
      (5) debtor can tell collector to stop contact at any time
    b. Third-party contact
      (1) can't notify others of debt
      (2) spouse and parents can be contacted
      (3) other parties can be asked for information but reason for information cannot be given
      (4) postcard contact is prohibited
    c. Prohibited acts
      (1) no harassment, oppression, or abuse
      (2) no physical force
      (3) no misrepresentation of authority
      (4) no threats of prison
  5. Penalties for FDCPA violations
    a. $1,000 actual damages - private
    b. FTC can issue complaint

 C. Suits for Enforcement of Debts
  1. Reduce to judgment
  2. Use garnishment for wages, accounts, and so on
  3. Consumer Credit Protection Act limits wage garnishments to 25 percent of wages (50 percent for child support)

 D. The End of the Line on Enforcement of Debts: Bankruptcy
  1. Bankruptcy Abuse Prevention and Consumer Protection Act of 2005
    a. Tightens up standards for declaring bankruptcy
    b. Tightens up exemptions
    c. Requires consumer debt adjustment plans as prerequisite to liquidations
    d. Defines disposable income as standard for bankruptcy
  2. Chapter 7 - Liquidation of all assets (personal or business)
  3. Chapter 11 - Reorganization (new plan for repayment)
  4. Chapter 13 - Consumer debt adjustment plan
  5. Can be voluntary or involuntary
  6. Debts discharged in bankruptcy except:
    a. Alimony
    b. Child support
    c. Student loans
    d. Taxes (three years)
    e. Willful and malicious acts

IV. International Credit Issues

 A. Differences Between Declaration of Bankruptcy in the U.S. and Japan

 B. Attitudes Toward Debt

KEY TERMS

Annual Percentage Rate
Bankruptcy
Bankruptcy Abuse
    Prevention and
    Consumer Protection
    Act (BAPCPA)
Chapter 7
Chapter 11
Chapter 13
Closed-End Transactions
Consumer Credit Protection
    Act (CCPA)
Consumer Leasing Act
Credit Repair Organization
    Act
Defense Authorization Act of
    2007
Equal Credit Opportunity Act

(ECOA)
Fair Credit and Charge Card
    Disclosure Act of 1988
Fair Credit Billing Act
Fair Credit Reporting Act
    (FCRA)
Fair Debt Collections Practices
    Act (FDCPA)
Federal Trade Commission
    (FTC)
Finance Charges
Garnishment
Home Equity Loan Consumer
    Protection Act of 1988
Home Ownership and Equity
    Protection Act (HOEPA)
Home Solicitation Sales
Judgment

National Defense Act of
2007
Open-End Credit
    Transactions
Predatory Lending
Regulation Z
Security Agreement
Security Interest
Service Members Civil Relief
    Act
Subprime Lending Market
Three-day Cooling Off
Period
Truth-in-lending Act (TILA)
Usury

MATCHING

a. Three-Day Cooling Off Period
b. Home Solicitation Sales
c. Regulation Z
d. Closed-End Credit Transaction
e. Fair Credit Billing Act
f. Consumer Leasing Act.

g. Fair Credit Reporting Act
h. Open-End Credit Transaction
i. Truth-in-Lending Act
j. Garnishment
k. Chapter 11
l. Equal Credit Opportunity Act

_____ 1. A credit card sale.

_____ 2. A car loan of $15,000 by a bank to a consumer to be repaid in 60 equal monthly installments.

_____ 3. Sales in which the buyer is first approached in his/her home by the seller.

_____ 4. Violated by a creditor who denies credit to a consumer because the consumer receives alimony and child support payments.

_____ 5. Violated by failure to disclose the annual percentage rate of interest charged in a consumer credit transaction.

_____ 6. Buyer's protection for "cold feet."

_____ 7. Applies only in the case of open-end credit transactions monthly statements.

_____ 8. Limits who may receive credit information about a debtor.

_____ 9. Form of bankruptcy in which a business is protected from creditors until a reorganization of the business obligations occurs.

_____ 10. Attachment of a debtor's bank account to satisfy a judgment.

_____ 11. Provides dollar limitations for debtor liability on stolen credit cards.

_____ 12. Requires disclosure of information such as amount due at lease signing, monthly payments, capitalized cost, excessive wear, use, and mileage provisions.

FILL-IN-THE-BLANK

1. When _____ occurs, a debtor turns over all non-exempt assets in exchange for release from debts.

2. If a creditor successfully sues a debtor on a debt, the court will issue a _____, which is the court's statement stating the debtor owes the money and the collector is entitled to be paid.

3. If a creditor charges 28 percent interest in a state where the maximum allowed interest rate is 24 percent, the creditor has violated the state's _____ law.

4. A creditor who refuses to extend credit to a woman unless her husband joins her in filing the credit application has violated the _____.

5. _____ prohibits creditors from sending an unsolicited credit card to a debtor.

6. The _____ applies to credit transactions in which the creditor takes a security interest in the debtor's residence.

7. The _____ provides disclosure protection for consumers who lease goods.

8. Additional disclosures by creditors are required in transactions where consumers use their homes as security for the credit under the _____.

9. A creditor is protected from harassment by a debt collector under the _____ Act.

10. A _____ is created by a _____ and once created, the creditor is given the right to repossess the pledged goods in the event the debtor defaults on repayment.

11. The _____ is characterized by high interest rates and high foreclosure rates.

12. A Chapter _____ bankruptcy is the liquidation of assets wherein the entity is dissolved or the individual's debts are discharged; a Chapter _____ bankruptcy is the consumer debt adjustment plan under which consumers can be given a new repayment plan for their debts; and a Chapter _____ bankruptcy is the reorganization of a business's obligations and in which a business has protection from collection and credits until a new plan for satisfying the business obligations is approved.

SHORT ANSWER

1. Under the Fair Credit Reporting Act, what information are consumer agencies prohibited from disclosing about a debtor?

    a. _____

    b. _____

    c. _____

2. What information, besides sex, race, color, religion, national origin, or age, cannot be considered in making a credit decision?

    a. _____

    b. _____

    c. _____

    d. _____

3. List the terms a creditor must include in a closed-end credit contract.

    a. _____

    b. _____

    c. _____

    d. _____

    e. _____

    f. _____

    g. _____

    h. _____

4. Under the Fair Credit Reporting Act, who can consumer reporting agencies disclose information to?

    a. _____

    b. _____

    c. _____

    d. _____

5. Explain whether the following questions on a credit application would violate the ECOA.

    a. Are you pregnant? _____

    _____

    b. Do you receive welfare payments? _____

    _____

    c. Do   you   have   a   criminal   record?
    _____

    _____

6. Under the Service Members Relief Act and the National Defense Act, what additional protections are afforded active duty service members?

    a. _____

    b. _____

    c. _____

    d. _____

    e. _____

Chapter 15

BUSINESS PROPERTY

CHAPTER OUTLINE

I.   What Can a Business Own? Personal Property: The Tangible Kind

    A.   Types of Personal Property - Fleet Vehicles, Machinery, Office Equipment

    B.   Transfer of Personal Property
        1.   Documents of title
        2.   Bills of sale

    C.   Lease - Right of Use and Possession

    D.   Bailments - Right of Possession
        1.   Parties
            a.   Bailor - property owner
            b.   Bailee - property possessor
        2.   Requirements
            a.   Property possession transferred
            b.   Intent to create a bailment
                Examples: valet parking, leasing in-line skates, coat check
        3.   Liability
            a.   Bailee liable for damages until return
            b.   Bailor must be certain property is in good condition

    E.   Creditors' Rights and Personal Property
        1.   Take security interest (lien) in personal property
            a.   Also called a chattel mortgage or collateral
            b.   Governed by Article IX of the Uniform Commercial Code (UCC)
        2.   Creation of security interest
            a.   Security agreement
            b.   Possession or some other perfection of the interest required
                (1) possession - creditor can waive security agreement
                (2) perfection by filing - each state's rules are different but all require some public filing
                      of a document (file a financing statement)
        3.   Enforcing a security interest
            a.   Debtor must be in default
            b.   Creditor may repossess without court action so long as there is no breach of the peace

II.   What Can a Business Own? Personal Property: The Intangible or Intellectual Kind

    A.   Patents, Copyrights, Trademarks, Trade Names, Trade Dress - Intangible Property: Has Value in Its Rights

B.   Protection for Business Intellectual Property
1.   Patents
     a.   Seventeen-year legal monopoly on products, processes, or machines with GATT; now 20 years
     b.   Exclusive rights to profits
     c.   Must be nonobvious, novel, and useful
     d.   Selling the idea without consent constitutes infringement
2.   Copyrights
     a.   Protect authors of books, magazine articles, plays, movies, songs, dances, photographs
     b.   Runs for lifetime of author plus seventy years
     c.   For material created while employed, copyright runs 120 years from the time of creation or 95 years from publication of the work, whichever is shorter
     d.   Sonny Bono Copyright Term Extension Act (CTEA)
          (1)   sponsored by the late Sonny Bono
          (2)   resulted from public appeal of Mickey Mouse losing its copyright
          (3)   Constitution prohibits granting copyright protection in perpetuity
     e.   Music - song plays controlled by the American Society of Composers, Authors and Publishers (ASCAP) and Broadcast Music, Inc. (BMI)
          (1)   songwriters register here
          (2)   users pay fee for each use
          (3)   royalties distributed to writers
     f.   Automatically a copyright but no suits can be filed until the copyright office is given a copy
     g.   Damages include profits, costs, attorney's fees
     h.   Technology has created new issues
          (1)   copying may not be for profit
          (2)   one case resulted in Digital Millenium Copyright Act
                (a)   criminalizes circumvention of protection technology
                (b)   criminalizes assisting others in circumventing technology
                (c)   criminalizes manufacturing products to circumvent
          (3)   Computer Software Copyright Act of 1980
                (a)   allows software to be copyrighted
                (b)   copyright source code and object code
3.   Fair use and copyrights
     a.   Short quotes
     b.   Research copies
     c.   Parody
4.   Trademarks
     a.   Words, pictures, designs, or symbols used to identify a product
     b.   Lanham Act of 1946 and subsequent amendments provide protection
     c.   Must be unique and nongeneric
     d.   Holder must maintain unique nature - Jell-O brand gelatin
     e.   Recent changes allow registration prior to use of the trademark - a practice followed in Europe for many years
     f.   Trademark Dilution Act of 1996 - protects against infringement
     g.   Consumer surveys are used to establish whether consumers will be misled
5.   Federal Trademark Dilution Act
     a.   Covers blurring of distinctive marks
     b.   Consumer surveys, used to see if there is confusion
6.   Trade Dress
     a.   Colors, shapes and designs associated with a product
     b.   Allowing their use is likely to create confusion

   c. *Two Pesos* case: Taco Cabana began business in 1978 in San Antonio, Texas, with patio eating areas, festive colors, and awnings and umbrellas. Two Pesos began business in 1985 in Houston with a similar look to its restaurants. Taco Cabana sued Two Pesos for infringement. The trial court held that Two Pesos had infringed Taco Cabana's trade dress and the court of appeals affirmed.

   d. In *Wal-Mart v. Samara,* 529 U.S. 205 (2000), the U.S. Supreme Court limited its ruling in *Two Pesos* to product packaging

    (1) no trade dress protection for product design unless it is registered

    (2) product packaging enjoys protection

   e. Chip piracy - e-commerce protection for chip design – Semi-Conductor Chip Protection Act

  7. Cyber Infringement

   a. Federal Trademark Dilution Act

   b. Applies to Internet

   c. Self-enforcing – parties can bring actions against others for the deception caused by the use of similar domain names

  8. Cybersquatting

   a. The common law notion of squatter's rights prevails

   b. Internet Corporation for Assigned Names and Numbers (ICAAN) approved the Uniform Domain Name Dispute Resolution Policy (UDRP)

   c. UDRP provides for arbitration to resolve disputes over domain names

   d. First UDRP decision was issued in January 2000 and granted the rights to worldwidewrestlingfederation.com to the WWF

   e. 591 UDRP proceedings commenced since then with 120 decisions

   f. Web site with decisions is at: www.icann.org/udrp/proceedings-list.htm and the registration site is at: www.domainmagistrate.com/faqs.html

III. International Intellectual Property Issues

 A. Patent Protection

  1. Some countries require opposition proceedings for defense of the patent

  2. Some countries impose working requirements (must produce it commercially or lose it)

  3. Trying to internationalize protection

 B. Trademark Protection

  1. Name, symbol, mark, letter, word or figure

  2. Must be registered in United States and other countries for full protection

  3. Protects the goodwill of the firm

  4. Common law countries establish trademark through establishing use and recognition

  5. Now in United States you can register trademark before you begin using it

  6. EU opened its Office for Harmonization on the International Market in Alicante, Spain on April 1, 1996; provides a one-step registration for all EU countries

  7. 1891 Madrid Agreement provides for international registry of trademarks - effective in all member countries for five years

  8. 1929 Pan American Convention provides protection for registered trademarks in all member countries

  9. Knock-off goods or goods carrying trademarks that are not produced by the trademark holder

  10. Gray market goods - actual trademark goods that are sold without authorization of trademark holder

C. Copyrights in International Business
1. Berne convention membership - registration in one is registration in all
2. Will be part of WIPO
3. Simultaneous publication in member country is protected

D. Differing International Standards
1. China's software piracy
2. China is on trade watch list because so much software is copied

IV. Enforcing Business Property Rights

A. Product Disparagement
1. Defamation for products/businesses
2. Elements
a. Statement about a business' reputation, honesty, or integrity that is untrue
b. Publication
c. Statement is directed at business with intent to injure
d. Damages

B. Palming Off
1. Company sells product by leading buyers to believe the product is something else
Example: Fake Rolex watches; Cabbage Patch dolls
2. Plaintiff must establish that confusion is likely

C. Misappropriation
1. Protects business trade secrets such as the customer list
2. Some theft or espionage is used to get it

V. What Can A Business Own? Real Property

A. The Nature of Real Property
1. Land/surface
2. Air rights
a. Airplane easements
b. Right to separate title and sell to others
c. Air rights can be sold and taxed
3. Mineral Rights
a. Can be sold/transferred separately
b. Oil, gas, coal, geothermal energy
4. Fixtures
a. Personal property becomes annexed to real property and is sold with the real property
b. Questions for determining whether an item is real or personal property:
(1) What did the parties intend?
(2) How is the property attached?
(3) Who attached the property? What was their interest in the land?
(4) Who wants to know? Insurer? Tax assessor? Buyer? Landlord?

B. Interests in Real Property
1. Fee simple - highest form of ownership
2. Life estate
a. Right to use and possession until death
b. Title goes back to grantor or remainderman

      3. Easement
        a. Right to use another's property for access
        b. Negative easement controls how another uses his land so as not to interfere with your use
        c. Easements in gross - utility easements
      4. Leases
        a. Periodic - month-to-month
        b. Fixed lease
        c. Issues of habitability controlled by statute

C. Transferring Real Property
    1. Transfer by deed
      a. Warranty deed - highest protection
        (1) title is good
        (2) transfer is proper
        (3) no encumbrances other than those noted
        (4) title insurance affords defense and protection against defects of record
      b. Special warranty or bargain and sale deed - same three warranties, but only for the time held by seller
      c. Quitclaim deed - no warranties; transfers title if you have title
    2. Recording - not required for transfer, but protects against future losses of title and rights
    3. Adverse possession - transfer of title through exclusive use and possession for statutorily-mandated period

D. Financing Real Property Purchases
    1. Borrow money and pledge land as security - mortgage
      a. Must be in writing
      b. Allows lender to take back (foreclose on) property if borrower defaults
    2. Other financing arrangement: deed of trust - third party holds title until debt is satisfied
    3. Both forms of financing documents should be recorded

KEY TERMS

Access Easements
Adverse Possession
Air Rights
Bailee
Bailment
Bailor
Bargain and Sale Deed
Berne Convention
    Implementation Act
Bill of Sale
Chattel Mortgage
Collateral
Community Trademark (CTM)
Computer Software Copyright
    Act of 1980
Copyrights
Cyber Infringement

Cybersquatting
Deed
Deed of Trust
Default
Design Patent
Digital Millennium Copyright
    Act
Disparagement
Documents of Title
Easement
Easements in Gross
Exculpatory Clause
Fair Use
Federal Anticybersquatting
    Consumer Protection Act
    (ACPA)
Federal Trademark Dilution Act

Fee Simple Interest
Financing Statement
Fixtures
Foreclosure
Function Patent
General Warranty Deed
Gray Market Goods
Infringement
Intangible Property
Internet Corporation for
    Assigned Names and
    Numbers (ICANN)
Knock-Off Goods
Lanham Act of 1946
Lease
License
Lien

Madrid Agreement	Quitclaim Deed	Trade Libel
Mineral Rights	Real Property	Trade Name
Misappropriation	Recording	Trade Secret
Mortgage	Security Agreement	Trademarks
Negative Easements	Security Interest	Uniform Commercial Code
Office of Harmonization of the	Slander of Title	(UCC)
Internal Market (OHIM)	Sonny Bono Copyright Term	Utility Patent
Opposition Proceedings	Extension Act (CTEA)	Warranty Deed
Palming Off	Special Warranty Deed	Working Requirements
Patents	Squatter's Rights	World Intellectual Property
Perfection	Tangible Property	Organization (WIPO)
Periodic Tenancy	Title Insurance	
Plant Patent	Trade Dress	
Product Disparagement	Trade Fixtures	

MATCHING

a. Fee Simple Interest   g. Digital Millennium Copyright Act
b. Chattel Mortgage   h. Trademark
c. Default   i. Cybersquatting
d. Bill of Sale   j. Working Requirements
e. Infringement   k. Copyright
f. Lease   l. Security Interest

_____ 1. Criminalizes the circumvention of protection technology in order to make copies of copyrighted materials.

_____ 2. Created when a security agreement is signed by a debtor for the extension of credit.

_____ 3. Contract showing the sale of personal property and provides proof of ownership.

_____ 4. Highest degree of land ownership.

_____ 5. The use of a patent, copyright, or trademark without the holder's consent.

_____ 6. Registering sites and domain names that are deceptively similar to existing trademarks that belong to others.

_____ 7. Protects the expression of ideas.

_____ 8. Words, pictures, designs, or symbols that businesses put on goods to identify them as their product.

_____ 9. A right of use and possession of property for a fixed or open-end period of time.

_____ 10. Imposed by some countries on a patent holder that requires that an idea or product must be produced commercially within a certain period of time or the patent is revoked.

_____ 11. Providing a lien or security interest in a property to the creditor.

_____ 12. Nonpayment of a debt.

FILL-IN-THE-BLANKS

1. _____ property is property you can see and touch; while _____ property comes in the form of patents, copyrights, trademarks, trade names, and trade dress.

2. If you leave your car with your auto mechanic, a _____ is created in which you are the _____ and the mechanic is the _____.

3. The colors, designs and shapes associated with a product are its _____.

4. If a company misleads buyers into thinking that they are buying a competitor's product, the competitor may successfully sue for the tort of _____, one of the oldest unfair methods of competition.

5. Wrongful use of a competitor's procedures, customer lists, or business processes, which are deemed to be _____, constitute the tort of _____.

6. Goods that are not actually produced by the firm, but carry the trademark or trade name of a firm's product are called _____.

7. One who converts a novel and useful idea into tangible form, marketable as a product, should apply for a _____.

8. A playwright who obtains a copyright to his or her successful Broadway play has a right to protect against _____ by others.

9. A _____, or a symbol that identifies a particular producer of a product, is protected by the _____ Act of 1946.

10. A professor's reproduction of a page from a copyrighted book does not constitute an infringement under the concept of _____.

11. Utility or _____ patents cover machines, processes, and improvements to existing devices; _____ patents protect the features of a product; and _____ patents are for new forms of plants and hybrids.

12. The protection of authors of books, movies, songs and so on is called _____.

SHORT ANSWER

1.   What are the elements for disparagement?

     a.   _____

     b.   _____

     c.   _____

     d.   _____

2.   What are the questions that are important in determining whether an item is a fixture and part of the real property?

     a.   _____

     b.   _____

     c.   _____

     d.   _____

3.   Name three forms of intangible property.

     a.   _____

     b.   _____

     c.   _____

4.   Define the following:

     a.   Fee simple   _____

     b.   Mortgage   _____

     c.   Easement   _____

     d.   Deed   _____

     e.   Warranty Deed   _____

     f.   Special Warranty Deed   _____

5. List which statutory protections would apply to each of these forms of intellectual property.

   a. Song _____

   b. Prescription drug _____

   c. Movie _____

   d. Software _____

6. Explain the Sonny Bono Copyright Term Extension Act.

   _____

   _____

   _____

Chapter 16

TRADE PRACTICES: ANTITRUST

CHAPTER OUTLINE

I. What Interferes With Competition? Covenants Not to Compete

    A. Early Common Law of Trade Restraints

    B. Covenants Not to Compete - Modern Common Law of Trade Restraints
        1. Initially were void
        2. Gradually became acceptable
            a. If necessary to protect the business
            b. If reasonable in time
            c. If reasonable in geographic scope
            Examples: Restriction on seller in sale of a business to protect goodwill, restrictions in shopping center leases to prevent identical tenants and too close proximity competition

II. What Interferes With Competition? An Overview of the Federal Statutory Scheme on Restraint of Trade

    A. Jurisdiction of Federal Antitrust Laws
        1. Must be some interstate commerce for federal laws to apply
        2. Sherman Act Jurisdiction
            a. Same standards for interstate as under the Commerce Clause
            b. Very broad standard
        3   Clayton Act Jurisdiction
            a. Narrower application
            b. To persons engaged in interstate commerce
        4. Robinson-Patman Act Jurisdiction
            a. Most stringent standards
            b. Seller must be engaged in interstate commerce
            c. Two claimed discrimination sales must be across state lines
            d. In-state firms are not subject to Robinson-Patman

    B. The Types of Activities Federal Antitrust Laws Regulate
        1. Horizontal vs. vertical
        2. *Per se* vs. Rule of Reason

III. Horizontal Restraints of Trade

    A. Designed to Lessen Competition Among a Firm's Competitors

    B. Sherman Act Restraints - Monopolization
        1. Section 2 prohibits monopolizing
        2. Some monopolies are permitted
            a. Newspapers - town can't support more than one
            b. Monopoly gained by nature of product - superior skill, foresight, and industry

3. Elements of monopolization
    a. Monopoly power
        (1) power to control prices or exclude competition in the relevant market
        (2) examine firm's market power
            (a) firm's product has inelastic demand curve (people are not willing to take substitutes)
            (b) firm's percent share of the market
        (3) examine relevant market
            (a) geographic market - national sales may be 10 percent for a beer while local sales are 75 percent (submarket)
            (b) product market - examine cross-elasticity of demand - how willing are consumers to substitute goods?
                Example: Hershey's chocolate chips for Nestle's chocolate chips? The greater the elasticity of demand, the broader the product market
            (c) decision on relevant market can control whether there is monopolization
                Example: Saran Wrap has 75 percent of clear plastic wrap market but only 20 percent of food wrap market
    b. Purposeful act required
        (1) show that monopoly has resulted from something other than superior skill, foresight, and industry
        (2) predatory pricing - pricing below cost for a temporary period to drive others out
        (3) exclusionary conduct - prevents competitor from entering the market
4. Attempts to monopolize - must show dangerous probability of monopolization

C. Horizontal Restraints - Price-Fixing
    1. Collaboration among competitors for the purpose of raising, depressing, fixing, pegging, or stabilizing the price of a commodity
    2. *Per se* violation - conduct is unreasonable and illegal; no defenses for such action
    3. Minimum prices - discourages competition
    4. Maximum prices - stabilizes prices
    5. List prices - exchange of price information hurts market
    6. Production limitations - controls supply and controls price
    7. Limitations on competitive bidding
        a. *Per se* violations
        b. Example: Engineers agreeing not to bid on projects
    8. Good intentions are not a defense
    9. Credit arrangement - universal agreement on charges is price-fixing

D. Division of Markets
    1. *Per se* violation
    2. Lessens competition in that market

E. Group Boycotts and Refusals to Deal
    1. May have the best intentions in the world but they are illegal
    2. Example: Garment boycotts on knock-offs

F. Free Speech and Anticompetitive Behavior
    1. *Noerr-Pennington* doctrine
        a. Competitors can work together for governmental action
        b. Lobbying and political efforts
        c. Cannot restrain this activity - First Amendment protections

     2.   Local Government Antitrust Act
         a.   Exempts state and local government from antitrust suits
         b.   Must have state policy to allow suit
     3.   Joint Venture Trading Act
         a.   Joint ventures for international competition permitted
         b.   Prior approval of Justice Department required
     4.   Shipping Act of 1984
         a.   Joint ventures among shippers
         b.   Allows better international competition on shipping

  G. Subtle Anticompetitive Behavior: Interlocking Directorates
     1.   Prohibits director of firm with $10 million or more in capital from being a director for a competitor
     2.   Lessens likelihood of exchange of anticompetitive information

  H. Merging Competitors and the Effect on Competition
     1.   Presumptively illegal to have horizontal mergers
     2.   Courts look at market share to determine true illegality
     3.   Exceptions
         a.   failing company doctrine - purpose is asset acquisition
         b.   small-company defense - two small companies merge to better compete with larger firms
     4.   Today Justice Department follows the Herfindahl-Hirschman index to evaluate market concentration

IV. Vertical Trade Restraints

  A. Covers Parties in Chain of Distribution: Manufacturer - Wholesaler - Retailer

  B. Resale Price Maintenance
     1.   Attempt by manufacturer to control price retailers charge for the product
     2.   Court has been reexamining
     3.   Court is also revisiting "suggested retail prices" and their enforcement

  C. Monopsony
     1.   A monopsony is price control by the buyer
     2.   *Weyerhaeuser v. Ross-Simons* – the court held that a buyer was not artificially driving up supplier prices through its large orders, it's manufacturing process was superior and it needed more supplies just because it could process more

  D. Sole Outlets and Exclusive Distributorships
     1.   Manufacturer appoints a distributor or retailer as the exclusive outlet
     2.   Subject to a rule-of-reason analysis:
         a.   Not automatically illegal
         b.   Violators can present justification
     3.   Factors examined in rule of reason analysis:
         a.   Manufacturers can pick and choose dealers
         b.   There must be interbrand competition
             Example: Coke can have exclusive distributors because there is plenty of soft drink competition from Pepsi, 7-Up, and so on
         c.   If there is little interbrand competition, then intrabrand competition is required
             Example: Car manufacturers and several dealerships

E. Customer and Territorial Restrictions
1. Restricting to whom and where a dealer can sell
2. Subject to a rule-of-reason analysis:
    a. Consider amount of interbrand competition
    b. Consider market power of manufacturer

F. Tying Arrangements
1. Sales arrangements that require buyers to buy an additional product in order to get the product they want
    a. Tying product = desired product
    b. Tied product = required product
        Example: Requiring buyer to buy nails in order to get the hammer he wants when there are other nails available
2. Generally illegal per se violation (Clayton Act, Section 3)
    a. Clayton Act - covers goods
    b. Sherman Act - Section 1 covers services, real property, and intangibles
    c. Violation depends on market and power - is tying product unique?
3. Defenses
    a. New-industry defense - needed to protect quality to establish product
        Example: Solar water heaters and requiring buyers to buy plumbing; in order to get solar technology to catch on it has to work
    b. Quality control for protection of goodwill - specifications are so detailed, could not be supplied by anyone else

G. Price Discrimination
1. Prohibited by Robinson-Patman Act
2. Selling goods at prices that have different ratios to the marginal cost of producing them
3. Required elements (if established, both buyer and seller are guilty):
    a. Interstate commerce
        (1) seller engaged in interstate commerce
        (2) at least one of two transactions occurs across state lines
    b. Price discrimination among purchasers
        (1) does not apply to leases and consignments
        (2) purchases must be made at about the same time
        (3) can be discrimination through additional terms
    c. Commodities of like grade and quality
        (1) no physical differences in the product
        (2) label difference does not make the goods different; generic brands versus brand name - would have to be different in quality for prices to be different
    d. Lessening or injuring competition
        Example: Predatory pricing differences
4. Defenses to price discrimination
    a. Legitimate cost differences
    b. Quantity discounts OK (if there is an actual savings)
    c. Market changes, inflation, material costs
    d. Meeting the competition

H. Vertical Mergers
    1. Mergers between firms with a buyer-seller relationship
    2. Illegality depends upon:
        a. Geographic and product markets
        b. Whether effect of merger hurts competition
    3. Failing firm defense
        a. No other offers to buy
        b. Chapter 11 bankruptcy wouldn't help
    4. States now have authority to step in and regulate mergers if feds do not

V. What are the Penalties and Remedies for Anticompetitive Behavior?

  A. Criminal Penalties
    1. Individuals – 10 years/$10 million
    2. Corporations - $100 million
    3. No penalties for FTC and Clayton Acts
    4. Robinson-Patman – some criminal penalties
    5. Employees, officers and directors can all be held liable

  B. Equitable Remedies
    1. Injunctions
    2. Divestitures

  C. Private Actions for Damages
    1. Treble damages
    2. Court is beginning to restrict application of antitrust laws
    3. *Prima facie* case is made by plaintiffs when they show government sanctions

VI. What Lies Ahead in Anticompetitive Behavior: The Antitrust Modernization Commission

  A. Released Its Findings in 2007 After Being Created in 2002

  B. Recommendations Tended to Favor Status Quo

  C. Courts Need to Refine on a Case-by-Case Basis, Considering the Economic Issues

VII. Antitrust Issues in International Competition

  A. U.S. Allows Joint Ventures in International Markets that Would Not Be Permitted in the U.S.

  B. Antitrust Laws Most Stringent in the United States

  C. Companies Doing Business in the United States Are Still Subject to U.S. Antitrust Laws

KEY TERMS

Antitrust Modernization
    Commission (AMC)
Celler-Kefauver Act
Clayton Act
Covenant Not to Compete
Cross-Elasticity of Demand
Customer and Territorial
    Restrictions
Equitable Remedies
Exclusionary Conduct
Exclusive Distributorship
    Agreement
Failing-Company Doctrine
Fair Trade Contracts
Federal Trade Commission Act
Geographic Market
Group Boycotts
Hart-Scott-Rodino Antitrust
    Improvements Act

Horizontal Mergers
Horizontal Restraints of Trade
Injunction
Interbrand Competition
Interlocking Directorates
Intrabrand Competition
Joint Ventures
Like Grade or Quality
Market Power
Meeting the Competition
Monopolization
Monopoly Power
Monopsony
Noerr-Pennington Doctrine
Per Se Illegal
Per Se Violation
Predatory Bidding
Predatory Pricing
Price Discrimination

Price Fixing
Prima Facie Case
Product Market
Relevant Market
Requirements Contracts
Resale Price Maintenance
Robinson-Patman Act
Rule of Reason
Sherman Act
Small-Company Doctrine
Sole Outlet Agreement
Submarket
Superior Skill, Foresight, and
    Industry
Treble Damages
Tying Sales
Vertical Mergers

MATCHING

a.   Superior Skill, Foresight, and Industry
b.   Resale Price Maintenance
c.   Equitable Remedy
d.   Failing-Company Doctrine
e.   Predatory Pricing
f.   Meeting the Competition

g.   Intrabrand Competition
h.   Sole Outlet Agreement
i.   Covenant Not to Compete
j.   *Noerr-Pennington* Doctrine
k.   Horizontal Restraints of Trade
l.   Monopsony

_____   1. Attempt by a manufacturer to control the price retailers charge for the manufacturer's product.

_____   2. A permissible form of price discrimination.

_____   3. Exclusive distributorship.

_____   4. Pricing a commodity below actual cost for a short period of time to drive a potential competitor out of business.

_____   5. Defense to a horizontal merger that allows a failing company's assets or inventories to be acquired by a competitor.

_____   6. Exception to Sherman Act violations where competitors are permitted to work together for the purpose of governmental lobbying and other political action.

_____ 7. Court order restraining or preventing anticompetitive conduct.

_____ 8. Competition among sellers of a manufacturer's product.

_____ 9. Permissible method of achieving monopoly power.

_____ 10. A trade restraint that is valid as long as it is reasonable in scope and length.

_____ 11. Designed to lessen competition among a firm's competitors.

_____ 12. Exists when the buyer, not the seller, has the ability to control market prices.

FILL-IN-THE-BLANKS

1. To prove monopolization, it must be shown that the defendant possesses _____ in the _____ and that this was acquired through illegitimate competition.

2. A relevant product market is determined by the market _____, or consumers' willingness to substitute other products in the event of unavailability or price change.

3. Section 8 of the Clayton Act prohibits _____, in an attempt to decrease the likelihood that anticompetitive information about price and markets will be exchanged between competitors.

4. If a buyer of a product merges with its seller, a _____ has resulted.

5. Damages allowed by the Clayton Act for any person whose business or property is injured as a result of an antitrust violation are _____ damages or "threefold the damages by him sustained."

6. A _____ or _____ agreement is one in which a manufacturer designates a particular retailer as the exclusive distributor for its product.

7. A _____ requires the buyer to take an additional product in order to be permitted to buy the one it needs.

8. Competition available for a manufacturer's product is _____ competition.

9. If a manufacturer sells the identical product to buyers in State A for $2.00 per unit and to buyers in State B for $2.75 per unit, it has engaged in the practice of _____, prohibited by the _____ Act.

10. In the situation described in problem #9, a defense that the manufacturer could raise is that it was engaged solely in _____, which is necessary because local and regional manufacturers in State A are marketing the same product at substantially below $2.75.

11. Conduct that prevents a potential competitor from entering a market is _____ conduct.

12. Under the _____ doctrine, small companies are allowed to merge in order to better compete with larger companies in the market.

SHORT ANSWER

1. List the four elements required in a price discrimination case.

    a. _____

    b. _____

    c. _____

    d. _____

2. To prove monopolization, what elements must be established?

    a. _____

    b. _____

3. Name six types of vertical trade restraints.

    a. _____

    b. _____

    c. _____

    d. _____

    e. _____

    f. _____

4. Name four types of horizontal trade restraints

    a. _____

    b. _____

    c. _____

    d. _____

5.   Explain whether the following would be price fixing.

   a.   Setting a minimum price. _____

   _____

   b.   Setting a maximum price. _____

   _____

   c.   Setting a suggested retail price. _____

   _____

6.   Two defenses are recognized for tying cases – what are they?

   a.   _____

   b.   _____

Chapter 17

MANAGEMENT OF EMPLOYEE CONDUCT: AGENCY

CHAPTER OUTLINE

I.   Names and Roles: Agency Terminology

    A.   Agency - Relationship is One in Which One Party Agrees to Act on Behalf of Another

       Examples: Sales clerks, real estate agents, sports agents

    B.   Principal - Employers

    C.   Agents - Party Hired By a Principal To Do a Task on Behalf of the Principal

    D.   Employers - Employees: Master/Servant Relationships
       1.   Master/principal exercises a great deal of control over the servant/agent
       2.   Factors that control whether this type of relationship exists:
          a.   Level of supervision
          b.   Level of control
          c.   Nature of agent's work
          d.   Regularity of hours and pay
          e.   Length of employment

    E.   Independent Contractors - Hired to Perform a Task but Is Not Directly Supervised

       Example: Lawyers

    F.   Agency Law
       1.   *Restatement of Agency* - common law followed by most courts
       2.   Three parts to agency law
          a.   Creating the agency relationship
          b.   Relationship between principal and agent
          c.   Relationships of agent and principal to third parties

II.   Creation of the Agency Relationship

    A.   Created When the Principal Hires Someone

    B.   Express Authority
       1.   Created by principal stating or writing that agency exists and the authority thereof
       2.   Requires oral or written agreement - must be in writing if statute of frauds requires
          Example: Agency contract is longer than one year

    C.   The Record - If the Agent's Contracts Must Be Evidenced by a Record, the Agent's Authority Must Be Evidenced by a Record

D. Capacity
    1. Principal must have capacity
    2. Age and mental capacity
    3. Unincorporated associations do not have capacity
        a. Have no legal existence
            Examples: Little League teams, some churches
        b. Members will be liable since there is no principal
        c. Uniform Unincorporated Nonprofit Association Act allows liability for organization, not those who sign
    4. Capacity of agent is not an issue but many firms are requiring drug testing for them

E. Implied Authority - The extension of express authority by custom
    Examples: Treasurer has authority to start bank accounts, order checks, and so on; apartment manager has authority to call for repairs and collect rent

F. Apparent Authority
    1. Arises from the way agents present themselves to third parties
    2. Also called agency by estoppel or ostensible authority
        Examples: Failure to notify of an agent's retirement, allowing bank to use your name for another's loan

G. Ratification
    1. Principal reviews contract and decides to honor it even though agent had no authority to enter into it
    2. Retroactive approval of agent's contract

III. The Principal-Agent Relationship

A. The Agent's Responsibilities
    1. Loyalty
        a. Agent can't represent both sides
        b. Can't make a profit at principal's expense
        c. Duty of loyalty - post-employment
            (1) covenants not to compete are enforceable for the most part
            (2) dot-com/e-commerce issues
                (a) note payment is given for covenant
                (b) confidentiality agreements are in addition to covenants not to compete
    2. Obedience
        a. Follows principal's instructions
        b. Need not do anything illegal
    3. Duty of care
        a. Give time and effort
        b. Follow through

B. The Principal's Rights and Responsibilities
    1. Duty to pay
    2. Except gratuitous agency
    3. *Del credere* agency - agent will be liability for payment if buyer does not pay

IV. Liability of Principals for Agents' Conduct: The Relationship With Third Parties
  A. Contract Liability
    1. Principal has full liability for authorized acts of agent and those done with apparent authority
    2. Issues of disclosure arise
       a. Disclosed principal - principal is fully liable; agent is not unless the agent had no authority
       b. Partially disclosed principal - agent indicates there is a principal but does not tell who it is; third party can hold either liable
       c. Undisclosed principal - agent does not disclose there is a principal; agent stands alone unless principal comes forward

  B. Liability of Principals for Agents' Torts
    1. Must have master-servant relationship
       a. Not independent contractor
       b. Degree of supervision is controlling
    2. Liable for torts of servants in scope of employment
       a. Scope = doing master's work
          Examples: Deliveries, sales calls, and so on
       b. Doctrine of respondeat superior - let the master answer
    3. Not liable for torts committed while on frolic - frolics include:
       a. Stops for personal reasons
       b. Going off-duty temporarily
       c. Liable for detours such as lunch break while employee is on the road
    4. Negligent hiring and supervision
       a. Hiring an employee without sufficient references/background checks is negligence
       b. Failure to supervise or take action with a dangerous or violent employee is negligent supervision
    5. Drug testing
       a. Necessary for certain situations: driving, machinery operation, any jobs where human safety is an issue
       b. U.S. Supreme Court has upheld right of employer/railroad to test employees because of public safety issues; public safety interest outweighs privacy interests
    6. Torts of independent contractors
       a. Principals generally not liable for torts of independent contractors
       b. However, they are liable for inherently dangerous activities done by independent contractors
          Example: Using explosives
       c. Also principals are liable for hiring an incompetent independent contractor
          Example: Abusive collection agency

V. Termination of the Agency Relationship

  A. Need to Give Public or Constructive Notice (Trade Publication) of the Termination in Order to Terminate Apparent Authority

  B. Also Give Private (Mailed) Notice (Letters) to Those That Have Dealt With the Agent

  C. Without Notice, Agent Will Have Lingering Apparent Authority (No One Knows They Have Left)

VI. Termination of Agents Under Employment at Will

    A. Has No Definite Ending Date

    B. Usually There Is No Formal Written Contract - Implied Contract

    C. Used to Be They Could Be Fired at Any Time; Courts Now Afford Protection

    D. The Implied Contract - Personnel Manuals Will Be a Contract If Employees Relied on Its Procedures

    E. The Public Policy Protection - Whistle-Blowers
        1. Protects employees who report illegal conduct or conduct that violates public policy
        2. Protects employees who refuse to participate in illegal conduct
            Examples: Price-fixing, FDA or FAA violations
        3. Peer review now used as a means for reviewing employee grievances

    F. The Antiretaliation Statutes: Protection for Whistle-Blowers
        1. Passed in many states and by federal agencies
        2. Prohibit firing, demotion, reprimands, and pay cuts of employees who report employer conduct
        3. Federal level - Energy Reorganization Act afford protection for employees involved in nuclear work (called EPS - Employee Protection Section)
        4. All 50 states have some form of protection for whistle-blowers
        5. Sarbanes-Oxley (SOX) provides antiretaliation protection against employees who raise financial reporting issues
            a. Criminal penalties for retaliation up to 10 years
            b. Employee damages are reinstatement, back pay and damages
            c. Also applies to analysts
        6. Many companies have created a peer review process for termination and other actions against employees

VII. Agency Relationships in International Law

    A. Complex Interrelationships Often Evade the Law - BCCI and Its Complex Structure Helped It Evade the Law

    B. Disclosure of Interrelationships Becomes Important for Conflicts, Compliance

KEY TERMS

Actual Notice	1978	Fiduciary Relationship
Agency	Constructive Notice	Gratuitous Agency
Agency by Estoppel	Disclosed Principal	Implied Authority
Agency Law	Employment at Will	Independent Contractor
Agent	Energy Reorganization Act	Inherently Dangerous
Apparent Authority	Express Authority	Activities
Capacity	Express Contract	Lingering Apparent Authority
Civil Service Reform Act of	False Claims Act	Master-Servant Relationship

Partially Disclosed Principal
Peer Review
Power of Attorney
Principal
Public Policy Exception
Ratification
Respondeat Superior

Restatement of Agency
Sarbanes-Oxley
Scope of Employment
Undisclosed Principal
Uniform Durable Power of
    Attorney Act (UDPAA)
Uniform Unincorporated

Nonprofit Association
    Act (UUNAA)
Unincorporated Association
Whistle-Blower
Whistle-Blower Protection
    Act of 1989

MATCHING

a. Whistle-Blower
b. Express Contract
c. Apparent Authority
d. Gratuitous Agency
e. Unincorporated Association
f. Implied Authority

g. Master-Servant Relationship
h. Independent Contractor
i. Power of Attorney
j. Scope of Employment
k. Ratification
l. Employment at Will

_____ 1. An agency relationship in which the principal exercises a great deal of control over the agent.

_____ 2. One hired by another to perform a task, but who is not directly controlled by the hirer.

_____ 3. The authority a company president would have to conduct salary reviews of company employees, when the contract between the company and president does not specifically list this as a duty of the president.

_____ 4. Agency by estoppel.

_____ 5. Employee who reports illegal conduct or refuses to participate in conduct which is illegal or a violation of public policy.

_____ 6. A group that acts as an entity but has no legal existence.

_____ 7. Conferring authority upon an agent retroactively.

_____ 8. Agent is working for the principal at the time a tort occurs.

_____ 9. An agency relationship in which the employee may be hired or fired at the discretion of the employer (if there is cause and documentation).

_____ 10. A relationship in which the agent has the authority to act for the principal but doesn't expect to be compensated.

_____ 11. Grants another authority to enter into transactions.

_____ 12. Specifies the limitations of an employee/agent's authority.

FILL-IN-THE-BLANKS

1. A principal won't be liable for the tort of his agent if the agent is classified as a(n) _____, or is not acting within the _____ of his or her employment.

2. _____ holds a principal liable if the principal allows others to think an agent has the proper authority to deal with them.

3. Even though a contractor has employed a firm to blast a tunnel through a mountain with explosives for the purpose of building a road, and exercises no control over this firm, the road contractor can still be held liable for the blasting firm's torts because use of explosives constitutes an _____.

4. An agent hired to find a piece of commercial property on which the principal plans to build a shopping center and who, without disclosure to the principal, purchases land for the principal from a partnership of which the agent is an active member, has violated his _____ duty to the principal.

5. Although express and implied authority of an agent had been terminated by mutual agreement of the principal and agent, _____ authority may still remain. Such authority will continue until _____ is given to third parties.

6. Giving notice to the public at large by publication of a fact in a newspaper or trade journal is referred to as _____ notice, and in most cases will be sufficient to give notice to third parties that an agent's authority has come to an end.

7. While a salaried personnel director of a corporation and a real estate broker hired by the corporation to sell some of its property are both considered agents, the personnel director is called a _____ while the real estate broker is called a(n) _____.

8. Under the _____ doctrine, a towing company can be held liable for injuries inflicted by the negligence of a tow truck driver who was on a call at the time of the accident.

9. A personnel manager's responsibility as set forth in his employment contract to enter into contracts with insurance companies to provide group benefits for employees is an example of _____ authority.

10. When a third party is aware there is a principal involved and knows the identity of that principal, the principal is _____ and is liable to the third party; whereas, when a third party knows there is a principal, but not the principal's identity, the principal is _____ and both the agent and principal can be held liable.

11. _____ are people hired by a principal to do a task on behalf of the principal.

12. The _____ Act provides antiretaliation protections for whistle-blowers.

SHORT ANSWER

1. What are the factors used to determine whether a master-servant relationship exists?

   a. _____

   b. _____

   c. _____

   d. _____

   e. _____

2. Name the two exceptions to the employment-at-will doctrine.

   a. _____

   b. _____

3. List three things an employer should do when laying people off.

   a. _____

   b. _____

   c. _____

4. Determine who is liable on contracts entered into by agents in the following situations:

   a. Undisclosed principal and agent with full authority

   _____

   b. Undisclosed principal and agent without authority

   _____

   c. Partially disclosed principal and agent with full authority

   _____

5.	Explain the protections and remedies given to whistle-blowers by Sarbanes-Oxley.

_____

_____

_____

6.	Explain the Uniform Durable Power of Attorney Act.

_____

_____

_____

Chapter 18

MANAGEMENT OF EMPLOYEE WELFARE

CHAPTER OUTLINE

I. Wages and Hours Protection

    A. Fair Labor Standards Act (FLSA) - Often Called "The Minimum Wage Law"
        1. Coverage
            a. Businesses engaged in interstate commerce
            b. Businesses engaged in production of goods to be shipped in interstate commerce
            c. Businesses engaged in interstate shipping
            d. Expanded to cover business enterprises with gross income of $362,500 or more
            e. Exemptions
                (1) independent contractors
                (2) agriculture, fishing, and domestic service
                (3) white-collar management
                (4) executive, administrative, and professional people
        2. FLSA minimum wage and overtime regulations
            a. Graduate increases in minimum wages
            b. Time-and-one-half pay for overtime (over 40 hours)
            c. White collar, professional, administrative employees are exempt
            d. New rules have created a great deal of ambiguity

    B. FLSA and Child Labor Provisions
        1. Age 18 years and over - any jobs
        2. 16-17 years old - any nonhazardous job (hazardous - mining, logging, roofing, excavation)
        3. 14-15 years old - any nonhazardous, non-manufacturing, and nonmining job during nonschool hours; limits on hours
        4. Recordkeeping - employers must keep records of hours and wages; fines for not doing so
        5. Child actors are subject to strict Screen Actors Guild rules

    C. Enforcement of FLSA
        1. Can begin by complaint filed with U.S. Labor Department
        2. Employer can seek interpretation from Department of Labor
        3. Labor Department can initiate its own investigation

    D. FLSA and Record-Keeping Requirements
        1. Employers must keep records of hours and wages of their employees
        2. Required formats

    E. Penalties for FLSA Violations
        1. Fines - $10,000 first conviction
        2. $10,000 and/or six months for second violation
        3. Employees can't be fired for reporting violations

F.   Liability for FLSA Violation
    1.   Corporation is liable
    2.   Officers can be held individually liable

G.   The Equal Pay Act of 1963
    1.   Illegal to pay different wages to men and women doing the same jobs
    2.   Equal Pay Act is not a comparable worth statute
        a.   Comparable worth requires equal pay for jobs that require equal skill, effort, and responsibility
        b.   Test case came from Washington when a licensed practical nurse discovered she earned less than the groundskeeper at a state hospital and less than men doing similar jobs in the prisons; trial judge found discrimination and ordered back pay but decision was later reversed
        c.   Presently, federal standards do not require comparable worth
    3.   Merit and seniority systems are exceptions

II.   Workplace Safety

A.   The Occupational Safety and Health Act
    1.   Passed to ensure workplace safety precautions
    2.   OSHA was agency created to enforce it

B.   OSHA Coverage and Duties
    1.   Employers covered - all with one or more employees
    2.   Basic responsibilities:
        a.   Know and follow OSHA's rules
        b.   Inspect for hazards and correct them
        c.   Post employee rights
        d.   Keep records of injuries
        e.   Post OSHA citations

C.   OSHA Responsibilities
    1.   Promulgating rules and safety standards
    2.   Can award variances for certain employers
    3.   Inspections
        a.   Have targeted industries (roofing, lumber)
        b.   Also have random inspections
        c.   Cannot retaliate against employee who notifies OSHA and requests an inspection
    4.   OSHA search warrant requirement
        a.   Either voluntary or require warrant
        b.   Surprise element still preserved even with warrant
        c.   Employees can accompany an OSHA inspector
        d.   Employees can file complaints
        e.   Right to notice if employer applies for variance
    5.   OSHA penalties
        a.   Fine and imprisonment escalate with seriousness of violation
        b.   Citation is first step
        c.   Many employers negotiate a consent decree after a citation
        d.   If no consent decree, there is a hearing before an administrative law judge (ALJ)
        e.   ALJ makes recommendations and OSHRC decides
        f.   Can then appeal to a court

   D. State OSHA Programs
       1. States share responsibility for safety with feds
       2. Secretary of Labor must approve state's plan

   E. Employment Impairment and Testing Issues - If Safety Is an Issue, U.S. Supreme Court Has Authorized Testing

III. Employee Pensions, Retirement, and Social Security

   A. Social Security Act of 1935
       1. Every employee, who is not an independent contractor, contributes to Federal Insurance Contributions Act (FICA)
       3. Benefits under Social Security depend on work and salary range

   B. Private Retirement Plans: Employment Retirement Income Security Act (ERISA)
       1. Coverage of ERISA: Applies to employers in interstate commerce
       2. Applies to medical, retirement, or deferred income plan
       3. Requirements of ERISA plans
           a. Must give employees an annual report
           b. Must disclose loans made from the fund
           c. ERISA does not require pension plans; it only regulates employers who offer them; levels of responsibility have caused some employers to drop the plans
       4. Employee rights under ERISA: get vesting rights in their pensions
       5. FASB 106, Retirees and Pensions - requires corporation to expense cost of benefits for retired employees
       6. Pension Protection Act of 2006
           a. Imposes new funding requirements
           b. New disclosure requirements

   C. Unemployment Compensation
       1. Benefits provided
           a. States determine amount
           b. States' rules on minimum and maximum
           c. States' rule on length
       2. Qualifying for benefits
           a. Must have been involuntarily terminated
           b. Must be able and available for work
           c. Must be seeking employment
       3. Who pays for unemployment benefits?
           a. States administer the program
           b. Funds deposited with state

IV. Workers' Compensation Laws

    A.   Compensation for Work-Related Injuries

    B.   Principles of Workers' Compensation
        1.   Employees injured in scope of employment are covered
        2.   Fault is immaterial
        3.   Independent contractors are not covered
        4.   Benefits include expenses, lost wages, and injury compensation
        5.   Employees do not have right of common law suit
        6.   Third parties can be sued to indemnify employers
        7.   Administrative agency handles program
        8.   Every employer must carry insurance or be self-insured

    C.   Employee Injuries
        1.   Primarily accidental injuries covered
        2.   Definition has been expanded
            a.   Back problems from lifting
            b.   Medical problems - heart attacks and nervous breakdowns
            c.   Stress
        3.   Co-worker injury
            a.   Covered if arises in scope of employment
            b.   Issue of rape is a problem; employer can be sued for the failure to screen employees adequately

    D.   Fault is Immaterial in Workers' Comp (Employee Can Even Disobey Instructions and Be Compensated)

    E.   Employee vs. Independent Contractors: Independent Contractors are Not Covered

    F.   Benefits
        1.   Lost wages
        2.   Medical expenses
        3.   Disability benefits
            a.   Partial disability - listed on schedule by rate
                 Example: 50 percent of wages
            b.   Total disability - generally 2/3 of salary
            c.   Unscheduled injuries are determined by board
            d.   Death benefits paid to family

    G.   Forfeiture of the Right of Suit: Benefits in Lieu of Suing Employer

    H.   Third-Party Suits: Can Sue Product Manufacturers, Other Third Parties, But Recovery Must First Go to Reimburse Employer

    I.   Each State Has an Administrative Agency for Administration of Benefits and Insurance

    J.   Insurance - Employers Must Have Some Form
        1.   Self-insurance
        2.   Private insurance
        3.   State fund insurance

    K.   Problems in Workers' Comp Systems
1. Extent of injuries covered
2. Fraud
3. Nature of injuries changing from manufacturing injuries to stress, heart disease, and repetitive motion
4. Long-term hazards
5. Relationship between Americans with Disabilities Act and Workers' Compensation

V. Labor Unions

    A.   History and Development of Labor Legislation
1. Norris-LaGuardia Act of 1932 (Anti-Injunction Act)
   a. Stopped federal courts from issuing injunctions to stop union strikes
   b. Some exceptions:
      (1) violence
      (2) lack of control - harm to public
2. Wagner Act - National Labor Relations Act (NLRA) of 1935
   a. Gave employees the right to unionize
   b. Prohibited employers from firing or discriminating against union members
   c. Established NLRB
      (1) created to conduct union election
      (2) created to remedy unfair labor practices
3. Taft-Hartley Act - Labor Management Relations Act of 1947
   a. Lists unfair labor practices for unions
   b. Addresses secondary boycotts
   c. Provides president with authority to have prestrike cooling-off period when public health and safety are at issue; has been used in coal and transportation strikes
4. Landrum-Griffin Act - The Labor Management Reporting and Disclosure Act of 1959
   a. Regulates union officials
   b. Gives union members a bill of rights
   c. Establishes penalties for misconduct

    B.   Union Organizing Efforts
1. Right to unionize
2. Selecting a union
   a. Once selected, union represents all employees
   b. Collective bargaining unit determined
      (1) can be a plant
      (2) can be workers doing same job in a company
      (3) NLRB decides based on:
          (a) type of union
          (b) duties, wages, and skills of employees
          (c) relationship to employer
          (d) wishes of employees
3. Petition, cards, and vote
   a. Petition for union representation filed
      (1) must be supported by signed, dated authorization cards from 30 percent of unit
      (2) cards must be signed willingly
   b. Election: NLRB monitors
      (1) restrictions on what employer can do just prior to election and during campaign
      (2) unions are subject to reasonable employer rules

4. Certification
    a. Exclusive right to represent employees
    b. Cannot hold another election for twelve months
    c. If collective bargaining agreement in place, cannot hold election during that agreement's effective time
    d. Union members have the right to not participate along with nonunion members in a strike
5. Nonunion members in the certified workplace
    a. Right to organize
    b. Cannot mandate membership
    c. Cannot force participation

C. Union Contract Negotiations
    1. Try to get employer contract - collective bargaining agreement
    2. Good faith bargaining required - 8(d) of NLRA
    3. Subject matter of good-faith bargaining
        a. Mandatory or compulsory subject matters
            (1) wages
            (2) hours
            (3) overtime
            (4) vacation
            (5) leaves
            (6) pay days
            (7) insurance
            (8) pensions
            (9) seniority
            (10) two-tier wage structure has been an issue in sports and air pilots' negotiations
        b. Permissive subjects for collective bargaining
            (1) strike roles
            (2) not unfair to refuse to bargain it
    4. Cannot bargain away statutory rights
        Example: Cannot agree to have a closed shop
    5. Failure to bargain in good faith
        a. Constitutes an unfair labor practice
        b. Can be the basis of a charge and complaint
    6. E-commerce and the use of e-mail for organizing

D. Protected Concerted Activities - Union Economic Pressure
    1. NLRA gives union right to engage in concerted activities
    2. Public advertisements - permitted
    3. Picketing - legal
    4. The strike - legal economic weapon
    5. The shareholders
        a. Unions have contacted shareholders for clout
        b. Allowed shareholders to bring public attention to the issues

E. Unfair Employee Practices
    1. Slowdown
        a. Not a strike or stoppage
        b. Employees refuse to do certain work or use certain equipment
    2. Featherbedding
        a. Payment for work not actually done
        b. Unfair labor practice

3. Secondary boycotts
   a. Illegal when coercion involved
   b. Third party involved

F. Employer Rights
   1. Freedom of speech: can explain their position to employees
   2. Right-to-work laws
      a. Prohibit closed shops
      b. Shops requiring union membership
   3. Right to an enforceable collective bargaining agreement

G. Economic Weapons of Employers
   1. Plant and business closings
      a. Congress has passed a plant closing law
      b. Many state and local governments have them as well
      c. Laws require notice and time frame before plant is closed
      d. Designed to eliminate shock to local economy
      e. Federal law is the Worker Adjustment and Retraining Notification Act of 1988
         (1) applies to employers with 100 or more workers
         (2) must give sixty days advance notice of closing that will affect fifty or more workers
         (3) must give sixty days notice of layoff that will affect 1/3 or more of work force for 6 months or more
         (4) some exceptions such as unforeseeable circumstances and seasonal businesses and construction
         (5) penalties include back pay and benefits and fines of $500 per day for each day notice not given
   2. Cannot use temporary closing or send work away (runaway shops)
   3. Plant flight - legal if there are economic reasons for transferring work
   4. Lockout - legal for economic reasons; legal to prevent strike but not to prevent union certification
   5. Conferring benefits - a violation if done temporarily
   6. Bankruptcy - legal

VI. International Issues in Labor

   A. Immigration Laws
      1. Immigration and Naturalization Act
      2. Immigration Reform and Control Act of 1986
      3. Illegal Immigration Reform and Immigrant Responsibility Act of 1996
      4. Antiterrorism and Effective Death Penalty Act
         a. Increased types and numbers of crimes that were grounds for deportation
         b. Decreased defense to deportation
         c. Department of Homeland Security has reported an increase in deportation
      5. Uniting and Strengthening America by Providing Appropriate Tools Required to Intercept and Obstruct Terrorism (USA Patriot Act)
      6. Homeland Security Act of 2002
         a. Created Department of Homeland Security
         b. Immigration controlled here
         c. Toughened security checks
         d. Require more employer vigilance on I-9s and hiring immigrants

7.   American Competitiveness in the Twenty-First Century Act of 2000
     a.   Restrictions on laying off U.S. workers
     b.   90-days after hiring immigrants
8.   American Competitive and Workforce Investment Act of 1998
9.   American Competitiveness in the Twenty-First Century Act of 2000

B.   Working Conditions and International Labor Laws
     1.   Moving to arbitration - Labor Management Cooperation Act - mediation as an alternative
     2.   Moving to international plants to avoid labor problems
     3.   Teams approach by companies has effect of mixing labor and management; breaks down union segregation
     4.   Foreign wage competition has moved jobs to Mexico

KEY TERMS

American Competitiveness in the Twenty-First Century Act of 2000
Antiterrorism and Effective Death Penalty Act
Boycott
Certification
Closed Shop
Collective Bargaining Agreement
Collective Bargaining Unit
Concerted Activities
Cooling-Off Period
Employment Retirement Income Security Act
Equal Pay Act of 1963
Fair Labor Standards Act
Family and Medical Leave Act
Featherbedding
Federal Insurance Contributions Act
Good-Faith Bargaining
Illegal Immigration Reform and Immigrant Responsibility Act of 1996
Immigration Act of 1990
Immigration and Customs

Enforcement
Immigration and Naturalization Act
Immigration Reform and Control Act of 1986
Independent Contractor
International Labour Organization
Labor Management Relations Act of 1947
Labor-Management Reporting and Disclosure Act of 1959
Landrum-Griffin Act
Lockout
Mandatory Bargaining Terms
Minimum Wage
National Institute for Occupational Safety and Health (NIOSH)
National Labor Relations Act
National Labor Relations Board
Norris-LaGuardia Act of 1932
Occupational Safety and Health Act
Occupational Safety and Health Administration
Occupational Safety and Health Review

Commission
Overtime Pay
Pension Protection Act of 2006
Picketing
Right-to-Work Laws
Runaway Shop
Scheduled Injuries
Slowdown
Social Security Act of 1935
Strike
Taft-Hartley Act
Unemployment Compensation
Unfair Labor Practice
Uniting and Strengthening America by Providing Appropriate Tools Required to Intercept and Obstruct Terrorism Act (USA Patriot Act)
Unscheduled Injuries
U.S. Department of Homeland Security
Wagner Act
Worker Adjustment and Retraining Notification Act of 1988 (WARN)
Workers' Compensation

MATCHING

a. Equal Pay Act	g. Occupational Safety and Health Administration
b. Lockout	
c. Overtime Pay	h. Fair Labor Standards Act
d. USA Patriot Act	i. Collective Bargaining Unit
e. Workers' Compensation Laws	j. Social Security Act
f. Mandatory Bargaining Terms	k. Norris-LaGuardia Act
	l. Unemployment Compensation

_____ 1. Provides wage benefits and medical care to victims of work-related injuries.

_____ 2. Employer's weapon in refusing to allow employee's to work.

_____ 3. Tightened security clearances and background checks on nonimmigrant and immigrant admittance into the United States.

_____ 4. Wages, hours, and other terms and conditions of employment.

_____ 5. Sets minimum wage requirements.

_____ 6. Federal law establishing disability, beneficiary and retirement benefits.

_____ 7. Rate of 1½ times the hourly rate for hours worked over 40 hours a week.

_____ 8. A group of employees recognized by the NLRB as appropriate for exclusive representation by a union for all employees in the group.

_____ 9. Funded by taxing employers in each state based upon the number of workers they employ and their wages.

_____ 10. Responsible for promulgating and enforcing the rules and regulations for workplace safety standards.

_____ 11. Makes it illegal to pay different wages to men and women for the same job.

_____ 12. Prohibits the use of injunctions as a remedy to labor disputes.

FILL-IN-THE-BLANKS

1. The _____ requires that every employer and employee contribute to social security programs based on their annual wage earned.

2. The _____ covers private retirement and pension plans set up by employers for the benefit of their employees.

3. In the case of a _____ OSHA offense, where there is no threat of serious injury, the penalty can be up to $7,000. A _____ offense may result in a fine of up to $70,000 and/or six months in prison.

4. The Equal Pay Act of 1963 covers only discrimination based on _____, but nevertheless allows for different pay rates for the same jobs so long as the differences are based on factors such as _____ and _____.

5. Under the child labor laws, a child may not work for unlimited hours in a manufacturing job until he or she reaches the age of _____.

6. A _____ is the refusal to work for or buy from an employer.

7. _____, such as loss of a body part, are injuries that carry a percentage disability figure in state disability statutes; _____ are injuries not listed in state statutes and the amount allowed for these injuries under workers' compensation is discretionary.

8. A _____ is an economic tool of employees that falls short of a strike but results in their refusal to perform certain work or use certain equipment that is in violation of their collective bargaining agreement.

9. _____ is the payment for work not actually done, and it is an unfair labor practice for a union to negotiate an agreement containing such a provision.

10. A business that requires union membership before an employee can be hired is a _____, and such a requirement is outlawed by the _____ Act.

11. The Taft-Hartley Act allows the President to invoke a _____ before a strike threatens public health or safety.

12. The _____ is the best known and most widely used weapon of unions.

SHORT ANSWER

1. Because of OSHA's limited manpower, the regulations provide for an order of priority on inspections. What are they?

   a. _____

   b. _____

   c. _____

   d. _____

   e. _____

2. Generally, eligibility requirements to receive unemployment compensation are:

   a. _____

   b. _____

   c. _____

3. Name five unfair labor practices that an employer is prohibited from doing.

   a. _____

   b. _____

   c. _____

   d. _____

   e. _____

4.   Although each state has its own workers' compensation system, what general principles are consistent for each state?

    a. _____

    b. _____

    c. _____

    d. _____

    e. _____

    f. _____

    g. _____

    h. _____

5.   Under the child labor provisions of the FLSA, what are the restrictions on the types of employment for the following age groups?

    a.   18 years old and older: _____

    _____

    b.   16-17 years old: _____

    _____

    c.   14-15 years old: _____

    _____

6.   List the penalties for each type of OSHA violation.

    a.   Willful _____

    b.   Serious _____

    c.   Nonserious _____

    d.   *De Minimis* _____

    e.   Failure to correct _____

Chapter 19

EMPLOYMENT DISCRIMINATION

CHAPTER OUTLINE

I. History of Employment Discrimination Law

    A. No Protection Under Common Law

    B. Civil Rights Act of 1866 (not really effective)

    C. Equal Pay Act of 1963

    D. Title VII of the Civil Rights Act of 1964 - Prohibited Discrimination in Employment on the Basis of Race, Color, Religion, Sex, or National Origin
        1. Amended by the Equal Employment Opportunity Act of 1972
            a. EEOC created
            b. Federal courts given jurisdiction for suits
        2. Amended by the Pregnancy Discrimination Act of 1975 - prohibited discrimination on the basis of pregnancy and childbirth

    E. Age Discrimination in Employment Act of 1967 - Expanded Title VII Protections to Include Age

    F. Rehabilitation Act of 1973 - Prohibits Federal Contractors from Discriminating Against the Handicapped

    G. Americans with Disabilities Act of 1990 - Provides Protection for Workers with Disabilities and Imposes Requirements for Access

    H. Family and Medical Leave Act of 1993 - Right to Take Twelve Weeks Unpaid Leave for Family Medical Emergency

    I. Executive Orders - Apply to Agencies and Federal Contractors

II. Employment Discrimination: Title VII of the Civil Rights Act (Fair Employment Practices Act)

    A. Prohibits Discrimination on Basis of:
        1. Race
        2. Color
        3. Religion
        4. National origin
        5. Sex
        6. Pregnancy

    B.   Application of Title VII
- 1.   Groups covered
  - a.   Employers with fifteen or more employees (for at least twenty calendar weeks)
  - b.   Labor unions with fifteen members or more and/or a hiring hall
  - c.   Employment agencies that work for covered employers
  - d.   State and local agencies
- 2.   Noncovered employers
  - a.   Employment of aliens outside the United States
  - b.   Religious corporations, and so on, when hiring for religious positions
  - c.   Congress
  - d.   Federal government (they have a separate scheme)
  - e.   Indian tribes
- 3.   Employment procedures covered
  - a.   Hiring
  - b.   Compensation
  - c.   Training
  - d.   Promotion
  - e.   Demotion
  - f.   Transfer
  - g.   Fringe benefits
  - h.   Rules
  - i.   Working conditions
  - j.   Dismissals
  - k.   For employment agencies - referrals

III.   Theories of Discrimination Under Title VII

    A.   Disparate Treatment
- 1.   Treating employees or potential employees differently on the basis of race
- 2.   *McDonnell Douglas Corp. v. Green* established the required elements (U.S. Supreme Court)
  - a.   Plaintiff belongs to a racial minority
  - b.   Plaintiff applied for and was qualified for job
  - c.   Plaintiff was rejected (despite qualifications)
  - d.   Job remained open
- 3.   Employer's burden of proof to show nondiscriminatory reason for the nonhire

    B.   Disparate Impact
- 1.   Not intentional discrimination
- 2.   Rule results in different effect on groups
  Example: Minimum height and weight requirement for prison guards had the effect of eliminating women
- 3.   Mostly statistical cases showing impact
- 4.   In *Wards Cove Packing, Inc. v. Atonio*, 490 U.S. 642 (1989), the Supreme Court put greater burdens of proof on Title VII plaintiffs

5.   In response to *Wards Cove* case, the U.S. Senate and House passed the Civil Rights Act of 1991 that has been called a "quota bill." Key provisions of the bill include a provision for jury trials in discrimination cases. This provision carried strong employer objections because presently only the Age Discrimination Act carries jury trial requirements and employees have been quite successful with recoveries under the Act due to the jury sympathy factor of "someday I'll be that age too." The act provides for compensatory damages whereas now the only remedies are back pay and reinstatement. In direct response to the *Wards Cove* decision, the legislation requires employers to carry the burden of business necessity in establishing a defense to a Title VII case.

6.   1991 Amendments also require the plaintiff employee to show causation between the practice of the employer and the disparate impact

C.   Pattern or Practice of Discrimination - Generally involves a statistical comparison

Example: 38 percent of work force in a community is black; 6 percent of an employer's work force is black

IV.   Specific Applications of Title VII

A.   Sex Discrimination
1.   "Protective" legislation is prohibited
Examples: Lifting (30 lbs.) restrictions, safety restrictions, height/weight requirements
2.   Proof same as under *Green*
3.   Ads cannot specify male or female
4.   Glass-ceiling issues
a.   "Mixed motives" in making decisions
b.   If race, gender, and so forth were a factor, it is discrimination
c.   Glass Ceiling Act - allows funding for research into why there is a problem
5.   Sexual harassment
a.   Covered by EEOC guidelines
b.   Employers must have policies on harassment
c.   Types of offenses:
(1)   demands for sexual favors - "quid pro quo"
(2)   environment of sexual suggestion
(3)   hostile conduct for refusal to provide sexual favors
(4)   verbal or physical suggestions
d.   Cannot be fired for refusal to accept sexual advances
e.   Managers and companies have liability for failure to take action on complaints of sexual harassment
f.   Pensions and sex discrimination
6.   Pregnancy
a.   Pregnancy Discrimination Act of 1974 added to Title VII
b.   Coverage and protections
(1)   can't require pregnant employee to quit
(2)   cannot demote upon return to work
(3)   cannot refuse to allow them to return to work
(4)   same sick rules for pregnancy as other ailments
(5)   same insurance coverage
(6)   no promotion or hiring refusals because of pregnancy

B.   Religious Discrimination
    1.   Permitted when religious organization is hiring people as pastors and so on
    2.   Employers must make reasonable accommodations for employees
        a.   Reasonable accommodation
        b.   Need not burden other employees
        c.   Need not restructure workplace or schedule

C.   Racial Discrimination
    1.   Some cases of reverse discrimination have been prohibited
    2.   Employers can, however, institute affirmative action plans

V.   Antidiscrimination Laws and Affirmative Action

A.   What Is Affirmative Action?
    1.   Prohibits discrimination against any group
    2.   Protects African Americans, Hispanics, Native Americans, Asians, women, persons with disabilities, and Vietnam veterans

B.   Who is Required to Have Affirmative Action Programs?
    1.   Those who have been subject to court orders or consent decrees
    2.   Those who are state and local agencies receiving federal funds
    3.   Those who are colleges and universities receiving federal funds
    4.   Government contractors

C.   Preparing an Affirmative Action Program
    1.   Begin with equal employment opportunity statement
    2.   Appoint an affirmative action officer
    3.   Conduct an internal audit and maintain good records
    4.   Establish overall goals and even goals for certain areas

D.   Affirmative Action Backlash: The Theory of Reverse Discrimination
    1.   California's proposition to eliminate programs in government agencies (including universities)
    2.   *Adarand* case requires affirmative action programs to withstand strict scrutiny
    3.   *Taxman v. Board of Education* – reverse discrimination case settled before it reached U.S. Supreme Court

VI.   Defenses to a Title VII Charge

A.   Bona Fide Occupational Qualification (BFOQ)
    1.   Qualification of sex, religion, or national origin necessary for job
        Examples: Pastor of Methodist churches must be Methodist, actors and actresses for parts
    2.   Customer preference is not a BFOQ

B.   Seniority or Merit Systems
    1.   Valid defense to Title VII sometimes
    2.   Must be bona fide
    3.   Must apply to all employees
    4.   Origins of the system cannot be discriminatory
    5.   Cannot be used to perpetuate discrimination

C. Aptitude and Other Tests
    1. Tests must be validated
        a. Job-related
        b. Do not eliminate certain races
    2. Validate by following employees for correlation between test scores and job performance

D. Misconduct
    1. Defense that there was a valid reason for termination or different treatment
    2. Employer could even use misconduct by employee discovered *after* termination

VII. Enforcement of Title VII

A. EEOC Is Responsible
    1. Five-member commission
    2. Appointed by president/approved by Senate
    3. No more than three from same political party

B. Steps in an EEOC Case
    1. Complaint
        a. Filed by employee or the EEOC
        b. Employee must file within 180 days from the violation
        c. Filed with EEOC or state agency
    2. Employer is notified of the charge
    3. EEOC has 180 days from filing of complaint to take action
    4. If case not settled within 180 days, employee gets right-to-sue letter
        a. Certifies administrative remedies are exhausted
        b. Employee can go to federal court
    5. In *Ledbetter v. Goodyear*, the court ruled that the 180-day limit started at time of discrimination
        a. It is not a running tab employee can postpone
        b. Cannot wait to leave before filing if it is over 180-days

C. Remedies Available Under Title VII
    1. Injunctions
    2. Back pay
    3. Punitive damages
    4. Affirmative action
    5. Attorneys' fees

VIII. Other Antidiscrimination Laws

A. Age Discrimination in Employment Act of 1967
    1. Applies to employers with twenty or more employees
    2. Protects those between the ages of 40 and 75

B. Equal Pay Act of 1963 - Equal pay for equal work

C. Communicable Diseases in the Workplace

      D.   Rehabilitation Act of 1973
          1.   Protection for handicapped
          2.   Enforced by Labor Department
          3.   Employers covered
              a.   Federal contracts over $2,500
              b.   States and municipalities
          4.   Covers:
              a.   Diabetes, epilepsy, heart diseases, cancer, retardation, blindness, deaf persons
              b.   Former drug addicts and alcoholics
          5.   Must make reasonable accommodations for handicapped

      E.   Americans with Disabilities Act
          1.   Applies to employers with fifteen or more employees
          2.   Required to make reasonable accommodations for handicapped
          3.   Cannot use tests to screen out handicapped applicants
          4.   Local governments required to make transportation available to handicapped

      F.   Family and Medical Leave Act
          1.   New (1993) law
          2.   Twelve weeks' unpaid leave each year for birth or adoption of child, illness of spouse, parent, or child
          3.   Must return to same job or equivalent

IX.   The Global Workforce

      A.   Companies Must Follow Restrictions of Host Country

      B.   UN Treaties Support Equal Pay and Nondiscriminatory Treatment

      C.   EU Follows All the Treaties

      D.   Conflicts Between U.S. Law and Most Country Law, Companies Follow Host Country Law

KEY TERMS

Affirmative Action
Age Discrimination in
    Employment Act (ADEA)
Americans with Disabilities
    Act (ADA)
Aptitude Tests
Bona Fide Occupational
      Qualifications (BFOQ)
Civil Rights Acts
Communicable Diseases
Disparate Impact
Disparate Treatment

Equal Employment
    Opportunity Act of 1972
Equal Employment
    Opportunity Commission
    (EEOC)
Equal Pay Act of 1963
Fair Employment Practices
    Act
Family and Medical Leave Act
    (FMLA)
Glass Ceiling Act
Merit Systems
Misconduct

Pattern or Practice of
    Discrimination
Pregnancy Discrimination Act
Quotas
Racial Discrimination
Rehabilitation Act of 1973
Religious Discrimination
Right-to-Sue Letter
Seniority Systems
Sex Discrimination
Sexual Harassment
Title VII

MATCHING

a. Equal Employment Opportunity Act of 1972
b. Federal Government and American Indians
c. Bona Fide Occupational Qualification
d. Right-to-Sue Letter
e. Equal Pay Act of 1963
f. Rehabilitation Act of 1973

g. Aptitude Testing
h. Affirmative Action Program
i. Family and Medical Leave Act
j. State agencies and labor unions
k. Age Discrimination in Employment Act
l. Preemployment Medical Examinations

_____ 1. The first federal legislation to deal directly with the issue of discrimination.

_____ 2. Provides employees with the right to take 12 weeks of leave for childbirth, adoption or family illness.

3. Gives the EEOC the right to file suits in federal district court.

_____ 4. Covered by Title VII.

_____ 5. Exempt from Title VII.

_____ 6. Sanctioned by the Supreme Court as a method for remedying past discriminatory treatment.

_____ 7. Job qualification based on sex, religion, or national origin that is necessary for the operation for the business.

_____ 8. Must be related to successful job performance and not have the effect of eliminating certain groups from the employment market in order to be a successful defense against alleged discrimination.

_____ 9. Certification from EEOC that an employee has exhausted his or her administrative remedies.

_____ 10. May protect a person with a history of drug abuse from employment discrimination.

_____ 11. Prohibits discrimination in employment based on age.

_____ 12. Prohibited under the ADA.

FILL-IN-THE-BLANKS

1. Treating individuals differently because of race, color, religion, nationality, or sex is referred to as _____.

2. If a local police force imposes height and weight requirements for its police force and these requirements have the effect of excluding most women applicants, a woman might successfully sue under the _____ theory of Title VII.

3. A court might conclude from circumstantial statistical evidence that an employer has engaged in discrimination against a group or class of persons over a period of time and order a remedy based on the _____ theory of discrimination.

4. Hostile conduct toward an employee for his or her refusal to grant sexual favors to a superior is called _____.

5. An employer's refusal to promote a woman to a management position because she has informed the employer of her plans to begin a family would violate the _____.

6. In discrimination law, the requirement that an applicant for rabbi of a congregation be a member of the Jewish faith is considered to be a _____, and therefore is not unlawful discrimination.

7. The elimination of discrimination against individuals with disabilities is the intent of the _____ Act.

8. After an EEOC complaint is filed, the EEOC has _____ days to take action in the case and if the complaint has not been settled within this time the employee has the right to demand a _____, which gives him or her the right to file suit.

9. The _____ created a commission to study barriers to women entering management and decision-making positions.

10. The correction of past discrimination against women and minorities cannot be achieved simply by the setting of _____, because such would be an unlawful infringement upon the rights of those who belong to the majority.

11. Remedies available under Title VII include _____, back pay, punitive damages and attorneys' fees.

12. Employees that are handicapped or receive federal assistance are protected under the _____.

SHORT ANSWER

1. What groups does Title VII cover?

    a. _____

    b. _____

    c. _____

    d. _____

    e. _____

2. What groups of employers are obligated to undertake affirmative action programs?

    a. _____

    b. _____

    c. _____

    d. _____

3. What acts are prohibited under the Pregnancy Discrimination Act?

    a. _____

    b. _____

    c. _____

    d. _____

    e. _____

    f. _____

4. What is the criteria used to determine whether a seniority or merit system is valid?

    a. _____

    b. _____

    c. _____

    d. _____

5. Certain employers and employment situations are not subject to Title VII. What are they?

   a. _____

   b. _____

   c. _____

   d. _____

   e. _____

6. Name and explain the two forms of sexual harassment.

   a. _____

   b. _____

Chapter 20

FORMS OF DOING BUSINESS

CHAPTER OUTLINE

I. Sole Proprietorships

    A. Formation
        1. Done by an individual
        2. May have a fictitious name
        3. No formal requirements for formation
        4. May have to publish d/b/a name

    B. Sources of Funding
        1. Loans
        2. Government help

    C. Liability (Full Personal Liability of Owner)

    D. Tax Consequences
        1. Owner claims all income and losses
        2. No separate filing requirement

    E. Management and Control (All Assets With One Person)

    F. Transferability of Interest
        1. Business can be sold - property, inventory, and goodwill
        2. Owner will usually sign a noncompete agreement

II. Partnerships

    A. Governed by the Uniform Partnership Act (UPA)
        1. Adopted in forty-nine of fifty states
        2. In absence of agreement UPA controls
        3. Revised Uniform Partnership Act (1994) - adopted most states now

    B. Definition - Voluntary Association of Two or More Persons/Co-Owners in a Business for Profit

    C. Formation
        1. Voluntary formation: by agreement - draw up articles of partnership
        2. Involuntary formation: partnerships by implication
            a. Sharing of profits
            b. Constitutes *prima facie* evidence that a partnership exists
            c. Exceptions - rent, wages, annuity to widow or estate, payment for goodwill
               Examples: Shopping center leases with percentage of profits, employee profit sharing plans
        3. Involuntary formation: partnership by estoppel (or ostensible partner)
            a. Results when someone allows the inference to be made that he/she is a partner
            b. Allowing name to be used to get a loan

D. Sources of Funding
    1. Capital contributions of partners
    2. Loans by partners
    3. Outside loans

E. Partner Liability
    a. Mutual principals and agents
    b. Partnership assets reachable by partnership creditors
    c. Personal assets reachable by partnership creditors when partnership assets are exhausted

F. Tax Consequences in Partnerships
    1. Partnership does not pay taxes
    2. Partnership files informational return
    3. Partners report income and losses on their returns

G. Management and Control
    1. Unless otherwise agreed, each has equal management authority
    2. May delegate day-to-day authority to one partner
    3. Each partner is mutual principal and agent of the others
    4. Borrowing - done routinely in most partnerships
    5. Unanimous consent required for
        a. Confession of judgment
        b. Selling goodwill
        c. Admission of another partner
    6. No compensation for work unless agreed
    7. Partner fiduciary duties
        a. Mutual principals and agents
        b. Each is to act in the best interests of the partnership
    8. Partnership property
        a. Property contributed to the firm or purchased with partnership assets
        b. Own property as tenants in partnership
            (1) equal rights to possession and use for partnership purposes
            (2) upon death of partner, rights automatically transfer to remaining partners
    9. Partner interests
        a. Personal property
        b. Transferable

H. Transferability of Interests
    1. Partner's interest is personal property
    2. Can be pledged to creditors and transferred
    3. Transferee does not become a partner
    4. Admission of new partner requires unanimous consent
    5. Transferring partner is not relieved of liability
    6. Some partnership agreements require partners to offer it first to remaining partners

I. Dissolution and Termination of the Partnership
    1. One partner no longer associated with the partnership
        Examples: Retirement, death
    2. Need not result in termination; can just be a change in structure or can proceed to termination

    3. Dissolution methods
        a. By agreement
        b. By operation of law: death of a partner, bankruptcy of partnership or partner
        c. Court order
    4. Termination
        a. Assets are liquidated
        b. Distribute in this order: outside creditors; partners' advances (loans); capital contributions; profits

III. Limited Partnerships

A. Governed by Uniform Limited Partnership Act (ULPA) - Recent Revision Is Called Revised Uniform Limited Partnership Act (RULPA)
    1. Adopted in nearly all states
    2. Use ULPA or RULPA when no agreement
    3. RULPA has limited adopters but will see more
        a. ULPA was drafted at a time when limited partnerships were not popular and size was smaller
        b. RULPA addresses the needs of the larger limited partnership

B. Structure
    1. Must have at least one general partner
    2. Must have at least one limited partner
    3. Liability of limited partner is limited to capital contribution
    4. Liability of general partner is all personal assets are subject to attachment

C. Formation
    1. Must meet statutory requirements; if not met a general partnership is created
    2. Must file certificate of limited partnership
        a. RULPA is much briefer
        b. Corrections can be filed by limited partners

D. Sources of Funding
    1. Limited partners provide most of the financing
    2. Limited partners can contribute services under RULPA
    3. Loans are used - called advances when made by partners
    4. Under RULPA, limited partners can use services already given as a contribution

E. Liability
    1. Limited partners have limited liability
    2. Cannot participate in management
    3. Cannot use their names in partnership name
    4. Must file correctly
    5. Under RULPA, can do the following and still retain limited liability status:
        a. Can be an employee
        b. Can consult with and advise the general partner
        c. Can act as a surety or guarantor for the limited partnership
        d. Can vote on amendments, dissolution, sale of property, and debt assumptions

F.   Tax Consequences
     1.   Taxed the same as general partnerships
     2.   Partners report profits and losses on individual returns
     3.   Limited partners get direct tax benefits with limited liability
     4.   IRS scrutinizes to be certain it is a partnership and not a corporation

G.   Management and Control - Management is Responsibility of General Partner
     1.   Profits and distributions
          a.   Authority belongs to general partner to make decisions here
          b.   Profits and losses are allocated on the basis of capital contributions
          c.   RULPA requires agreement for splitting profits and losses to be in writing
     2.   Partner authority
          a.   General partner has same authority as in general partnership
          b.   Can restrict by agreement
          c.   Consent of limited partners required for:
               (1)   admitting a new general partner
               (2)   admitting a new limited partner (can give authority in the agreement)
               (3)   extraordinary transactions (selling assets)
          d.   Limited partners have right to inspect books and records

H.   Transferability of Interests
     1.   ULPA allows transfer of interests
     2.   May have significant restrictions on transfer to prevent liability under federal securities laws
     3.   The more easily an interest can be transferred, the more likely the IRS is to label it a corporation
     4.   Transfer of a limited partner's interest does not dissolve the partnership
     5.   Under RULPA, assigning limited partner can be given the authority to make the assignee a limited partner

I.   Dissolution and Termination of a Limited Partnership
     1.   RULPA provides for the following means:
          a.   Expiration of time period in agreement or event as provided in agreement
          b.   Unanimous written consent of all partners
          c.   By court order
          d.   Withdrawal of general partner
     2.   If termination is elected, assets are distributed as follows:
          a.   Outside creditors
          b.   Partners' distributions
          c.   Return of capital contributions
          d.   Remainder split according to agreement

IV. Corporations

     A.   Characteristics
          1.   Unlimited duration
          2.   Free transferability of interest
          3.   Limited liability
          4.   Centralized management
          5.   Legal existence
               a.   Can hold title to property
               b.   Can sue or be sued

B. Types of Corporations
1. Profit
2. Not for profit
3. Domestic - in the state of incorporation
4. Foreign - everywhere else
5. Government corporations - like FNMA
6. Professional corporations - limited liability on everything except professional malpractice
7. Close or closely held corporations
    a. Limited number of shareholders
    b. Subject to less formality
8. Subchapter S or S corporation
    a. IRS election to be treated as partnership for tax purposes
    b. Still have limited liability
    c. Limits on size for this election

C. The Law of Corporations: Model Business Corporation Act (MBCA)
1. Liberal statute
2. One-third of the states have adopted
3. Revised in 1984

D. Formation
1. Must comply with statutory requirements
2. File articles of incorporation
    a. Name
    b. Names and addresses of all incorporators
    c. Capital structure of the corporation
        (1) types of stock
        (2) classes of stock
        (3) rights of shareholders
        (4) voting rights
    d. Statutory agent
3. Where to incorporate
    a. Status of state's corporation laws
    b. State tax laws
    c. Ability to attract employees
    d. Incentives
4. Incorporators
    a. Idea people - also called promoters
    b. Will be personally liable for contracts entered into before incorporation
    c. Corporation can ratify contracts - promoter is secondarily liable
    d. Corporation can enter into a novation with the third party - promoter or incorporator is released from liability
5. Must hold initial meeting after incorporation
    a. Elect new directors
    b. Adopt bylaws (day-to-day procedures)

E.   Capital and Sources of Corporate Funds
   1.   Short-term financing - loans from banks
   2.   Debt financing - bond market
   3.   Equity financing - shareholders
       a.   Common stock
            (1)   usually most voluminous
            (2)   get dividends
            (3)   voting shares
       b.   Preferred stock
            (1)   priority for payment of dividends and liquidation of corporate assets
            (2)   cumulative preferred - guaranteed certain amount for dividend (if not paid one year, carried over to the next year)
       c.   Cost of financing
            (1)   must be registered with SEC
            (2)   dealers' and underwriters' fees
            (3)   additional reports filed each year

F.   Liability Issues
   1.   Must make full payment for shares - if not, there is liability
        Examples: Promising to pay, paying with undervalued property
   2.   If corporate veil is pierced, there is shareholder liability
       a.   Means corporate immunity from liability is set aside
       b.   Reasons for piercing
            (1)   inadequate capitalization - must put enough money at the risk of the business
            (2)   alter ego theory - separate nature of corporation is disregarded; no formalities - personal and corporate properties are mixed together
            (3)   ignoring corporate formalities
            (4)   forming to perpetrate a fraud on creditors

G.   Corporate Tax Consequences
   1.   Double taxation
       a.   Corporation pays on income
       b.   Shareholders pay tax on dividends
   2.   S Corporation is an alternative

H.   Corporate Management and Control - Directors and Officers
   1.   Election of directors
       a.   Board - hires officers and sets policy
       b.   Executive Committee - delegated authority in between board meetings
   2.   Director liability
       a.   Fiduciary
       b.   Business judgment - must give time and effort
   3.   Corporate opportunity doctrine
       a.   Director has duty to give opportunities first to corporation
       b.   If they do not, profits belong to corporation
   4.   Officer liability
       a.   Increasing personal liability
       b.   Increasing prosecutions
   5.   Officers, boards and Sarbanes-Oxley
       a.   Sarbanes-Oxley brought substantial reforms
       b.   Reforms go beyond MBCA

6. Prohibitions on loans to officers
7. Code of ethics for financial reporting
   a. Separate from regular codes
   b. 97% of publicly held companies have codes
   c. Stiffer penalties for false financial information
8. Role of legal counsel for corporations
   a. Must investigate whether violations have occurred
   b. Lawyer must inform the CEO of the investigation
   c. Lawyer must report material violations to CEO
   d. If no action is taken, lawyer must go up the ladder to the board (independent members)
   e. Company must create a legal compliance committee

I. Corporate Management and Control: Shareholders
   1. Board is governing body
      a. Can have executive committee for day-to-day issues
      b. Board elects officers and decides salaries
   2. Voting shareholders
      a. Elect the board
      b. Can demand an annual meeting if one not held in thirteen months
   3. Shareholder voting
      a. Can give a proxy
         (1) voting authority
         (2) good for eleven months
      b. Pooling agreements - group of shareholders agrees to vote a certain way
      c. Voting trust
         (1) title to shares signed over to trustee
         (2) trustee does the voting
         (3) shareholders still have dividends
         (4) trust agreement must be filed in corporate office
   4. Shareholders rights in business combinations
      a. Board resolution required for:
         (1) merger
         (2) consolidation
         (3) asset sale
      b. Notice given to shareholders of resolution and meeting
         (1) each shareholder gets notice
         (2) even nonvoting shares will vote in these major changes
      c. Shareholder approval
         (1) majority under MBCA
         (2) all shares vote
         (3) not required for short-form mergers - merger between subsidiary and parent that owns 90 percent of the subsidiary
      d. Dissenting shareholders
         (1) those who don't vote for the merger
         (2) entitled to appraisal rights
            (a) demand value of their shares
            (b) must have filed a written objection to the merger before the sale
            (c) given fair value of shares as of the day before the vote
         (3) freeze-outs - mergers undertaken to get rid of minority shareholders
            (a) courts require business purpose for freeze-out (other than getting rid of minority shareholders)
            (b) majority shareholders owe fiduciary duty to minority shareholders

5. Shareholders have access to books and records
   a. Under revised MBCA, no ownership requirements
   b. Must have proper purpose
      (1) business motivation
      (2) not political or philosophical motivation
6. Transfer restrictions
   a. Must be noted or referenced on stock certificates
   b. Must serve a necessary purpose
   c. Must be reasonable

J. The Dissolution of a Corporation
   1. Voluntary
      a. Board resolution
      b. Shareholder approval
   2. Involuntary
      a. Forced by court or state agency
      b. Example: Fraud

V. Limited Liability Companies

A. History
   1. Been in existence internationally for some time
   2. GMBH - Europe
      Limitada - South America
   3. LLC - U.S.

B. Nature
   1. Aggregate organization
   2. Liability shield
   3. Income flows through

C. Formation
   1. Articles of organization
   2. Filed centrally
   3. Name must disclose status

D. Sources of Funding - Members Contribute Capital

E. Liability - Members Stand to Lose Capital Contributions, But Their Personal Assets are Not Subject to Attachment

F. Tax Consequences - Income Passes Through to Members; LLC Does Not Pay Taxes

G. Management and Control
   1. Operating agreement - specifies voting rights
   2. One member or an outside consultant can have operating authority delegated to him or her

H. Transferability of Interest
  1. Interest can be transferred
  2. They do not become a member unless majority of remaining members approve

I. Dissolution and Termination
  1. Upon withdrawal, death, or expulsion of a member
  2. Judicial dissolution
  3. By agreement

VI. Limited Liability Partnerships

  A. Formation
    1. Strict formal requirements exist
    2. Filing requirements:
      a. The name of the LLP
      b. Registered agent
      c. Address
      d. Number of partners
      e. Description of business

  B. Sources of Funding - Partners Make Capital Contributions

  C. Liability
    1. Limited liability for all
    2. Some exceptions for professionals

  D. Tax Consequences: Flow-Through/Pass-Through Status

  E. Management and Control - Can Manage Without Liability Exposure

  F. Transferability: Restricted

  G. Dissolution and Termination - Same as for Limited Partnership

VII. International Issues in Business Structure

  A. Joint Ventures Increasing

  B. Joint Ventures with Countries Themselves

  C. Business Structure Varies

KEY TERMS

Advances	Fiduciaries	Professional Corporations
Alter Ego Theory	Foreign Corporations	Profit Corporations
Appraisal Rights	Freeze-Out	Proper Purpose
Articles of Incorporation	General Partner	Proxy
Articles of Limited Partnership	Government Corporations	Publicly Held Corporations
Articles of Organization	Incorporators	Ratification
Audit Committees	Initial Meeting	Revised Uniform Limited
Board of Directors	Joint Ventures	Partnership Act
Business Judgment Rule	Limited Liability Company	Revised Uniform Partnership
Bylaws	Limited Liability Partnership	Act
Close Corporations	Limited Partner	S Corporation
Common Stock	Limited Partnership	Sole Proprietorship
Corporate Opportunity	Limited Partnership Agreement	Subchapter S Corporation
Doctrine	Model Business Corporation	Tenancy in Partnership
Corporate Veil	Act (MBCA)	Transfer Restrictions
Corporations	Nonprofit Corporations	Uniform Limited Partnership
Cumulative Preferred Stock	Novation	Act
Debt Financing	Partnership	Uniform Partnership Act
Dissenting Shareholder	Partnership by Estoppel	Voting Trust
Dissolution	Partnership by Implication	Watered Shares
Domestic Corporations	Partnership Property	
Equity Financing	Pooling Agreement	
Executive Committee	Preferred Stock	

MATCHING

a.	Limited Partner	g.	Professional Corporations
b.	S Corporation	h.	Limited Liability Partnership
c.	Dissolution of Partnership	i.	Limited Liability Company
d.	Government Corporation	j.	Sole Proprietorship
e.	Board of Directors	k.	General Partner
f.	Corporation	l.	Partnership by Estoppel

_____ 1. Form of business in which the sole owner of the business is liable for all debts as well as receiving all the profits of the business.

_____ 2. Involuntary formation of a partnership by which an individual is held to be a partner, and therefore liable for partnership debts, because the individual has led others to believe that he or she is a partner and such belief is relied upon.

_____ 3. Limited partners are not held liable for the negligence, wrongful acts, or misconduct of their general partners.

_____ 4. Provides limited liability to its "members" and tax treatment like a partnership where members are taxed at their level of income and not at the business level.

_____ 5. Will automatically occur upon the death of a partner.

_____ 6. Elected directors who control the operations and management of the corporation.

_____ 7. Full liability and full responsibility for the business.

_____ 8. Limited liability for shareholders/owners.

_____ 9. Taxed like a partnership, avoiding double taxation.
_____ 10. Exists to achieve social goals.

_____ 11. Have liability limited to their contribution to the partnership.

_____ 12. Corporations organized by doctors, dentists, lawyers, etc.

FILL-IN-THE-BLANKS

1. The parties forming a corporation, known as _____, will be personally liable for contracts entered into during the pre-incorporation stage until the corporation assumes liability through a _____ of the incorporators' acts.

2. A court may pierce the corporate veil under the _____ theory when the corporation is in reality not an entity separate from the shareholder and personal and corporate property are mixed together freely.

3. If a shareholder received $2,000 worth of a corporation's stock in exchange for personal property valued at $500, he is the owner of _____ and is personally liable for $1,500.

4. A director of a corporation may be held personally liable if he or she violates the _____ by failing to carefully study documents and information available to him or her or failure to consult experts when expert analysis is required.

5. A contract among shareholders to vote their shares in a certain way is a _____.

6. A corporate requirement that shares of its stock must first be offered to the board of directors before they can be sold to others is a _____.

7. _____ carries voting rights, but does not have a fixed dividend rate; _____ has priority in the payment of dividends and in asset distribution.

8. In the state in which it was incorporated, a corporation is known as a _____ corporation; in all other states it is known as a _____ corporation.

9. A corporation is formed by the filing of _____ with the state; the _____ comprise the operational rules of the corporation and are adopted by the officers at their _____ meeting.

10. _____ of a partnership means a change in the structure of the partnership (such as death or retirement); while _____ of the partnership means that all business stops, assets are liquidated, and the proceeds are used to pay off the debts of the partnership.

11. _____ serve a watchdog role for corporations and are required of all stock exchange companies. They are made up of independent outside directors and at least one financial expert under Sarbanes-Oxley.

12. Officers and directors may not take an opportunity for themselves that the corporation may be interested in taking under the _____.

SHORT ANSWER

1. List the four reasons that the presumption of partnership by profit sharing can be overcome.

   a. _____

   b. _____

   c. _____

   d. _____

2. Limited partners can engage in what activities and not lose their limited liability status?

   a. _____

   b. _____

   c. _____

   d. _____

3. List the requirements for the articles of incorporation under the MBCA.

   a. _____

   b. _____

   c. _____

   d. _____

4. What are the four ways that a limited partnership can be dissolved?

   a. _____

   b. _____

   c. _____

   d. _____

5. Compare the income tax liability issues for partnerships, limited partnerships, corporations, limited liability companies, and limited liability partnerships.

   Partnerships: _____

   _____

   Limited partnerships: _____

   _____

   Corporations: _____

   _____

   Limited liability companies: _____

   _____

   Limited liability partnerships: _____

   _____

6. List the types of entities/business structure in which its owners can have limited liability.

   _____

   _____

   _____

   _____

Chapter 21

SECURITIES LAW

CHAPTER OUTLINE

I.   History of Securities Law

    A.   Initially Regulated at the State Level

    B.   1929 Stock Market Crash Precipitated Federal Regulation

II. Primary Offering Regulation - The 1933 Securities Act

    A.   Regulates Primary Offerings (First-Time Offerings) of Securities

    B.   What Is A Security?
       1.   Investment in a common enterprise with profits to come from the efforts of another
       2.   Includes stocks, bonds, warrants, debentures, voting-trust certificates, oil wells, and so forth
       3.   Pension plans are not covered

    C.   Regulating Primary Offerings: Registration
       1.   Securities and Exchange Commission (SEC)
       2.   SEC - issue injunctions, institute criminal proceedings, enter into consent decrees, handle enforcement and promulgate rules
       3.   First time public offering is called an IPO

    D.   Regulating Primary Offerings: Exemptions
       1.   Exempt securities
          a.   Securities issued by federal, state, county, or municipal governments
          b.   Commercial paper (less than nine months)
          c.   Banks, savings and loans, religious and charitable organizations
          d.   Insurance policies
          e.   Annuities
          f.   Common carriers (ICC regulates)
          g.   Stock dividends and splits
       2.   Exempt transactions
          a.   Intrastate offerings
             (1)   issuer must be domestic business in state where offering is made
            (2)   offerees must all be residents of the state
            (3)   triple 80 requirements
               (a)   80 percent of assets in the state
               (b)   80 percent of its income earned in the state
               (c)   80 percent of sale proceeds will be used on operations in the state
            (4)   transfer restrictions apply (Rule 147 – 9 months)
          b.   Regulation A - small offering exemption
             (1)   shortcut method of registration
            (2)   S-1 filed
            (3)   issues of $5 million or less during any twelve-month period
            (4)   SEC can use *integration* - can group offerings in a year and then exemption is not met

      c.   Regulation D

          (1)   Rule 504 - $1 million or less only transfer restrictions

          (2)   Rule 505 - $5 million to limited number and types of investors

          (3)   Rule 506 - no amount limit but limits on types of investors

          (4)   limits on types of investors - accredited investors

               (a)   private business development firm

               (b)   directors, officers, partners (general) of issuer

               (c)   banks

               (d)   purchasers of $150,000 or more

               (e)   natural persons with net worth greater than $1 million

               (f)   persons with income of greater than or equal to $200,000/year

          (5)   limits on advertising

          (6)   all must carry restrictions on transfer

      d.   Stock issued pursuant to corporate reorganization is also exempt

E.   What Must Be Filed - Documents and Information for Registration

    1.   Issuer/offeror files a registration statement

    2.   SEC has twenty days from date of filing to act

      a.   If no action, effective after twenty days

      b.   Can issue a comment or deficiency letter during that time

          (1)   must remedy deficiencies

          (2)   first-time offerings generally take six months for approval

    3.   SEC follows full disclosure standard

    4.   Materials include

      a.   Description of securities

      b.   Audited financial statement

      c.   List of assets

      d.   Nature of business

      e.   List of management and their shares

    5.   Before registration statement is effective

      a.   Can run tombstone ad

      b.   Can issue red herring (sample) prospectus

      c.   Cannot make offers to sell

    6.   Can do shelf registration

      a.   File and get approval

      b.   Can go to market any time within 2-year period

      c.   Must update information in filing

F.   Violations of the 1933 Act

    1.   Section 11 violations - civil liability for inaccurate information in registration statement

    2.   What is required for a violation?

      a.   Failure to make full disclosure

      b.   Registration statement contains a material misstatement or omission

    3.   Who is liable for a violation?

      a.   Officers

      b.   Directors

      c.   Anyone who signed registration statement

      d.   Experts (lawyers, accountants, appraisers, geologists)

4. Defenses for Section 11 violations
   a. Immaterial misstatement
   b. Investor knew of misstatement and bought anyway
   c. Due diligence - acted with prudence and had no reason to believe there was a problem
5. Due diligence and Sarbanes-Oxley
   a. Auditors' independence
   b. Public Company Accounting Oversight Board (PCAOB) (Peek-a-Boo)
      (1) consists of five presidential appointees
      (2) nonprofit organization
      (3) no more than two members who are CPAs
      (4) will develop registration system for public accounting firms
      (5) establish rules to ensure quality, ethics and auditor independence
      (6) will inspect firms to determine compliance with Sarbanes-Oxley
      (7) will investigation violations and impose discipline
      (8) will encourage high standard in the accounting profession
   c. All firms must register if doing audits for publicly traded companies
   d. Auditor independence – cannot do audits of company and do its:
      (1) bookkeeping
      (2) information systems
      (3) appraisals
      (4) actuarial services
      (5) management or human resources services
      (6) broker, dealer services
      (7) legal services
      (8) expert services
      (9) other as PCAOB dictates
   e. Must rotate audit partner every five years
   f. Audit firms must have internal systems to monitor conflicts
6. Penalties for violations of Section 11
   a $10,000 and/or five years imprisonment
   b. Injunctions to stop sales
   c. Civil suits
7. Securities Litigation Reform Act of 1995
   a. Limits attorneys' fees
   b. Addresses "professional plaintiff"
   c. Allows "safe harbor" protection for financial predictions

G. Section 12 Violations
   1. Selling without registration (unless exempt)
   2. Selling before the effective date
   3. False information in the prospectus
   4. Same penalties as Section 11

III. The Securities Exchange Act of 1934

A. Regulates Secondary Market

B. Securities Registration
   1. All traded securities on exchanges must be registered
   2. All securities of firms with over $10 million in assets and 500 or more shareholders must be registered

C. Periodic Filing - Same Firms: National Stock Exchange and/or 500 or More Shareholders and $10 Million or More in Assets
1. 10-Q - quarterly financial report
2. 10-K - annual report
3. 8-K - unusual events, spinoffs
4. Periodic filings must be certified under Sarbanes-Oxley
    a. Both CEO and CFO must sign
    b. Certify that they have reviewed the report
    c. Certify that the report contains no untrue statements
    d. Certify that the financials represent fairly all material aspects of the company's financial performance
    e. Certify that they are responsible for sufficient controls on company financial systems
    f. Penalties of $1 million and/or ten years

D. The Antifraud Provision 10(b) and Regulation 10(b)-5
1. Fraud or misrepresentation in the sale of securities
2. Applies to all firms (only requires interstate commerce)
3. How corporations run afoul
    a. Failure to give information or giving overly pessimistic information results in violation
    b. Examples: Failure to disclose pending merger, failure to disclose a rich mineral strike
    c. What should be disclosed?
        (1) pending takeovers
        (2) drops in quarterly earnings
        (3) pending large dividend
        (4) possible lawsuits
    d. When to disclose?
4. How individuals run afoul
    a. Applies to insiders who trade on nonpublic information
    b. Applies to tippees of insiders
5. Running afoul with timing
    a. Must allow information to go public
    b. *Texas Gulf Sulphur* case and adequate disclosure
6. Running afoul with e-commerce
    a. Pump and dump facilitated by internet
    b. Posting of false information can be very damaging
7. Sarbanes-Oxley and disclosure
    a. Must use caution on classification of revenues and expenses
    b. "Earnings Management" issues present concerns under new standards
    c. Must work for honest and ethical conduct
    d. Give full, fair, accurate, timely and understandable information
    e. Must comply with all laws, rules and regulations
8. Standing to sue - must have been an actual seller or purchaser to sue
9. Mental state - need scienter - intent to defraud
10. Penalties include $100,000 and up to five years per violation (Insider Trading and Securities Fraud Enforcement Act of 1988)

E.   Section 16 - Insider Trading and Short-Swing Profits
1.   Applies to officers, directors, and 10 percent shareholders
2.   Liable to corporations for profits made on sales and purchases or purchases and sales during any six-month period
3.   SEC matches highest sale with the lowest purchase
4.   Sarbanes-Oxley era: two-day notification of activity in stock

F.   Regulating Voting Information - Section 14
1.   Idea is to have full disclosure
2.   Proxy materials registered with the SEC
a.   Who is soliciting
b.   How the materials will be sent
c.   Who is paying
d.   How much has and will be spent
e.   Purpose of proxy - an annual meeting
3.   Shareholder proposals
a.   Management must include a 200-word proposal if subject matter is appropriate
b.   Can get list for solicitation
4.   Shareholders and executive compensation
a.   Major concern
b.   Compensation committees are now composed of independent directors
5.   Remedies for Section 14 violations
a.   Invalidate proxies
b.   Invalidate actions at meeting

G.   Shareholder Rights in Takeovers, Mergers, and Consolidations
1.   Definitions
a.   Mergers - combination of two or more corporations
(1)   horizontal mergers - merger of two competitors
(2)   vertical mergers - merger of two firms in the chain of distribution
(3)   conglomerate mergers - merger between two unrelated companies
b.   Consolidations - two or more companies form a new firm
c.   Tender offer
(1)   not a business combination
(2)   method used to get a combination
(3)   publicly advertised offer to buy stock
(4)   generally offer is higher than market to make it attractive
d.   Takeovers
(1)   can be friendly - management favors
(2)   can be hostile - management opposes
e.   Asset acquisitions
(1)   no change in corporate structure
(2)   shareholder approval not required
f.   Filing requirements under the Williams Act
(1)   passed in 1968
(2)   enforced by SEC
(3)   applies to all offers to buy more than 5 percent of another's securities
(4)   filing requirements
(a)   tender offer statement filed with SEC
(b)   disclosure information to shareholders

(c) target company opposing the takeover (hostile) must file its materials with the SEC

(d) required to be disclosed
    i. name of offeror
    ii. source of funding
    iii. plans for company if takeover is successful
    iv. number of shares now owned

(e) time requirements so shareholders aren't forced into action

(f) definition of tender offers done by courts

  (5) penalties for violations
    (a) failure to disclose
    (b) fraudulent information in the materials

  (6) proposed changes - Congress is debating more regulation

  (7) hostile takeovers
    (a) management must do the following (within ten days of offer)
      i. recommend acceptance or rejection
      ii. no opinion (remains neutral)
      iii. unable to take a position
    (b) can take action to stop

g. State laws affecting tender offers
  (1) states are enacting statutes to protect their companies
  (2) types
    (a) voting-right restrictions - can accumulate shares but don't get voting rights: Hawaii, Indiana, Minnesota, Missouri, New York, Ohio, Wisconsin
    (b) redemption-rights laws - raiders subject to same redemption price: Maine, Utah, Pennsylvania
    (c) fair price laws - all shareholders get a fair price: Connecticut, Georgia, Illinois, Kentucky, Louisiana, Maryland, Michigan, Mississippi, Virginia, Washington
    (d) third generation statutes (Wisconsin and Pennsylvania) require three-year waiting periods before a merger can take place (see above note on PA)
  (3) Future of State Antitakeover Statutes
    (a) seventh circuit has stated economic arguments do not invalidate the statutes
    (b) U.S. Supreme Court refused to grant certiorari - impliedly approved the decision

h. Proxy regulations
  (1) must follow SEC regulations
  (2) if not, action at meeting can be set aside
  (3) proxy costs can be reimbursed by directors

IV. The Foreign Corrupt Practices Act

V. State Securities Laws

  A. Blue Sky Laws (state registration requirements)

  B. Can Follow a Merit Review Standard - Securities Reviewed for Their Merit Must be "Fair, Just, and Equitable"

VI. International Issues in Securities Laws

    A. United States Has Most Stock Exchanges

    B. European Union Has Regulations on Disclosure

    C. Insider Trading Becoming More Vigorously Regulated in Other Countries

    D. Only United States Has Proxy Disclosures

KEY TERMS

Accredited Investor
Asset Acquisition
Blue Sky Law
Comment Letter
Consolidation
Deficiency Letter
Due Diligence
8-K Form
Exemption
Exempt Securities
Exempt Transactions
Fair-Disclosure Rule
Foreign Corrupt Practices Act
   (FCPA)
Friendly Takeover
Full-Disclosure Standard
Hostile Takeover
Howey Test
Initial Public Offering (IPO)
Insider Trading and Securities
   Fraud Enforcement Act

Insiders
Intrastate Offering Exemption
Material Misstatement
Merger
Merit Review Standards
Primary Offering
Prospectus
Proxy Solicitations
Proxy Statement
Public Company Accounting
   Oversight Board (PCAOB)
Red Herring Prospectus
Registration Statement (S-1)
Regulation A
Regulation D
Regulation FD
Rule 504
Rule 505
Rule 506
Rule 10(b)-5
Sarbanes-Oxley

Scienter
Section 10(b)
Section 11
Section 12
Section 16
Securities
Securities Act of 1933
Securities and Exchange
   Commission (SEC)
Securities Exchange Act of 1934
Shelf Registrations
Short-Swing Profits
Small-Offering Exemption
Standing
Tender Offer
10-K Form
10-Q Form
Tippees
Tombstone Ad
Williams Act

MATCHING

a. Tender Offer
b. Standing
c. Consolidation
d. Exempt Security
e. Merger
f. Exempt Transaction

g. Merit Review Standard
h. Sarbanes-Oxley
i. Material Misstatement
j. Accredited Investor
k. Rule 504
l. Regulation A

_____ 1. A bond issued by a state government.

_____ 2. A corporate issue of stock of less than $1 million in a twelve-month period.

_____ 3. A person who purchases at least $150,000 of the securities in an issue.

_____ 4. An offer that is publicly advertised to shareholders for purchase of their stock, usually offering a higher than market price.

_____ 5. Must be shown to prove a violation of Section 11 of the 1933 Act.

_____ 6. The actual sale or purchase of stock in reliance upon information given.

_____ 7. Requires audit firms to change audit partners at least once every five years.

_____ 8. A combination in which two or more companies combine into a new company and neither of the old companies continues in existence.

_____ 9. Requirement that an offering be fair, just, and equitable.

_____ 10. Combination of two or more corporations, after which only one corporation continues to exist.

_____ 11. Not a true exemption, but applies to issues of securities of $5 million or less in a 12-month period.

_____ 12. Applies to offerings of $1 million or less in a 12-month period.

FILL-IN-THE-BLANKS

1. The _____ is an initial public offering of corporate securities by the corporation itself.

2. The _____ is the federal administrative and enforcement agency in the area of securities regulation.

3. In order for the _____ exemption to apply, the investors and issuer must all reside in the same state.

4. Under the 1933 Act, an issuer must file a _____ and a _____ with the SEC prior to an initial offering. Normally, the SEC will issue a _____ within twenty days of the filing.

5. Prior to the effective date of an SEC registration, an issuer may run a _____ ad and send out a _____ prospectus disclosing that the securities will be sold, but the registration is not yet effective.

6. The _____ is a federal statute requiring an offeror to file a tender offer statement with the SEC and the target company. Shareholders must also be given all the information and details of the offer if the tender offer is made with the purpose of acquiring more than _____ percent of another corporation's securities.

7. A _____ occurs when management favors the takeover; whereas, a _____ occurs when the management opposes the takeover.

8. National stock exchange companies or a company with 500 or more shareholders and $10 million in assets must file a quarterly _____, an annual _____, and a _____ upon an unusual event.

9. Section 10(b) and Rule 10(b)-5, the _____ provisions of the 1934 Act, have been interpreted to prohibit insider trading by corporate insiders or _____.

10. _____ requires accounting firms to set up internal systems for developing and monitoring professional ethics and for discussing ethical issues that arise while auditing clients.

11. Anyone selling securities must complete certain filing requirements before the sale unless an _____ applies.

12. Permitting sales without registration, _____ creates a three-tiered exemption structure that consists of Rules _____, _____, and _____.

SHORT ANSWERS

1. An accredited investor includes any investor who, at the time of the sale, is:

    a. _____

    b. _____

    c. _____

    d. _____

    e. _____

    f. _____

2. What information does the SEC require in the registration statement?

    a. _____

    b. _____

    c. _____

    d. _____

    e. _____

    f. _____

3.   What are the three defenses for Section 11 violations?

    a.   _____

    b.   _____

    c.   _____

4.   Describe the nature of these securities laws.

    a.   Section 10(b) _____

    b.   Section 14 _____

    c.   Section 16 _____

    d.   Section 11 _____

    e.   Section 12 _____

    f.   Regulation D _____

5.   What are some of the tactics used by a target company to fight a takeover?

    a.   _____

    b.   _____

    c.   _____

    d.   _____

6.   Sarbanes-Oxley created the PCAOB – what are its responsibilities?

    a.   _____

    b.   _____

    c.   _____

    d.   _____

    e.   _____

ANSWERS
TO
STUDY GUIDE
QUESTIONS

CHAPTER 1

MATCHING

1. g
2. b
3. a
4. i
5. d
6. h
7. c
8. e
9. f
10. j
11. l
12. k

FILL-IN-THE-BLANKS

1. jurisprudence
2. public; private
3. criminal; civil
4. common; *stare decisis*
5. Equity
6. constitutions
7. uniform laws
8. procedural; substantive
9. Expropriation; appropriation
10. bilateral; multilateral; universal
11. party autonomy
12. act of state doctrine

SHORT ANSWER

1. a. Flexibility
   b. Consistency
   c. Pervasiveness
2. a. Keeping order
   b. Influencing conduct
   c. Honoring expectations
   d. Promoting equality
   e. Providing compromises
3. a. Constitutional laws
   b. Federal laws
   c. State laws
   d. Local laws
   e. Private laws
4. a. Custom
   b. Treaties
   c. Private law or party autonomy
   d. International organizations
   e. Act of state doctrine
   f. Trade law and policies
   g. Uniform international laws
   h. European Union
5. a. Federal law; passed by Congress
   b. State uniform law; panel of experts, adopted in each state
   c. Review of trial decisions; precedent
6. a. Aristotle – "the law is reason unaffected by desire" and that "law is a form of order, and good law must necessarily mean good order"
   b. Holmes – "law embodies the story of a nation's development through many centuries"
   c. Blackstone – "that rule of action which is prescribed by some superior and which the interior is bound to obey"
   d. Black's Law – "a body of rules of action or conduct prescribed by the controlling authority, and having legal binding force"

CHAPTER 2

MATCHING
1. g
2. j
3. a
4. e
5. k
6. b
7. h
8. l
9. c
10. i
11. f
12. d

FILL-IN-THE-BLANKS
1. inherence
2. social responsibility
3. Front-Page-of-the-Newspaper Test
4. Is it legal? Is it balanced? How does it make me feel?
5. Tone at the Top
6. Reporting lines
7. Enlightened Self-Interest
8. Invisible hand
9. Laura Nash
10. *Wall Street Journal*
11. inherence
12. Sarbanes-Oxley

SHORT ANSWER
1. a. "Everybody else does it."
    b. "If we don't do it, someone else will."
    c. "That's the way it's always been done."
    d. "We'll wait until the lawyers tell us it's wrong."
    e. "It doesn't really hurt anyone."
    f. "The system is unfair."
    g. "I was just following orders."
    h. "You think this is bad, you should have seen…"
    i. "It's a gray area."
2. a. Inherence
    b. Enlightened Self-Interest
    c. Invisible Hand
    d. Social Responsibility
3. a. Taking things that don't belong to you
    b. Saying things you know are not true
    c. Giving or allowing false impressions
    d. Buying influence or engaging in conflict of interest
    e. Hiding or divulging information
    f. Taking unfair advantage
    g. Committing acts of personal decadence
    h. Perpetrating interpersonal abuse
    i. Permitting organizational abuse
    j. Violating rules
    k. Condoning unethical actions
    l. Balancing ethical dilemmas
4. a. Blanchard and Peale
    b. Laura Nash
    c. Front-Page-of-the-Newspaper Test
    d. The *Wall Street Journal* Model
5. a. Competition is so intense that business survival is threatened.
    b. Managers make poor judgments.
    c. Employees have few or no personal values.
    d. Employees respond only to earnings demands, with no constraints on how the earnings are achieved.
    e. Managers and executives have been touting to analysts, investors, and the business media how well their company has been doing.
6. a. A code of ethics
    b. Training for employees in the code and in ethics
    c. A means for employees to report misconduct anonymously
    d. Follow-up on reports employees make on misconduct
    e. Action by the board, including follow-up and monitoring, on complaints and reports made by employees
    f. Self-reporting and investigation of legal and ethical issues
    g. Sanctions and terminations for those within the company who violate the law and company rules
    h. A high-ranking officer, with the ability to communicate with the CEO and board, who is responsible for the code of ethics and ethics training in the company

CHAPTER 3

MATCHING
1. b
2. l
3. k
4. j
5. h
6. e
7. f
8. d
9. a
10. g
11. c
12. i

FILL-IN-THE-BLANKS
1. subject matter; *in personam*
2. limited
3. diversity of citizenship; federal district
4. Plaintiffs; defendants
5. minimum contacts; long-arm statute
6. affirm; modify
7. Appellate; trial; brief; oral argument
8. reverse; remand
9. appellant; petitioner; appellee; respondent
10. attorney-client privilege
11. dissenting opinion
12. precedent; *stare decisis*

SHORT ANSWER
1. a. Trial courts
   b. Appellate courts
2. a. Plaintiffs
   b. Defendants
   c. Lawyers
   d. Judges
3. a. Those in which the United States is a party
   b. Those that involve a federal question
   c. Those that involve diversity of citizenship
4. a. Small claims court
   b. Traffic court
   c. Justice of the Peace
   d. City courts
   e. Probate courts
   f. Tax court
   g. Bankruptcy court
   h. U.S. Claims court
   i. U.S. Court of International Trade
   j. Indian Tribal court
5. Trial = evidence, jury, verdict
   Appellate = review of trial court's procedure and verdict
6. The International Court of Justice is comprised of fifteen judges, no more than two of whom can be from the same nation, who are elected by the General Assembly of the UN. The court has contentious jurisdiction, which means that the court's jurisdiction is consensual – the parties agree to submit their dispute to the ICJ.

CHAPTER 4

MATCHING

1. b
2. h
3. d
4. i
5. c
6. g
7. j
8. e
9. f
10. a
11. k
12. l

FILL-IN-THE-BLANKS

1. mediation
2. summons; process server; answer; default; counterclaim
3. motion to dismiss
4. motion for summary judgment
5. minitrial
6. legal, equitable, injunction
7. opening statement
8. class action suit
9. closing argument; instructions
10. arbitration; arbitrator
11. binding; nonbinding
12. summary jury trial

SHORT ANSWER

1. a. Arbitration
   b. Mediation
   c. Medarb
   d. Minitrial
   e. Rent-a-Judge
   f. Summary Jury Trial
   g. Early Neutral Evaluation
   h. Peer review

2. a. Motion for judgment on the pleadings (made after answer and complaint are filed)
   b. Motion for summary judgment (made before, during, or after discovery)
   c. Motion to dismiss (made any time, but usually part of the defendant's answer)
   d. Motion for directed verdict (made after plaintiff's case)
   e. Motion for judgment NOV (made after the verdict)

3. a. Open lines of communication
   b. Parties can agree to anything
   c. Creative remedies permitted
   d. Parties set timetable
   e. Privacy
   f. Control by parties (or mediator/arbitrator)
   g. Cheaper
   h. More flexibility
   i. Parties select mediator/arbitrator
   j. Positions examined for validity
   k. Enforcement by good faith

4. a. Complaint
   b. Summons
   c. Answer

5. a. E-mail
   b. Depositions
   c. Documents
   d. Records

6. The International Chamber of Commerce is a private organization that handles arbitration cases from parties in 123 countries. The World Bank has established the International Center for Settlement of Investment Disputes to arbitrate disputes between investors and the nations in which they have investments. The American Arbitration Association created the International Centre for Dispute Resolution to provide an international AAA service for global U.S.-based companies.

CHAPTER 5

MATCHING
1. e
2. k
3. j
4. i
5. b
6. l
7. f
8. c
9. g
10. d
11. a
12. h

FILL-IN-THE-BLANKS
1. Equal Protection Clause; Fourteenth Amendment
2. checks and balances
3. interstate commerce
4. commercial speech
5. Bill of Rights
6. police power
7. balancing test
8. eminent domain; public purpose; taking; just compensation
9. procedural due process
10. Equal Protection Clause
11. legislative; executive; judicial
12. eminent domain; public purpose

SHORT ANSWER
1. a. Legislative Branch
   b. Executive Branch
   c. Judicial Branch
2. a. Public purpose
   b. Taking or regulating
   c. Just compensation
3. a. Tax cannot discriminate against interstate commerce
   b. Tax cannot unduly burden interstate commerce
   c. There must be some connection between the state and the business being taxed
   d. The tax must be apportioned fairly
4. a. What does the legislative history indicate?
   b. How detailed is the federal regulation of the area?
   c. What benefits exist from having federal regulation of the area?
   d. How much does a state law conflict with federal law?
5. a. First Amendment - freedom of speech
   b. Fourth Amendment - privacy
   c. Fifth Amendment - due process and self-incrimination
   d. Sixth Amendment - jury trial
   e. Fourteenth Amendment - equal protection
6. a. Through financial support such as political candidate donations
   b. Through financial support such as party donations
   c. Through direct communications and ads about issues, ballot propositions, and funding proposals
7. Courts are concerned with two factors: (1) whether federal regulation supersedes state involvement, and (2) whether the benefits achieved by the regulation outweigh the burden on interstate commerce.

CHAPTER 6

MATCHING	FILL-IN-THE-BLANKS
1. k	1. Freedom of Information Act
2. h	2. Code of Federal Regulations; U.S. Government Manual; Federal Register
3. c	3. public comment period
4. f	4. *ultra vires*
5. e	5. zero-based budgeting
6. i	6. intervenor
7. d	7. consent decree; nolo contendere
8. b	8. administrative law judge; hearing officer; hearing examiner
9. j	9. formal; informal
10. l	10. substantial evidence
11. a	11. commission
12. g	12. social goal

SHORT ANSWER

1. a.   Specialization
    b.   Protection for small business
    c.   Faster relief
    d.   Due process
    e.   Social goals
2. a.   Enabling Act by Congress
    b.   Agency study and research of need for regulation
    c.   Proposed regulations published in *Federal Register*
    d.   Public comment period
    e.   Hearings held regionally
    f.   Modification of proposed regulation
    g.   Public comment period on modification
    h.   Rule is promulgated or withdrawal of proposed regulation
    i.   Court challenges
3. a.   Administrative Procedures Act (APA)
    b.   Freedom of Information Act (FOIA)
    c.   Federal Privacy Act
    d.   Government in the Sunshine Act
    e.   Federal Register Act
4. a.   It is arbitrary, capricious, an abuse of discretion, or is in violation of some other law
    b.   Regulation is unsupported by substantial evidence
    c.   It did not comply with the APA requirements of notice, publication, and public comment or input
    d.   Regulation is unconstitutional
    e.   Regulation is *ultra vires* or beyond the authority given to the agency
5. a.   Regulation not based on evidence and study
    b.   Period during which anyone can provide input to agency on the proposed rules
    c.   Settlement of a regulatory issue with a nolo contendere plea
    d.   Following all processes of an agency before going to court
    e.   Laws that require public meetings with advance notice
6. a.   Nonprosecuting: (1) Regulation, (2) Licensing, (3) Inspections
    b.   Prosecution
    c.   Penalties and Sanctions
    d.   Consent Decrees
    e.   Hearings
    f.   Appeal of Agency Action

CHAPTER 7

MATCHING

1. c
2. g
3. e
4. a
5. j
6. f
7. b
8. h
9. i
10. d
11. l
12. k

FILL-IN-THE-BLANKS

1. World Trade Organization
2. North American Free Trade Agreement
3. International Court of Justice
4. International Monetary Fund
5. common law; civil law; code law; Islamic legal
6. Export Trading Company Act
7. Foreign Corrupt Practices
8. Contracts for the International Sale of Goods (CISG)
9. European Court of Justice (ECJ)
10. World Bank; Special Drawing Rights
11. Most Favored Nation
12. tariffs

SHORT ANSWER

1. a. Primary trade sanctions or boycotts - companies based in home country are prohibited from doing business with certain countries
   b. Secondary boycott - companies from other nations doing business with a sanctioned country will also experience sanctions for such activity
2. a. If the parties choose which law applies, that law will apply
   b. If no provision is made, the law of the country where the contract is performed will be used
3. a. Language
   b. Environment and technology
   c. Social organization
   d. Contexting
   e. Authority
   f. Nonverbal behavior
   g. Time concept
4. Bringing profits from business back to the local government
5. Officials of foreign countries are not subject to criminal trials in the U.S.
6. a. Criminalize bribery of foreign public officials
   b. Define public officials to include officials in all branches of government, whether appointed or elected; any person exercising a public function, including for a public agency or public enterprise; and any official or agent of a public international organization
   c. Include as public functions any activity in the public interest
   d. Cover business-related bribes to foreign public officials made through political parties and party officials
   e. Include as illegal those payments made to someone who will become a public official in anticipation of favorable treatment
   f. Provide for "effective, proportionate and dissuasive criminal penalties" to those who bribe foreign public officials
   g. Authorize the seizure or confiscation of the bribe and bribe proceeds, or property of similar value, or impose monetary sanctions of comparable effect
   h. Prohibit the establishment of off-the-books accounts and similar practices used to bribe foreign public officials or to hide such bribery
   i. Establish jurisdiction over acts that take place in their countries even if there is not extensive physical contact by those paying the bribes
   j. Pledge to work together to provide legal assistance relating to investigations and proceedings and to make bribery of foreign public officials an extraditable offense

CHAPTER 8

MATCHING   **FILL-IN-THE-BLANKS**
1.   e   1.   Fourth
2.   h   2.   grand jury proceedings; preliminary hearing; indictment; information
3.   b   3.   Miranda; Fifth; Due Process
4.   f   4.   Sarbanes-Oxley
5.   a   5.   culpability multiplier
6.   k   6.   omnibus hearing
7.   j   7.   *mens rea*; *actus rea*
8.   d   8.   Economic Espionage
9.   g   9.   Counterfeit Access Device and Computer Fraud and Abuse
10. l   10.   No Electronic Theft Act
11. c   11.   racketeering
12. i   12.   USA Patriot Act

SHORT ANSWER
1.   a.   Intent to take property
     b.   Actual taking of property for permanent use
     c.   No authorization to take property
2.   a.   Warrant and/or arrest
     b.   Initial appearance
     c.   Preliminary hearing or grand jury
     d.   Arraignment
     e.   Discovery
     f.   Omnibus hearing
     g.   Trial
3.   a.   Records are being destroyed - burning warehouse exception
     b.   "Plain view" exception - can seize items because privacy was not protected - allowed the world access to the items
4.   a.   Have a code of ethics in place
     b.   Conduct training on the code of ethics
     c.   Have a company hotline and ombudsperson for employees to use anonymously to report violations
     d.   Protect employees who report violations
     e.   Investigate all allegations regardless of their sources
     f.   Report all violations immediately and voluntarily
     g.   Offer restitution to affected parties
     h.   Cooperate and negotiate with regulators
     i.   Admit your mistakes and shortcomings
     j.   Be forthright and public with your code of ethics
5.   Officers and managers who directed the activities as well as those actually engaging in the conduct.
6.   The new obstruction section makes it a felony for anyone, including company employees, auditors, attorneys, and consultants, to alter, destroy, mutilate, conceal, cover up, falsify, or make a false entry with the "intent to impede, obstruct, or influence the investigation or proper administration of any matter within the jurisdiction of any department or agency of the United States."

CHAPTER 9

MATCHING

1. j
2. d
3. b
4. c
5. k
6. h
7. i
8. e
9. f
10. l
11. g
12. a

FILL-IN-THE-BLANKS

1. tort
2. Slander; libel
3. published
4. ordinary and reasonably prudent person
5. absolute privilege
6. contract interference
7. false imprisonment
8. intentional infliction of emotional distress
9. contributory negligence
10. Comparative negligence
11. strict tort liability
12. Health Insurance Portability and Accountability Act

SHORT ANSWER

1. a. A statement about a person's reputation, honesty, or integrity that is untrue
    b. Publication
    c. A statement that is directed at a particular person
    d. Damages
    e. In some cases, proof of malice
2. a. Truth
    b. Opinion and analysis
    c. Privileged speech
3. a. Duty
    b. Breach of duty
    c. Causation
    d. Proximate cause
    e. Damages
4. a. Assumption of risk
    b. Contributory negligence
    c. Comparative negligence
5. False imprisonment; shopkeepers generally have a statutory defense: so long as they act reasonably, they are not liable for false imprisonment.
6. A tort is a private wrong. When a tort is committed, the party who was injured is entitled to collect compensation for damages from the wrongdoer for the private wrong. A crime, on the other hand, is a public wrong and requires the wrongdoer to pay a debt to society through a fine or by going to prison.

CHAPTER 10

MATCHING	FILL-IN-THE-BLANKS
1. a	1. *caveat emptor*
2. d	2. consent decree
3. g	3. express warranty
4. h	4. merchantability
5. e	5. fitness for a particular purpose
6. i	6. disclaimers
7. j	7. Wheeler-Lea Act
8. f	8. negligence
9. c	9. contributory negligence; assumption of risk; product liability
10. b	10. comparative negligence
11. l	11. Consumer Product Safety Commission
12. k	12. assumed

SHORT ANSWER

1. a.   Seller has skill or judgment in use of the goods
    b.   Buyer is relying on that skill or judgment
    c.   Seller knew or had reason to know of the buyer's reliance
    d.   Seller makes a recommendation for the buyer's use and purpose
2. a.   Misuse or abnormal use of product
    b.   Contributory negligence
    c.   Assumption of risk
3. a.   To protect the public against unreasonable risks of injury from consumer products
    b.   To develop standards for consumer product safety
    c.   To help consumers become more informed about evaluating safety
    d.   To fund research in matters of product safety design and in product-caused injuries and illnesses
4. a.   Design defects
    b.   Dangers of use that were not warned about or dangers because unclear use instructions were given
    c.   Errors in manufacturing, handling, or packaging of the product
5. Advertising a cheaper product to get customers into the store and then, by not having the cheaper product, sell them a more expensive one.
6. a.   The celebrity must ascertain the truth of the ad claims.
    b.   The celebrity cannot make any claims about product use unless the celebrity has actually used and experienced the product.
    c.   If any claims are being made that are not the celebrity's, the source of the information must be disclosed as part of the ad.

CHAPTER 11

MATCHING	FILL-IN-THE-BLANKS
1. h	1. nonattainment; prevention of significant deterioration
2. j	2. bubble
3. l	3. effluent
4. e	4. National Pollution Discharge Elimination System
5. i	5. best conventional; best available
6. c	6. Community Right-to-Know Substance
7. k	7. Comprehensive Environmental Response, Compensation, and Liability; Superfund
8. b	8. Toxic Substances Control
9. a	9. Federal Water Pollution Control Administration
10. f	10. Safe Drinking Water Act
11. d	11. injunction
12. g	12. BANANAs (Building Absolutely Nothing Anywhere Near Anything)

SHORT ANSWER

1. a. The new plant must have the greatest possible emissions controls
   b. The proposed plant operator must have all other operations in compliance with standards
   c. The new plant's emissions must be offset by reductions from other facilities in the area
2. a. Proposed action's environmental impact
   b. Adverse environmental effects (if any)
   c. Alternative methods
   d. Short-term effects vs. long-term maintenance, enhancement, and productivity
   e. Irreversible and irretrievable resource uses
3. a. Conventional
   b. Nonconventional
   c. Toxic
4. a. Owners and operators of a contaminated piece of property
   b. Owners and operators at the time the property was contaminated
   c. Those who transport hazardous materials
   d. Those who arrange for the transportation of hazardous materials
5. a. Monitor or enforce terms of the security agreement
   b. Monitor or inspect the premises or facility
   c. Mandate that the debtor take action on hazardous materials
   d. Provide financial advice or counseling
   e. Restructure or renegotiate the loan terms
   f. Exercise any remedies available at law
   g. Foreclosure on the property
   h. Sell the property
   i. Lease the property
6. "Brownfields" are sites defined by the EPA as "real property, the expansion, redevelopment, or reuse of which may be complicated by the presence or potential presence of a hazardous substance, pollutant, or contaminant." Brownfields often contribute to urban blight and present barriers to economic development and revitalization.

CHAPTER 12

MATCHING
1.   l
2.   f
3.   c
4.   k
5.   a
6.   i
7.   g
8.   b
9.   j
10. e
11. d
12. h

FILL-IN-THE-BLANKS
1.   offer; offeror; offeree
2.   counteroffer
3.   bilateral; unilateral
4.   implied-in-law; quasi
5.   implied
6.   unenforceable
7.   executed; executory
8.   Revocation
9.   Consideration
10. charitable subscriptions
11. Parol evidence
12. Implied-in-fact

SHORT ANSWER
1.   a.   The Parties
     b.   The Subject Matter of the Contract
     c.   The Price
     d.   Payment Terms
     e.   Delivery Terms
     f.   Performance Times
2.   A contract is a promise or set of promises for breach of which the law gives a remedy, or the performance of which the law in some way recognizes as a duty.
3.   a.   Contracts for the sale of real property
     b.   Contracts that can't be performed in one year
     c.   Contracts to pay the debt of another
     d.   Contracts for sale of goods for $5,000 or more
4.   a.   Rejection
     b.   Counteroffer
     c.   Death of offeror
     d.   Time lapsed
5.   Mailbox rules applies in acceptance and determines when an acceptance becomes valid.
6.   CISG has fewer product liability protections; requires more terms in offer to be valid; follows mirror image rule.

CHAPTER 13

MATCHING

1. e
2. a
3. g
4. c
5. b
6. d
7. j
8. i
9. f
10. h
11. l
12. k

FILL-IN-THE-BLANKS

1. void
2. duress
3. undue influence
4. commercial impracticability
5. impossibility
6. Exculpatory
7. compensatory damages; consequential damages
8. liquidated
9. Age capacity; mental capacity
10. Contract defense
11. *scienter*
12. conditions concurrent

SHORT ANSWER

1. Some statutes are enforceable against minors, e.g., student loan agreements, military service, necessities such as food, clothing, and medical care.
2. a. Capacity
   b. Misrepresentation
   c. Fraud
   d. Duress
   e. Undue influence
   f. Illegality and public policy
3. a. Compensatory damages
   b. Incidental damages
   c. Liquidated damages
   d. Consequential damages
4. a. Misstatement of a material fact (or the failure to disclose a material fact)
   b. Reliance by the buyer on that material misstatement or omission
   c. Resulting damages to the buyer
5. A clause in a contract that excuses performances due to events beyond the parties' control.
6. Companies can use a bill of lading to control access to the goods and payments for them. The bill of lading is a receipt for shipment issued by the carrier to the seller, it also provides evidence of who has title to the goods. The bill of lading is often used in conjunction with a letter of credit that is issued by the buyer's bank and is sent to the corresponding bank where the seller is located. The letter of credit lists the terms and conditions under which the seller can draw on the letter of credit or be paid.

CHAPTER 14

MATCHING
1. h
2. d
3. b
4. l
5. i
6. a
7. e
8. g
9. k
10. j
11. c
12. f

FILL-IN-THE-BLANKS
1. bankruptcy
2. judgment
3. usury
4. Equal Credit Opportunity Act
5. Regulation Z
6. three-day cooling off period
7. Consumer Leasing Act
8. Home Equity Loan Consumer Protection Act
9. Fair Debt Collection Practices
10. security interest; security agreement
11. Subprime Lending Market
12. seven; thirteen; eleven

SHORT ANSWER
1. a. No disclosure of bankruptcies that occurred more than ten years ago
   b. No disclosure of lawsuits finalized more than seven years ago
   c. No disclosure of criminal convictions and arrests that have been disposed of more than seven years ago
2. a. Marital status of the applicant
   b. Applicant's receipt of public assistance income
   c. Applicant's receipt of alimony or child support payments
   d. Applicant's plans for having children
3. a. The amount the debtor is financing
   b. The finance charges
   c. The annual percentage rate
   d. The number and amount of payments and when they are due
   e. The total cost of financing
   f. Whether there are any additional penalties such as prepayment penalties or late payment penalties
   g. Any security interest the creditor has in the goods sold by credit
   h. The cost of credit insurance if the debtor is paying for credit insurance
4. a. A debtor who asks for his own report
   b. A creditor who has the debtor's signed application for credit
   c. A potential employer
   d. A court pursuant to a subpoena
5. a. Illegal (sex discrimination)
   b. Illegal (public assistance income)
   c. Valid question
6. a. A 6% interest limit on ARMs while service members are on active duty
   b. A maximum of 36% interest APR on all debt to all service members
   c. No delinquency reports on service members to credit agencies while they are on active duty
   d. No repossession of cars during active duty without a court order
   e. Continuing protection that prevents foreclosure during active duty

CHAPTER 15

MATCHING
1. g
2. l
3. d
4. a
5. e
6. i
7. k
8. h
9. f
10. j
11. b
12 c

FILL-IN-THE-BLANKS
1. Tangible; intangible
2. bailment; bailor; bailee
3. trade dress
4. palming off
5. trade secrets; misappropriation
6. knock-off goods
7. patent
8. infringement
9. trademark; Lanham
10. fair use
11. function; design; plant
12. copyrighting

SHORT ANSWER
1. a. Statement about a business's reputation, honesty, or integrity that is untrue;
    b. Publication
    c. Statement that is directed at a business and is made with malice and the intent to injure that business
    d. Damages
2. a. What did the parties intend?
    b. How is the item attached to the real property?
    c. What is the relationship between the attacher and the property?
    d. Who wants to know?
3. a. Patents
    b. Copyrights
    c. Trademarks
    d. Trade Names
    e. Trade Dress
4. a. Highest form of land ownership
    b. Lien on real property to secure debt
    c. Right to use another's property (access) or right to control use of another's property
    d. Document that transfers real property
    e. Highest level of title protection in real property transfer
    f. Promises of title protection only for grantor's period of ownership
5. a. Copyright
    b. Patent
    c. Copyright
    d. Copyright or patent
6. The Sonny Bono Copyright Term Extension Act was sponsored by the late Sonny Bono. Representative Bono was concerned because copyrights he held and many others, such as the copyright on the cartoon character Mickey Mouse were about to expire. Even though the Constitution prohibits granting copyrights in perpetuity, the Act extended the copyright for the life of a creator plus 70 years.

CHAPTER 16

MATCHING

1. b
2. f
3. h
4. e
5. d
6. j
7. c
8. g
9. a
10. i
11. k
12. l

FILL-IN-THE-BLANKS

1. market power; relevant market
2. cross-elasticity of demand
3. interlocking directorates
4. vertical merger
5. treble
6. sole outlet; exclusive distributorship
7. tying sale
8. interbrand
9. price discrimination; Robinson-Patman
10. meeting the competition
11. exclusionary
12. small-company

SHORT ANSWER

1. a. Seller engaged in commerce
   b. Discrimination in price among purchasers
   c. Commodities sold are of like grade or quality
   d. Substantial lessening of competition in any line of commerce or a tendency to create a monopoly; or competition is injured, destroyed, or prevented
2. a. Possession of market power in the relevant market
   b. Intentional or willful abuse of that power
3. a. Resale price maintenance
   b. Monopsony
   c. Sole outlets and exclusive distributorships
   d. Customer and territorial restrictions
   e. Tying arrangements
   f. Price discrimination
4. a. Monopolization
   b. Price-fixing
   c. Division of markets
   d. Group boycotts and refusals to deal
   e. Joint ventures
5. a. Price fixing if done among competitors
   b. Price fixing if done among competitors
   c. So long as done vertically and not enforced via boycott, it is not a violation
6. a. New Industry Defense – the manufacturer of the tying product is permitted to have a tied product to protect initially the quality control in the start-up of a business
   b. Quality Control for the Protection of Goodwill – this defense is rarely supportable, the only time it would apply is if the specifications for the tied goods are so detailed that they could not possibly be supplied by anyone other than the manufacturer of the tying product

CHAPTER 17

MATCHING
1. g
2. h
3. f
4. c
5. a
6. e
7. k
8. j
9. l
10. d
11. i
12. b

FILL-IN-THE-BLANKS
1. independent contractor; scope
2. Apparent authority
3. inherently dangerous activity
4. fiduciary
5. lingering apparent; actual notice
6. constructive
7. servant (employee); independent contractor
8. respondeat superior
9. express
10. disclosed; partially disclosed
11. Agents
12. Sarbanes-Oxley

SHORT ANSWER
1. a. Level of supervision of agent
   b. Level of control of agent
   c. Nature of agent's work
   d. Regularity of hours and pay
   e. Length of employment
2. a. Public policy exception
   b. Implied contract exception
3. a. Conduct regular reviews of employees, using objective, uniform measures of performance
   b. Give clear, business-related reasons for any dismissal, backed by written documentation when possible
   c. Seek legal waivers from older workers who agree to leave under an early-retirement plan, and make sure they understand the waiver terms in advance
   d. Follow any written company guidelines for termination, or be prepared to show in court why they're not binding in any particular instance
4. a. Agent and principal
   b. Agent
   c. Agent and principal
5. Sarbanes-Oxley provides specific protections for whistle-blowers who disclose financial fraud. Section 806 prohibits a publicly traded company from discharging or otherwise discriminating against an employee because the employee: (1) assists in an investigation of prohibited conduct, and the investigation includes both federal and internal or board investigations; or (2) files or participates in a suit or other action for fraud by the company against shareholders. Remedies for whistle-blowers under Sarbanes-Oxley include reinstatement, back pay, and compensatory damages.
6. Under the Uniform Durable Power of Attorney Act, individuals can execute a type of power of attorney that comes into existence in the event of disability or incapacity of the principal. This authority then "kicks in" when needed. The act is helpful for children who are trying to manage their parents' financial affairs when their parents become mentally or physically disabled.

CHAPTER 18

MATCHING		**FILL-IN-THE-BLANKS**
1.	e	1. Federal Insurance Contributions Act (FICA)
2.	b	2. Employment Retirement Income Security Act (ERISA)
3.	d	3. nonserious; willful
4.	f	4. gender; merit; seniority
5.	h	5. sixteen
6.	j	6. boycott
7.	c	7. Scheduled injuries; unscheduled injuries
8.	i	8. slowdown
9.	l	9. Featherbedding
10.	g	10. closed shop; Taft-Hartley
11.	a	11. cooling-off period
12.	k	12. strike

SHORT ANSWER

1.
   a. Hazards or conditions that could cause death
   b. Investigations of fatal accident sites
   c. Employee complaints
   d. Particularly hazardous industries
   e. Random inspections

2.
   a. Employee must have been involuntarily terminated
   b. Employee must be able and available for work
   c. Employee must be seeking employment

3.
   a. Refusal to bargain in good faith
   b. Refusal to bargain on a mandatory issue
   c. Violation of collective bargaining agreement
   d. Interference with joining a union
   e. Timing of benefits
   f. Observation of union activities
   g. Domination of labor union
   h. Discrimination in promotion of union members
   i. Blacklisting

4.
   a. An employee who is injured in the scope of employment is automatically entitled to certain benefits
   b. Fault is immaterial
   c. Coverage is limited to employees and does not extend to independent contractors
   d. Benefits include partial wages, hospital and medical expenses, and death benefits
   e. In exchange for these benefits, employees, their families, and dependents give up their common law right to sue an employer for damages
   f. If third parties are responsible for accident, recovery from third party goes first to employer for reimbursement
   g. Each state has some administrative agency responsible for administration of workers' compensation
   h. Every employer who is subject to workers' compensation regulation is required to provide some security for liability

5.
   a. No restrictions
   b. This age group can work any "nonhazardous" job for unlimited hours
   c. This age group can work only in nonhazardous, non-manufacturing, and non-mining jobs, and only during non-school hours

6.
   a. Willful – up to $70,000 and/or six months imprisonment
   b. Serious - $7,000
   c. Nonserious – Up to $7,000
   d. *De Minimis* – Up to $7,000 per violation
   e. Failure to correct - $7,000 per day

CHAPTER 19

MATCHING

1. e
2. i
3. a
4. j
5. b
6. h
7. c
8. g
9. d
10. f
11. k
12. l

FILL-IN-THE-BLANKS

1. disparate treatment
2. disparate impact
3. pattern or practice
4. sexual harassment
5. Pregnancy Discrimination Act
6. bona fide occupational qualification (BFOQ)
7. Americans with Disabilities
8. 180; right-to-sue letter
9. Glass Ceiling Act
10. quotas
11. injunctions
12. Rehabilitation Act

SHORT ANSWER

1.
   a. Employers with at least 15 workers during each working day in each of 20 or more calendar weeks in the current or preceding year
   b. Labor unions that have 15 members or more or operate a hiring hall that refers workers to covered employers
   c. Employment agencies that procure workers for an employer who is covered by the law
   d. Any labor union or employment agency provided it has 15 or more employees
   e. State and local agencies

2.
   a. Employers who, pursuant to consent decree or court order, must implement plans to compensate for past wrongs
   b. State and local agencies and colleges and universities that receive federal funds
   c. Government contractors
   d. Businesses that work on federal projects

3.
   a. Forcing a resignation
   b. Demoting or limiting an employee's job upon her return to work
   c. Refusing to allow a mother to return to work after pregnancy
   d. Providing different sick leave rules for pregnancy and other medical ailments
   e. Providing different medical insurance benefits or disability leave for pregnancy and other ailments
   f. Refusing to hire or promote on the basis of pregnancy or family plans

4.
   a. The system must apply to all employees
   b. Whatever divisions or units are used for the system must follow the industry custom or pattern
   c. The origins of the system cannot lie in racial discrimination
   d. The system must be maintained for seniority and merit purposes and not to perpetuate racial discrimination

5.
   a. Employment of aliens outside the United States
   b. Religious corporations, associations, educational institutions, or societies
   c. Congress
   d. Federal government and corporations owned by the federal government
   e. American Indian peoples and departments or agencies

6.
   a. *Quid Pro Quo* – cases in which an employee is required to submit to sexual advances in order to remain employed, secure a promotion, or obtain a raise.
   b. *Atmosphere of Harassment* – cases in which the invitations, language, pictures, or suggestions become so pervasive as to create a hostile work environment.

CHAPTER 20

MATCHING

1. j
2. l
3. h
4. i
5. c
6. e
7. k
8. f
9. b
10. d
11. a
12. g

FILL-IN-THE-BLANKS

1. incorporators; novation
2. alter ego
3. watered shares
4. business judgment rule
5. pooling agreement
6. transfer restriction
7. Common stock; preferred stock
8. domestic; foreign
9. articles of incorporation; bylaws; initial
10. Dissolution; termination
11. audit committees
12. corporate opportunity doctrine

SHORT ANSWER

1. a. Profits paid to repay debts
    b. Profits paid as wages or rent
    c. Profits paid to widow or estate representative
    d. Profits paid for the sale of business goodwill
2. a. Being employed by the general partnership as an employee or contractor
    b. Consulting with or advising the general partner
    c. Acting as a surety or guarantor for the limited partnership
    d. Voting on amendments, dissolution, sale of property, or assumption of debt
3. a. The name of the corporation
    b. The names and addresses of all incorporators
    c. The share structure of the corporation
    d. The statutory agent
4. a. Expiration of the time period in the agreement or the occurrence of an event causing dissolution, as specified in the agreement
    b. Unanimous written consent of all partners
    c. Withdrawal of a general partner
    d. Court order after application by one of the partners

5. Partnerships:

    Flow-through - partnership
    Tax - partners

    Corporations:

    Tax - corporation
    Tax - shareholder

    Limited Partnerships:

    Flow-through - partnership
    Tax - partners

    Limited Liability Companies:

    Flow-through - partnership
    Tax - partners

    Limited Liability Partnerships:

    Flow-through - partnership
    Tax - partners

6. Corporation, limited partners in limited partnership, limited liability companies, limited liability partnerships

CHAPTER 21

MATCHING
1. d
2. f
3. j
4. a
5. i
6. b
7. h
8. c
9. g
10. e
11. l
12. k

FILL-IN-THE-BLANKS
1. primary offering
2. Securities and Exchange Commission (SEC)
3. intrastate offering
4. registration statement; sample prospectus; comment or deficiency letter
5. tombstone; red herring
6. Williams Act; five
7. friendly takeover; hostile takeover
8. 10-Q form; 10-K form; 8-K form
9. antifraud; tippees
10. Sarbanes-Oxley
11. exemption
12. Regulation D; 504; 505; 506

SHORT ANSWER
1.
   a. Any bank
   b. Any private business development company
   c. Any director, executive officer, or general partner of the issuer
   d. Any person who purchases at least $150,000 of the securities being offered
   e. Natural persons who's net worth is greater than $1 million
   f. Any person whose individual income exceeded $200,000 in the last two years or who expects income with that person's spouse greater than $300,000 in the current year
2.
   a. A description of what is being offered, why it is offered, how the securities will fit into the business's existing capital structure, and how the proceeds will be used
   b. An audited financial statement
   c. A list of corporate assets
   d. The nature of the issuer's business
   e. A list of those in management and their shares of ownership in the firm
   f. Other relevant and material information such as pending lawsuits
3.
   a. Immateriality
   b. Investor Knowledge
   c. Due Diligence
4.
   a. Insider trading
   b. Proxy solicitation
   c. Short-swing profits
   d. False information in registration statement
   e. Selling in advance of SEC approval; false prospectus
   f. Small offering exemption
5.
   a. Persuading shareholders that the tender offer is not in their best interests
   b. Filing legal suits or complaints on the grounds that the takeover violates provisions of the antitrust laws
   c. Matching the buy-out with a target company offer
   d. Soliciting a "white knight" merger
6.
   a. Developing a registration system for public accounting firms that prepare audit reports for companies that issue securities.
   b. Establishing rules to ensure audit quality, ethics, and auditor independence.
   c. Conducting inspections of public accounting firms to determine their compliance with Sarbanes-Oxley requirements.
   d. Investigating violations and imposing disciplinary sanctions where necessary for members of the profession.
   e. Encouraging the highest professional standards among public accounting firms and auditors.

FLOWER SHADOWS

FLOWER SHADOWS

A Novel

Terry Farish

WILLIAM MORROW AND COMPANY, INC. NEW YORK

Grateful acknowledgment is made for use of the following previously published material:

Kenneth Rexroth. *One Hundred Poems from the Chinese*. Copyright © 1971 by Kenneth Rexroth. Reprinted by permission of New Directions Publishing Corporation. All rights reserved.

Isaac Rosenberg. "Girl to Soldier on Leave." Collected in *The Penguin Book of First World War Poetry*. Chatto & Windus. All rights reserved.

Library of Congress Cataloging-in-Publication Data

Farish, Terry.
   Flower shadows / by Terry Farish.
     p. cm.
   ISBN 0-688-10973-X
    1. Vietnamese Conflict, 1961–1975—Fiction. I. Title.
PS3556.A7155F57   1991
813'.54—dc20   91-8816
                                  CIP

Printed in the United States of America

First Edition

1 2 3 4 5 6 7 8 9 10

BOOK DESIGN BY LISA STOKES

For Elizabeth

Acknowledgment

Grateful acknowledgment is made to Minh Hoang Thi Chau, Elaine (Lane) Querry Stallings, Rodger Martin, Raymond Beauregard, and Stephen Farish for their contributions to the accuracy of facts represented.

I have already drained and broken
The cup of Spring.
Flower shadows lie heavy
On the translucent curtains.

Li Ch'ing-chao

Chapter 1

Pearly and I were half of the Red Cross Unit at Cu Chi. If you counted Hoa, our hooch girl, there were five girls in the unit, and in the telling, Hoa is always there. She came to us tiny and fawnlike, with her rice bowl and fruit for her meals and wearing her sun hat made of coconut leaves. She slipped in and made a place for herself partly because we befriended her and partly because we were easy to steal from. Hoa was maybe sixteen. We weren't sure. She said she was eighteen, but she looked more like twelve. Her job was to scrub our blue uniforms clean. She put sheets on our metal-frame beds and washed our underwear, which came back more stained every time she washed it, if it came back at all. Sometimes she took our earrings, and sundresses our mamas sent from home. Sometimes she went in and out of our rooms, through the rows of blue and orange beads we had strung for bedroom doors, with a backless sundress over her black silky pajamas.

When we caught her with our stuff, she'd say gently, "I fuck GI instead?," meaning she needed the money. Pearly would say, "You fuck any goddamn GIs, I'm gonna fire you," and gave Hoa something she would resell in the Vietnamese black market.

Hoa taught us things, even though we counted days like beads the way all Americans did and waited to be short. Short as in having done our time.

We Red Cross girls were noncombatants protected in a sandbagged hooch, but when the war pressed between the grains of sand and vaulted the concertina wire around our compound, Hoa knew what to do. She needed some fruit, bananas or a pineapple, to feed Pearly's spirit, and she packed Pearly's red bathrobe and her pop beads that she wore to general's mess. These were for the journey to the other world. She said we had to consult a wizard to know what day to bury her, but there wasn't any time. She only had time to whisper a Buddhist prayer in Pearly's ear, and the army didn't take the bananas to Graves Registration. Even though Hoa was a little thief, she was good to Pearly and me.

This story is Pearly's. I am responsible for her. She is always with me. I can see her Italian boy haircut and her long, slim neck and hear her telling some incredible story. Her life was one catastrophe after another long before I met her coming to Vietnam. It was her style. It was in her walk. It was in her eyes and made you hold your breath when you watched her. She had lived in a mill town with a boy who got drafted. Staid folk in that mill town, and then Pearly, who totaled their trucks and Rototillers. She told me stories. That's how she lived, and she transformed a chopper ride, serving in a mess tent, even a Kool-Aid

run—these being normal things we did in Vietnam—
into life-or-death situations.

Hoa told me a story about how you only get to
live so many days. Everybody gets so many days allotted. She said she knows for a fact that if you die
by mistake too soon, the King of the Dead will send
you back to earth because you weren't finished. She
says nothing in the stars can be changed or altered.
She said Pearly had finished her allotted days and I
had not. This story is still for Pearly. I am like the
girl with the little fish who died, and she loved the
fish, so she saved his bones because "cherished bones
keep love alive." I'm holding on to you, Pearly, for
dear life, but I need to stop hearing the blood gurgle
in your throat. It should have been my blood. Sometimes I would take a beating, physical pain, instead
of always wishing it had been my own throat and my
blood. But here I am. You told me, Say good things,
so that's what I'm doing. Could you let go of me a
little?

Pearly said telling stories is a courage. And Pearly
never shut up. She called it whaffling on, though
Pearly hardly whaffled. I'm going to hardly whaffle
like Pearly and tell how we two American girls who
weren't nurses and didn't sing onstage and didn't get
paid for our looks (whatever part of which we had
that was good, we lost over there) came to be in Vietnam. It was 1969, and we were there along with more
GIs than had been in country the whole war, and
along with the monsoon rains, which had come to the
South where we were near the Delta.

I was leaning up against the saltwater-taffy dis-
play, all the crinkly pink and blue and tangerine

wrappers, in Jack's Cafe on the seawall. I was watching to see what would come in off the boulevard from out of the rain. Jack's was on stilts to keep the dining room dry when the water rises high. It overlooked Galveston Bay and was tucked in among a dozen shell shops along Stewart's Beach. Jack would give me hours of waitressing whenever I came to Galveston. I could just show up. He didn't care. He said his take was better those hours.

There was hardly a rush now at nightfall, and I ate one of the green-tinted taffies. The girls at college had shown me how to do my hair up in a bulky French twist that I did for work at Jack's, but I wasn't especially careful with it, and lots of strands fell down my neck. Jack's was the kind of place you could waitress in jeans, so he didn't care about the hair. I didn't have on jeans, though. I had on a crop top and striped pants that Mama sewed, matching up the stripes where the bell sleeves fit into the bodice. I wore them that night because I wished I were home for spring vacation instead of Galveston, but I wouldn't give Mama the satisfaction of going home. She had a boyfriend, a real stiff who she had all but married, and not going home was my revenge.

"Fine, Mama," I had said. "Fine. I really don't care."

I was rehearsing "Fine" and looking in the mirror above the counter, noticing how well Mama matched up stripes. There wasn't anything she couldn't do. She even smoked well. She had just the right way of bringing a cigarette to her lips with her deft seamstress's fingers. I never smoked in front of her because it made me feel like a little child in her mama's high heels. I couldn't fill them, and I didn't feel deft.

"Fine, Mama," I said into the mirror.

I saw a boy in the mirror behind me and caught my breath. The screen door hadn't slammed. He was just there. I knew him right off, and at the same time the boy was a stranger. He was the boy I made a fool of myself over in the eighth grade. Jesse De Witt. He walked like Jesse walked, like a gorilla, being all arms and stockylike. But when I looked straight into his face in the mirror, it wasn't the right face. It was Jesse in a plaster mask.

He looked at me, and he didn't say, "Hey, Long Tall Di." That's how I got separated from Diana-the-Shy, another Diana in our hometown who was less long and tall and rhapsodic. And I didn't answer, "Hey, Jess." This boy's eyes didn't know me. We were from a town a little way north of Galveston. We couldn't have not talked if we'd met at the Post Office Drug at home. But there were lots of strangers in Galveston, and the waves were so loud you didn't have to talk by the water. I think of Galveston as a place to nestle you in huge arms. It makes you feel nestled to the universe.

I stopped lounging over the candy and watching the rain. Most of the kids were down on the beach and didn't care if rain blasted against their cheeks and poured through their cutoffs. From the café we could hear their shouts and screams over the rush of traffic, rain, and surf. Just one kid, this Jesse-Ghost kid, came up from the beach. I wished there were other customers, because he didn't have anything better to do than watch me with eyes that didn't know me.

Jesse-Ghost riffled through his pocket and pulled out a bill that wasn't American money. Jack shrugged and gave him what he wanted anyway. He slid a coffee across the counter, and Jesse grabbed at it. I watched his hands shake. The guys on the beach had hair to their shoulders or curls like Garfunkel. Jesse-Ghost was cut to the scalp, so I guessed the draft had gotten him.

I went back to naming just causes for me to hold Mama to blame. She called me flighty, unmotivated, and the cause of there being too many boys hanging around the front porch with her peacocks. When she hugged me, she would sniff my cheek for clues to anything about me, because I would not talk. She would only know that I had just eaten peanut butter or sneaked her Merle Norman translucent face powder. Seeing Jesse reminded me of the time when I liked him and he had sneaked in through our back-yard and snapped the palmated leaves off Mama's prize banana tree. Jesse had not left a single clue to be sniffed on my cheek when Mama came into my room to talk about her banana crop.

I wondered if she'd like Jesse more at twenty than she had liked him at fourteen, since he had gone to Vietnam and came back with ghostly eyes. She considered soldiers to be noble. My father had been one. He had died from wounds he got in North Africa in the Second World War. I could never understand how wounds could take so long to kill someone. The war had been over five years, but mama always said he died for his country. When I smell butterscotch, I think of him. I remember he liked hard butterscotch candies. I talk to him in my head, and I see him most clearly as the man in khakis in front of an armored personnel carrier. I have a picture. He is in a horse-shoe of men, and my eyes follow along until I find my father's pale eyes.

Mama had a reverence for our country. I could swear my first memory was the roar of delegates and the ritual calling of each state's name to hear how they cast their votes at the Republican National Convention. I believe America was Mama's religion. I heard of people doing almost anything to keep from getting sent to Vietnam. But to question the morality of going was like questioning the morality of my mother.

I always wanted to tell you, Pearly, that coming to Vietnam was a lot more for my mother than for President Nixon or the generals. It was more personal. But then, I bet there isn't anything people do that's not for personal reasons. I was a patriot for personal reasons.

"They send you back tongue-tied?" I asked Jesse, passing by him.

He looked at me stone-faced and mumbled something about how he didn't think I'd remember him. It'd only been a couple years.

The rain let up. It was six-thirty at night. I lit a cigarette, let the smoke fill my lungs, and blew it slowly into the sea air and thought of Mama. That's when Jesse started to talk.

"They called them Delta Deltas," Jesse was saying at the counter.

"Who?" I said.

"Girls there I was telling you about. Or doughnut dollies, same thing," he said. "But I never saw no damn girl in Nam. I never saw no damn doughnut. I heard about them, though."

I wiped off the counter and dried my hands on the towel that was tied like an apron around my waist.

Jesse kept on talking. He only wanted to talk about Vietnam. "Just left Tan Son Nhut." He looked at his watch. "Five days ago. Monday, 1500 hours. Christ Almighty," he said.

I would give Jack another twenty minutes. I

thought of last August when I spent my afternoons under the orange sun, letting my hair bleach out as pale as the sand. I had shaken sand out of my shoes and my bathing suit, but it stayed in my belly button and between my toes all August. I half listened to Jesse and wondered what I would do between spring and when the sun beat down and warmed the sand. Jack was playing Dionne Warwick on the kitchen radio. He was playing "Walk On By."

The war in Vietnam was real enough even for a Texas girl studying at a poor women's college. My college butted up against an army post. Butted up? This was Texas, and Mineral Wells butted up against Denton in a Texas sort of way. The guys who cruised the campus on weekends learned to fly helicopters in business hours.

A WOC, what they called Warrant Officer Candidates, came and took me to cold motel rooms in the Texas heat where Texas girls—I was true to this myth—maybe drank and maybe danced and maybe sweet-talked, but only down as far as the lace of their underwear, and leaving the rest of themselves to the imagination. My WOC played Dionne Warwick, "Anyone Who Had a Heart," on my dorm piano. He was a Georgia boy with an accent as thick as cream. I could hear his voice now, in Jack's, as I was looking out on the bay. I wondered what happened to him. It wasn't that I didn't have a heart that I only wondered. It was just that I only saw WOCs in their jeans, not flight suits, and part of college was always saying good-bye, and my WOC was one more good-bye while I was trying not to flunk chemistry.

A girl down the hall in my dorm married a WOC. They had Thursday, Friday, and Saturday, and then he flew out of San Francisco on a C-130. Letters were life-and-death matters. The girl—Kate—clicked through the combination on her mailbox and wept when there was a flimsy tissue-paper airmail envelope shaded with the crescent-moon shape of Vietnam. The weeping came from her throat, not from her eyes, like it had its roots in her belly and heart. But it was worse when there wasn't any letter, because then she didn't have the relief of tears, and the pain stayed tight inside. I could see that on her face.

For sure, the war was around us. But this was a woman's college that, if it hadn't been for the WOCs, would have been a nunnery. Farm girls came to study nursing. Black girls came, and Hispanics from Harlingen. If they had a lot of money, they probably weren't at this school. Either that or they were pulled out of party schools and sent there as penance.

If girls questioned the war, their protests were romantic. They played "Leaving on a Jet Plane" on their dorm record players. I had watched Kate who married the WOC sunbathing on the roof the summer he was flying dust-off choppers out of Phu Bai. The girl was a little hairy, and we all thought she had better learn how to rid herself of that fur on her legs before he came back.

The war was all around. People even knew it in North Texas. It was happening then, while girls were getting mono and falling in love and straightening their hair or trimming each other's ends and eating enormous amounts of food sent from home and vowing, an oath with raised fists, to lose weight tomorrow. And then there'd be the odd truth that the WOC I dated from Georgia with an accent as thick as cream and with whom I howled, nose to nose at the piano, all the words in perfect sync to "Walk On By," was fighting a guerrilla war.

A lot of girls had maps on their walls with colored pins to mark where their boyfriends were. By
1969 everybody pretty well knew where Vietnam was,
and down the dorm corridors Mary of Peter, Paul,
and Mary lamented "Where Have All the Flowers
Gone?" It was heart-wrenchingly romantic.

"You got a light?" It was Jesse. I stepped back
inside. It was nearly seven and almost dusk. I gave
him a book of matches with a sketch in black strokes
of Jack's on stilts. It looked like a house on crutches.
He lit up. "I bought a bike," he said. "First thing
I did." He pointed out the door at a Kawasaki bike
half under the stairs. It was shiny and a lot more
spiffy than Jesse. He was the exact opposite of Mama's boyfriend, Manfred. Jesse eased off the stool and
stood by the door, looking not as stocky as he used
to. I remembered him in a white tux going to our
prom. Now he sat on the top of the steps to the boulevard and watched the waves spread over the rocks.
He seemed to like the roar. He leaned a little into it,
and when a family with four kids climbed over him
to come inside, he didn't notice. He watched the gulls
fight for crumbs from a little boy's cookie. The gulls'
screeches were faint and drifted in and out on the
wind.
      When I walked past the open door again to take
chicken in a basket and mugs of cocoa to all the little
kids, I saw Jesse was still sitting on the step leaning
into the roar of the waves. I decided if he was there
when I got off, I'd ask him for a ride on his bike. I
couldn't think of anything that would make Mama
and Manfred angrier.
      Manfred was a smooth-skinned blowhard. I hated
him without remorse or any desire to be reasonable.

Manfred would take one look at the guy in the wind and begin a discourse on the political ramifications of Vietnamization and land-use reform, and the guy in the wind would cease to exist. Once Manfred gave a descriptive, informative account of the way a person had died in battle, how the person's legs stood there after his body was blown away.

Maybe Mama thought he was worldly because he didn't talk about feed grain. I know that's what she pined for, worldliness. Or maybe her bed was too cold and even Mama needed someone to preen for, and here came Manfred buying stamps at her post office every noon and no one to write to.

I took off my apron. The family was finishing their supper in the dark because Jack was impatient to close. The children thought that was wonderful and squealed about the trace of moonlight that appeared. Jack stayed to finish clearing up. I came out with the customers and climbed over Jesse on the step. I stopped and sat a few steps down from him.

"How about a ride on your bike?" I said.

Jesse didn't look at me. I kicked off my shoes and squeezed my eyes shut so I could smell the night better. My striped pants were my baggy ones. My best ones were too tight. I was fasting, if it hadn't been for the taffy. I had these puff sleeves and this sash at the waist. The sash felt prissy next to Jesse, and I untied it and stashed it under the stairs. I leaned into the railing.

I wondered if he remembered the time I had called him up in the eighth grade and said, "Jesse, do you like me?," and he had said, "Yeah, I guess," and I had hung up, stunned by his lack of ardor. But then a football player offered to let me wear his suspen-

ders on game day. That was ardor in the eighth grade.
I had called Jesse because he had crinkly eyes like
Roy Rogers when he smiled. He had not smiled once
tonight.

I looked across at the seawall. It was a seven-foot
concrete breakwater that stretched for miles up and
down the beach to protect the people. But in the end
it was a come-on, something to tempt people down
the steep staircases that cut through the wall so they
could get nearer the sea.

Jesse was on his bike, ramming the starter with
the heel of his boot. He got it going and glanced up
at me. It wasn't strictly an invitation. Guys were rarely
so subtle. I couldn't figure it, but it was a beautiful,
dark spring night, and I could smell the redbud trees
in bloom down the boulevard. I went with him. The
rain had stopped, and I wanted to be close to somebody that night.

I sat on the seat behind him. He smelled like an
old man, like he was wearing his grandfather's undershirt seeped in the smells of cooking fat and tobacco
and salves for his pains. But I told him, "I always
thought you were real cute. You know I aways did."
Loose talk, but I was feeling fine. I was remembering
him as my old crush who I believe I even went trick-
or-treating with once. Kids together.

Then he took me on a hell ride. I held the metal
back of his seat. On the boulevard he picked up speed,
and we flew. The seawall was a streak of gray. We
weren't past the first staircase to the sea before I
lurched forward and gripped Jesse around the middle
and pressed myself tight to his back for fear of being
fired into the night by our sheer speed. I remembered
pressing my cheek against his shoulder blade and he
was a skinnier kid then and the blade caught my

cheekbone. There was a lot of clashing of bones. That's how I remembered it.

The ride never stopped. The bike streaked the length of Seawall Boulevard. It cut corners around the fishing piers. It spanned the causeway when all there was, was blue and back again, until it bumped, exhausted, on a sand road to the sea. It cruised along the beach two or three times between Jack's Cafe and the glass ponies in Myra's Gift Shop window on the other side of the wall.

When it stopped, I couldn't let go right away. My hair was blown across my face and stuck into my mouth. After a while I peeled my hair away. Jesse got off the bike. He dropped his sleeping bag on the sand, and I knew he would lie under the moon, and that's when I saw his eyes in the moonlight.

They had changed, and they were awful, begging blue eyes.

I should have run then. I should never have been there. But I walked with him, bowlegged—that's how I remembered it after gripping astride the bike—to the water. I took the cigarette he offered. The wind kept the ashes trimmed to the ember. I crossed my arms over my puffy-sleeved blouse to cover myself from the wind. He kept looking at me with those awful begging eyes. He talked about Vietnam, not the way WOCs talked about it, like it gave them a rush. WOCs couldn't wait to fly. Jesse talked about it with his eyes begging me to fix something. He said it stunk there. He said he couldn't get the stink of death away. It had started to rain again, and the air was wet and cool and salty and the arms of my universe and it made me strong. But Jesse couldn't breathe it. I believe if I had touched the palm of my hand over his mouth, I could have suffocated him. I never had that much power over anybody. He could have been a toad in a gully, and me with a mound of fist-sized rocks.

"I was a door gunner before I got shot. I was gunning down anything that moved."

"Have you been home, Jesse?" I said.

"I got shot down by Nui Ba Den. We were carrying bodies, and I was one more body."

"Does your mama know you're home?"

"I knew I was dead. When you're a gunner, you're a wide-open target. I was giving myself about twenty minutes to start to stink in that heat."

His eyes terrified me. They were awful. They were like having your grandfather beg, and I was too young to have people beg me. What could I do for him? Mama should have made me come home. She should have made me sit through a meal of malevolently hating Manfred.

I ran. I couldn't hold myself back anymore. I needed to run so badly that even if I'd still been on the bike, I'd have jumped. I ran down the beach and up the stone steps of the seawall. I was sure I could hear his footfalls, but the world was clear to me and I could breathe the air without trying and he didn't catch me. I had time to slip my fingers in the crevice of my stone. There was a stone I claimed at the top of the third stone staircase from the café, and I never ran past without touching it. Tag.

When I finally did go home, I heard more stories about Jesse from my friend Opal, namely that Jesse had lost his important parts. Well, there was gossip on account of his behavior and we all knew he lost something.

Chapter 2

I grew up hearing Opal read my soul. Opal was our next-door neighbor, and even though she was a student of the stars, she was Mama's best friend anyway. During that first year of college sometimes I waited for a waxing moon to get started on something because Opal said that's when you have the benefit of the planet's energy to work with. That's one reason I didn't get a lot of essays written, but I met a lot of WOCs.

When I went back to school, girls were talking about getting engaged. They were talking about the lottery and whose boyfriend was going to have to go. And then one day a woman in a blue pinstripe skirt and hideous hip-length jacket was seen spreading a rumor in the student union. She said the Red Cross was looking for girls to work in a mobile recreation unit in Vietnam. When we were back in the dorm that night rolling our hair and doing our nighttime sit-ups and feeding our faces all at the same time, some girls who had WOCs were talking about what if they did go?

I didn't go for a WOC. I went for no particular reason I could say except that I was in a desperate need of knowing about life beyond Texas and how a person got eyes like Jesse's. Girls gave lots of reasons after it was over. All I knew for sure then was that the crescent-moon shape of Vietnam seemed to spill across the state of Texas.

Maybe I went because I was a nutrition major. I couldn't believe the number of nutrition courses I was going to have to endure in the next semester. I was going to plan menus. Bland ones, liquid, high protein, low sodium, no mustard, food, food, food. Get real good at something, Mama said. Get a practical skill. You could be the county extension agent. I thought of myself as poetical. I was a potential poet. Mama said nobody earned a living brooding.

She in fact had taken the postal-clerk exam when she was already thirty-three, and she became the town's postmistress. And with Manfred she didn't seem to have a huge empty place for me, now that I was about to be able to give her tips on how to thicken up her jams.

The Red Cross said I was what they were looking for, and they hired me to begin after I finished my finals. Mama read everything the Red Cross sent in June and July before I left. We went shopping for the four navy-blue head scarves, the one navy sweater, the nice dresses for evening, the washcloths, the trunk. We went down the Red Cross list.

Mama read about the Red Cross like she was reading the Bible. She read the history of Supplemental Recreational Activities Overseas to Opal when

Opal was out planting azaleas. She said, "My kid's going to Vietnam." Then she shook her head and went back to counting socks for my trunk.

Mama had her shoes off and her crocheting in her lap when I went indoors to finish packing the day before I left. Mama took the day off, which was unprecedented. She was listening to the TV show *Jeopardy!*, whipping off the answers as quick as she poked her hook in the yarn and pulled up the loops. Who was Mao Tse-tung? What is Marrakech? What was the Battle of Dien Bien Phu? Under, pull, through. She was making an afghan for Opal's baby. Mama swore by *Time* magazine. She knew all the ministers of Asia and the capital of Nepal. I wondered if Mama was impressed that I was traveling through thirteen time zones to Southeast Asia in a war. She didn't look it. She was focused on the socks.

Opal stomped in. She was a real big woman, and she always wore her husband's striped short-sleeved shirts, and she always had a baby on her hip. I thought she was beautiful. Opal was a half-step generation between Mama and me, being ten-and-a-half years older than me and ten-and-a-half years younger than Mama.

Opal came, balancing a cake on one palm. She'd baked it in her glass baking dish and decorated it with pink paper umbrellas and the words *Bon Voyage* in deco-green icing. Mama turned off *Jeopardy!* and took the cake before Opal lost her balance between the cake and the baby. We all sat down at the kitchen table, the baby, Jacob, still squirming under Opal's arm. She was unmindful of him. She cut the cake with one hand the way women with babies get accustomed to doing things. I had lugged all Opal's babies—she'd had three—around that way whenever I baby-sat, and

imagined being a housewife and knew no way could
I be that. Now I was impatient. I wasn't thinking
anything at all about Mama and Opal, because I was
getting on the airplane in Houston in sixteen hours.

Opal said, "It rains all the time there. That's what
I hear."

"Where do you hear that?" Mama said.

"At the Post Office Drug. That's where I heard
about the kid who got his balls blown off. You know
him, Diana. He was just a year ahead of you."

"Yup," I said. "Is that true?"

"In Tay Ninh Province," Opal went on. Vietnam names fell off people's lips like Texas names.
She could have been saying New Braunfels, where I
rode the rapids and got my first period, which seemed
like a curse from the black pine shade, the only shade
in Texas. And it came to me there, and I had put on
a sweater and felt the ribbed cuffs tight around my
wrists and felt what was going on inside my body
and felt womanly and walked very carefully—in awe
of it all. I felt like I had to be the first woman, the
absolutely first woman, and would never call a boy
and say, "Jesse, do you like me?"

"Kid's name was Jesse," Opal told Mama.

Mama got the Funk & Wagnalls because she didn't
want to hear about Jesse's balls. She read us about
Vietnam's rainfall. I licked a dot of frosting off my
fork, but I had a hard time making myself chew cake.

"Could have had a certificate in nutrition and you
go and join a touring USO show in Vietnam." Opal
winked at me. She said *Nam* to rhyme with *Sam*.

"It's not a USO show," Mama said. "Tell her."

"It's not a USO show," I said. Mama narrowed
her eyes on me, so I kept going. "We go to Washington tomorrow, and then they'll teach us what we're

doing. There's something about a four-week program progression."

"I read you about that, Opal," Mama said.

"I'm dense," she said with her mouth full. "What kind of programs?"

Mama dug through the pamphlets around the cake. "Well, like this." And she read to her. " 'Let's Go Sleuthing—good for the hot summer weather. Girls read mysteries, and the men solved them. An hour of fun, a relaxing break for servicemen in the busy military schedule, something to look forward to each week—these are the goals we try to attain through the Red Cross Clubmobile personnel. We try to assist commanders in maintaining a high degree of morale.' "

I licked my fork. Opal stuck an umbrella in my hair. I laughed and stuck an umbrella in the curl over Mama's ear and in Opal's heavy dark hair that hung down her back. We went back to work on our cake with the silly umbrellas bobbing in our hair.

I glanced at Opal. "You haven't read my soul since that day I went for the behind-the-wheel test. Remember?" I said. "Remember how you used to tell me when it was a good time to do things? They always came true."

"Well, I always could read your character. It was clear in your chart."

This was the part that irritated Mama. If this hadn't been a sort of party, Mama would have turned *Jeopardy!* back on real high. I could read her mind. Mama would somehow have gotten in that it was on account of Opal marrying a Mexican that she was getting into ignorant thought patterns and how it was his fault she kept having babies with their method of birth control. ("You know, that high school stuff, like pulling out.")

"She wasn't ever wrong, Mama," I said. "Everything Opal ever said came true."

Mama went to get something for us to drink.

"How's it look?" I said. "The future."

Opal pulled her hair back and held it in her fist to think about that. Jacob had gone to sleep, tummy down, across her lap. "One of your problems is that you're so psychic."

"Don't go telling her she's psychic," Mama said.

"Everybody's psychic." Opal never heard a measure of Mama's testiness. That's why I loved her, somebody so sure of herself that Mama could not even make a dimple in her hide. Opal picked some people to love, and she picked my mother, and nothing my mother did would stop her. Opal said she saw things in people they didn't see in themselves. She said Mama paid her dues. That made no sense to me.

"Well," she said, "I was fixing to mention some things which you'll know about soon enough because you just will. You just know things in a subconscious way." Mama knocked the ice tray against the sink. "You're going to have close calls. But you've got Mercury for backup. Just remember it's important to feed yourself positive thoughts because so much is unconscious. You have a divine mind."

"I have a divine mind," I told Mama.

"You are a peach," Mama said back. She kept her lips pursed.

"What are you setting me up for?" I asked Opal.

Opal shook her head.

"What do you mean, divine mind?"

"You absorb other people's cultures."

"She hasn't absorbed her own," Mama said.

"I'm young," I suggested.

Opal shrugged. She heaped cake on her fork. She

said, "Women will lead men out of confusion. Women are the light of the world."

I thought of Jesse's eyes.

Love! you love me—your eyes
Have looked through death at mine.

I read that somewhere in a class that was a reprieve from counting milligrams of sodium. The poem was called "Girl to Soldier on Leave," and I thought of the photos of soldiers kissing girls on city streets, bending them with their hands in the smalls of girls' backs.

Mama sat down with a pitcher of peach nectar. "Well," she said, "I'd be very obliged if you'd write and not leave me wondering." I wanted to go to my room so I could smoke a cigarette. "Nobody knows what you're getting into for certain," Mama said. "Nothing's certain."

I thought the seawall was certain. But that was too poetical a thought for Mama, and I didn't know what I could say so that her eyes wouldn't look so tense. I wanted to go check my suitcases and my trunk that Mama would ship as soon as I got my assignment in Saigon. But there wasn't anything I could do about my mother's eyes. Mama told me to hold out my hands, and she filled them with small bottles of vitamins to put in my suitcase.

"Open your mouth and shut your eyes, I'll give you something to make you wise."

"Mama, I might throw up," I said.

"You won't throw up," Opal said.

"All right, honey," Mama said, "don't open your mouth. Just shut your eyes." So I did, and I felt my mama's and Opal's lips kissing my cheek.

Chapter 3

Pearly used Pond's beauty cream that advertised it would make you beautiful in seven days. She told me she had been using it for six days, and there was no sign that she would be beautiful on the seventh. I met Pearly in training. She said things like that without a trace of a smile because she was not especially interested in beauty. She had ironwood-black curly hair that could have been shiny if she'd done anything with it. You could see a little bit of a space between her front teeth, which was odd and suited her and somehow made her whole self easy on the eye even if she was unremitting on the ear because Pearly was music and could not stop talking. I, on the other hand, did not talk. I told myself my thoughts were of more consequence than anybody's chatter. I held myself above, but I was fascinated with Pearly.

Sometimes when I saw Pearly, she had done up her eyes with black eyeliner, but I don't think it was for beauty so much as for shock. She galloped down the maroon-carpeted stairs of the Presidential Hotel in Washington—that's when I saw she didn't shave her legs—to make last-minute calls to a dozen people. Pearly was from New Hampshire, and I believe she was on friendly terms with the entire population of that state. Later I knew she was the kind of person to call anybody up, even people she horrified, even old mill-town folk. She didn't hold out to be adored.

I only called Mama. And I sent her a picture of myself in my Red Cross blues with my wispy hair up in a ponytail so it didn't touch my collar. Thinking about whether or not her hair touched her collar was not something Pearly spent any time on. Pearly was not a brooder. She took care of everything to suit herself. This made her not universally popular. People are scared of that much presence. I was.

We sat in circles of girls together in Washington, D.C., to learn how to develop a program.

We sat in a circle of girls on our suitcases at Travis Air Force Base, waiting with hundreds of troops for our flight to Saigon. Each girl wore her navy-blue high heels, dress blues, and a hat shaped like a boat propped cockeyed on the side of her head.

We rode together on the bus from Tan Son Nhut to headquarters, which they called MACV, Military Assistance Command, Vietnam. The bus had metal gridwork over the windows so no one could lob a grenade inside. A GI who rode with us said it was for our protection. I thought he wanted to impress us. I was impressed. He said depending on where we went, they'd probably give us flak jackets, but nobody knew what flak jackets were. He said they were made of steel on the inside and would protect you from incoming, but no one knew what incoming was.

"Rounds," he said. "Rockets. Mortars."

I was very impressed. He said he was a Spec 2, which I knew later was a lowly rank, but he was the most impressive person in terms of what he knew. He said, Don't walk in groups. He said Saigon might be the most dangerous place we were in. He reminded us about Tet. While people were shooting firecrackers and honoring the dead during the Tet celebration, tanks started rolling in and nearly took the capital. Mama and I had seen it on the news. I watched for tanks through the metal diamonds over the windows. I saw millions of black-haired people in the street. They did all their business in the streets and on the sides of the streets, their buying and selling and washing and eating.

Pearly sat beside me. She said, "I wonder if the war could have been over last year at Tet if they'd just managed to overrun us."

I looked at her. How annoying, I thought. Just what these guys needed, some girl to say the VC should have won.

"What are you, some Jane Fonda?" I said.

She said she came to South Vietnam, not North Vietnam, as if I didn't know where we were, and sitting beside her snide face with its straight, chiseled nose was beginning to irk me. I stared through the metal grid at the stream of armed troops and fortressed stucco buildings.

I had the window seat, and Pearly was leaning over me to see. "Christ," she said when we were both looking at the barricaded city. "Christ," she said again nearly in my ear, "you read the papers, and everybody already knows it's over except for more people to die. We can't win here."

I remembered the fighting I saw on TV, and how the men were proud of a victory, and Mama and I cried when we watched that. I thought of the WOCs who were so proud to come. "So what'd you come for?" I said because I have Mama's testiness and I can go right to the end of an argument without any discussion in between, like going with the fist to the belly. "Yeah, so what'd you come for," I jabbed. "If you don't believe in any of this," I said with my Georgia WOC clearer than Pearly before my eyes. "I came because I believe in us."

Pearly continued staring out the window at the beautiful pastel French-looking buildings surrounded by oil drums, sandbags, and wire. "Innocence is a kind of insanity," she said like she was quoting somebody, and no doubt she was, being so learned and perfect, and meaning me and all the rest of us were innocent and insane. I got up and sat nearer the Spec 2 to learn relative facts.

At MACV we sat in a circle of girls with Mary Ann Dunne, who was the head girl in all Vietnam. I didn't give Pearly the pleasure of my noticing her, because I knew I wouldn't have the pleasure of her noticing me. To be really accurate, I'd say Mary Ann Dunne was a mahogany bureau. She was that solemn, and she looked something like a bureau in that she stood forthright before us when she talked and only moved her lips. Our body clocks were confused. Who knows what time it was in Texas. But I was wide awake and running on excitement. I watched Mary Ann's deliberate lips and wrote the words she said in my notebook and knew Mama would be pleased that we were led by such a fortress.

The first training had more to do with our presence than with what we actually did. Mary Ann said, "You'll be working closely with the army. Avoid

compromising appearances." I smiled at her. I didn't
even know what a compromising appearance was. I
was nineteen and concerned about how my uniform
fit. I was concerned about how I looked in a ponytail
when I liked myself better with my hair brushed out.
I wondered when they were going to let us eat, and
when they did, if it would be better than dorm food
or camp food. My cheeks burned with excitement and
enthusiasm and Vietnam's heat. It reminded me of
Texas summer camp where we hung a mirror on the
bark of a black walnut tree to look in while we teased
and sprayed our hair, and we only wore bras and
panties at the girls' tent because sweat was dripping
between our breasts and our scalps were always wet
with sweat and we always picked one boy to love that
summer. I believed in everybody. I was there to support American GIs and I already loved them and
would work twelve-hour days to entertain them. I
didn't know what a compromise was.

I looked at Pearly. Pearly was watching me, which
made me squirm. We were going around the room
introducing ourselves to Mary Ann. Pearly was Pearly
Boudreau. She accented the first syllable of her last
name and gave it a puff of air to make the *Bou* part
fly. She irritated the class from D.C. to Saigon. There
were fourteen girls and twelve units, and everybody
hoped that if any girls went in pairs, it wasn't herself
and Pearly. If they were talking about her, all any
girl had to say to describe her was, You know, the
one with the attitude problem. She still hadn't shaved
her legs, and wore leather thongs when she should
have been wearing regulation tennis shoes.

I thought about Opal. Opal would be figuring
what sign that girl, Pearly, was. Opal had always told
me, "Ah, you are very intelligent." I believed her,

heart and soul, and took that with me for truth. I wondered what was the truth of Pearly.

"Do you believe your future is foretold before you ever live it?" It was Pearly. It was the middle of that first night in Saigon, and I couldn't sleep. The room was stifling. I could feel sweat trickle down my neck. The generator was broken, so our room was airless. A single light hung in the bathroom by the carafe of potable water, but it didn't work.

Some fluke got Pearly and me in the same room, and I knew she was awake. Our beds were in a line head to toe under the window that was blocked by the air conditioner that didn't run. There were six girls to a room along with our cots, curler bags, cigarettes, makeup, Red Cross culottes, dog tags, and love letters from boyfriends back home.

"What?" I whispered.

"I said, do you believe in fortune-telling, divination, things like that? How you can see your life in the palm of your hand?"

"Yeah," I whispered back. I couldn't see her straight-on eyes. Maybe she was human and sad to be awake in a stifling Q—for Quarters—room in Saigon. So I told her, "Yeah, I grew up next door to somebody who tells me things. I grew up with her saying, 'Honey, don't lie to me. You oughta know better than to lie to a psychic.' "

Pearly's head was at the foot of my bed. She held out her hand in the dark. "Read my palm," she said.

I shook my head. "I don't know how," I said, but I didn't want Pearly to go away. The girl smelled like Fritos, which she'd been eating in the dark. Having her there made it seem less still and less airless.

Pearly wasn't busy sneering. She could as easily be my roommate in Denton on a steamy summer night. There could be shrieks of silly girls.

Pearly sat up cross-legged at the foot of my bed, cramming her mouth with Fritos. She wore a guy's shirt.

"Read my palm," Pearly said. "I always wanted somebody to do that."

"It's too dark," I whispered.

Pearly pulled a bag up from the floor and set it on top of the bag of Fritos in the triangle between her legs. She fished out a flashlight and snapped it on.

"I'm no good at it," I said.

Pearly shined the light into my face. It didn't wake the others. It was just a Brownie penlight, and I was so exhausted I lay absolutely still and looked at the particles of light it formed. Then I got up and knelt beside her and looked out over the air conditioner that didn't work, into the street. I saw Military Police in helmets—the Spec 2 called them steel pots and said we'd get issued them too. I watched an MP pacing in a sort of dugout with a radio and an M-16 rifle. It was very still. It was 3:00 A.M. Mary Ann Dunne had told the girls there would be breakfast later across the street where the MPs were. Across the street was a stucco building like the one we slept in. French pink stucco that was now an American enlisted Q and a mess hall. We were all supposed to walk across for breakfast, but not en masse. We were told not to walk in groups. We'd be a target that way, though Mary Ann said no Red Cross girl had been shot walking in a group. It was just American SOP. Standard Operating Procedure, they said. They said. They said. I was learning a foreign language.

I sat down. Pearly was digging through her bag, and came up with a notebook.

"I can read your sign," I offered. Pearly liked that idea. "What are you?" I said.

"August. Leo."

"Well, Leos are self-centered, egotistical, and brainy, and you probably want to teach college or something when this is over."

"What are you?" she said.

"Gemini. Half of the time they are one person, and half the time they are not, they're somebody else, but they're always trying to be the one they're not. Geminis are real dissatisfied, and they're gypsies. It's hard to be in one place." I paused.

"Don't stop."

"I'm thinking."

"You have a real nice voice."

"No I don't."

"Yeah you do."

"Where are you from?" I asked.

"New Hampshire," Pearly said. "Where folks mostly grunt. What else about me?"

"Well, Leos don't want a lot of people hanging on them. They like their freedom."

"I won't have lots of kids?" Pearly asked.

"No," I said. I didn't know why I was so sure.

Pearly crammed the bag of Fritos into her duffel. There was not the smallest amount of daylight, but our eyes let in all available light, and we both sat with our arms wrapped around our knees making predictions until one of the sleeping girls hissed, "Would you shut up?"

"What about guys?" Pearly whispered.

"What about them?"

"Oh, anything."

"You'll have them like beads," I said.

"I'll have them like beads," she repeated, the same way she had said the beauty cream hadn't worked yet. "Oh, shit."

The girl, Maria, yelled at us, and Pearly and I muffled our belly guffs in our pillows.

We must have rolled over and dozed for a while. At least I did, because I remember opening my eyes and seeing a dull light creep through the space above the air conditioner. Saigon street noise came through the cracks. I knelt at the window as I had before, and watched a woman in a black turban who set out brass vases and a supermarket variety of American soaps right on the side of the street. Pearly knelt beside me.

"Her teeth are black," I said, watching the woman.

"From chewing betel nut," Pearly said.

"What's betel nut?"

"From a betel-nut tree. They do that like Americans drink coffee."

"How do you know?"

"I used to get postcards from Nam. Each one had Another Amazing Fact of Vietnam. I know the women have black teeth and the men have gold."

The market woman wore black pants and a loose top to her waist. The girls at MACV wore long silk gowns over their black pants. The old women who sold American soap did without the gown.

"Black market," Pearly said. "A guy I knew brought one of those vases home. They're artillery shells. The Vietnamese take the Americans' shells and make them into vases and sell them back to the Americans."

"I don't believe you," I said. I lay down and

pulled the sheet up as far as my ears.

"I know from Peter who used to live in our house. A bunch of us had an old red house by a falls. It was a thousand years old, and it was built into a granite wall. Living there was like living in a cellar. Dead town," she said.

I pulled the sheet down from my ears. I didn't know what she was talking about, but I didn't want to miss it.

"You lived in a house with boys?"

"In a cavern, really. The barn was attached, and it could have been a dance studio, it was that big. It had a ceiling that touched the sky. I was the baker," she said. "I used to bake corn bread from scratch from our own corn."

"You lived in a house with boys," I repeated. Mama called that shacking up. She thought that was worse than being a draft dodger or being fat, both of which she thought were horrible things and showed lack of willpower.

"The most excitement we had was the falls, having them there out your bedroom window. But the next best thing was going to the Laundromat on Saturday morning. We all got in the truck with our dog and our sheets and a bag of muffins and turned that Laundromat full of schizos into a party."

I never was in a Laundromat in my life. Mama kept a laundry room where she sorted the whites so she could bleach them, and my whites came back whitewashed white and reeking of Clorox. Maybe that's why I was still a virgin. I knew Pearly would find that a hysterical fact.

Pearly had stopped being obnoxious, and looked homesick about walking in her cornfield and mushing corn with a mortar and pestle. She said they hoed zucchini, sprouted beans in the dark of their musky pantry, and that one girl had a baby in her own bed. "And we wore black armbands to say the government doesn't stand for us."

I sat up. "Pearly," I said. "I believe you could talk the night away, but would you tell me this? What are you doing here in an army Q in Vietnam?"

Pearly spoke slowly. Everything she said seemed important because of the way she told things so slowly and calmly. Listening to Pearly there in the almost-dark was like listening to something that runs deep and sure. It was Pearly like a river from that morning on. Pearly loved to tell a story. Mama always said, ". . . well, to make a long story short . . ." Pearly made a short story long.

"I lived by the falls with these three boys and two other girls. So one Saturday, you know, when everybody in New Hampshire puts their living-room furniture on their front lawn and tries to sell it . . . the state's a flea market. Run by trolls. French-Canadian trolls. Joyless people, and they carry picks and they always wear gray. And they never buy large, economy-size anything, because they could die and it would be such a waste. God, you want to hear doom, meet a New Hampshire troll.

"So anyway, that Saturday. God, it was beautiful. They were sending tour buses around to see how beautiful we are by the falls, and our relic cut into the granite. God, even the poison ivy is beautiful in New Hampshire, and that day the draft man caught up with us, and everything crumbled."

I watched the outline of her face and her curls that looked sketched in and tried to place the little space between her teeth as she talked.

"We'd had it pretty good. We ate pretty good.

We listened to Peter preach. He preached from Tho-
reau and *The Glass Bead Game*. And we listened to the
crickets inside because our house had gone back to
nature. So Peter had to go to Fort—some fort, some
fuckin' fort—and Henry the other guy went up to
Montreal, and I was pissed.

"I told Peter I hated his guts. He told me he'd
be home in two years. I told him he didn't have to
go. We should have gotten married and had babies.
And he said yeah, and I could have shot my foot.
And I told him, Shut up and leave me alone, I hate
your guts."

Pearly lay down, and I thought she must have
worn herself out, but she hadn't. After a while she
said, "So that was the end of Peter."

"He died?"

"I don't think so. No such luck. He was a JAG
clerk. He worked with the lawyers because he was
pre-law. He finagled a good job. Mostly it was the
end of this really sweet and carefree life for me. We
used to sit around bitching. All the time. That's all
we did was bitch about if I ran the world, if you ran
the world. So I thought, How is anybody going to
run the world from a kitchen by a falls and buried in
granite? I came for a firsthand look."

Pearly paused and gestured to the guards across
the street and the sand-filled oil drums that barricaded the hotel.

"But I don't know if I can take it. These lifer
people are killing me. We were wearing out, and
there's no going back. But I miss them, and I hate all
this shit they're putting us through here."

The room was stifling, and I had a sense of what
the army was doing to Pearly, how boxed in she felt.
Pearly and I looked at the dribbling of stars above

the hotel. Then I stretched out on my belly. I had hardly slept in three nights. My eyes burned, and my body seemed like it moved in slow motion or double motion. I was a double exposure. Pearly had told me so much. It was like she gave me a gift, and I wanted to give her one thing back.

"Before I came here," I said, "I met a soldier who just got home. There was something about him that was different. I could tell he'd done something I'd never done. It was spring vacation, and all these kids were in Galveston. I went with this guy I met at the diner where I work. He was nice-looking. He had a motorcycle. I went back with him to the beach. He was camped out on the beach, him and about a thousand more kids.

"He was real nice. We had a normal conversation. I used to know him in my hometown. He played fullback in high school. But he looked at me in such a funny way. I just had this class in poetry, and he made me think of a poem about World War One, something about 'your eyes have looked through death at mine.' " I paused. I could smell the fumes from the motorcycle that had lingered on my fingers and hear the waves break and the screams of all the kids camped on the beach. "I know lots of guys who were coming here."

The air conditioner at that moment kicked on. The light bulb in the ceiling burned. The bathroom light shined on the water carafe. The generator hummed from some secret interior place of the old stucco building. It was enough to make me believe spirits moved in that room besides us six live girls.

My hair felt so heavy and damp, and I pulled all of it back off my face and neck. I got Pearly's features straight in the brightness. She hadn't taken off her makeup. Black liner smeared her cheeks. Her hair was thick and dense with curls. Mine stuck out in clumps, and Mama used to spend hours trying to untangle it when I was little.

Pearly tapped the sole of her bare foot playfully on the bed, and with her head back, she laughed as if the Metropole Q were the biggest joke. Maria stomped out of bed, tripped over her radio, and pulled the cord on the overhead light.

Pearly stood up. "Come on," she said. I looked at her.

"What do you mean, come on? We're under a curfew. There's nowhere to come on to."

"Just come."

I followed Pearly, who brought the bag of Fritos and a bag of M&Ms too. We went in the bathroom and shut the door and sat knee to knee on the bathroom floor. Pearly displayed her palm in the yellow glow of the bathroom light. "All right, fortune-teller," she said, "read my palm."

I laughed. "Let me see," I said, "I had a boyfriend . . ."

"Oh, God, not another boyfriend."

"This was a long time ago. We were walking on the beach, and he said, You want me to read your palm? And I thought, Sure, why not, this will be good for a laugh." We laughed crazily in a Frito haze in the narrow, tall white-tiled bathroom.

"So what did he tell you? What does this line mean?"

"That's your heart line. See all the lines that come across? Ooooh, girl, every one of them stands for a lover. You love easily. You are sensuous. You can see why a boy wants to read your palm on the beach. Oh, and see, here's the mount of Venus." I touched the soft roundness beneath Pearly's thumb. Pearly raised the bag of M&Ms to her mouth, and chocolate mixed with the stillness and the whiteness. "I always eat when I'm homesick," she said. "What's this line?" She poured M&Ms in my palm so that M&Ms mixed in with the lines and flavored the reading.

I made a face at this funny girl, Pearly, who I'd only sat in circles with but I was feeling closer to than anybody else here.

"Oh, that's your head line. You're highly imaginative. You can tell, well, that's what that boy told me, because your head line veers into the mount of the moon, there." I pushed my hair off my face with the circle of my elbow. "You have a lot of willpower and nearly always get your way."

"And what's this line?" Pearly said. "Is this where you tell that I will live to be a hundred?"

"Your life line," I said. We each ate some more M&Ms, and I rubbed chocolate off the frail lines. I held Pearly's hand up in the yellow light and rubbed it clean with my own palm. "Oh my God," I laughed. "You've barely got one, honey. I don't believe you're alive." Then we both laughed, and Pearly swooned and lifted the back of her hand to her forehead.

There was a knock on the door. "There's a line forming out here," someone called.

"All right, just a minute," Pearly yelled.

In the bathroom the pipes were exposed. We were eye level with the water pipes. We could hear the water cut on and off from other parts of the Q.

"This is stupid. This stuff is truly dumb," I said through laugh tears. "We're running on no sleep." In my trancelike haziness I giggled through a chant I used to jump rope to:

"Apple tree, pear tree, plum tree pie,
How many children before I die?
One, two, three, four, five . . ."

"It's like believing in ways to charm a guy," Pearly said between fits of laughing. "You know, like a girl should spray her perfume on her letters to him so he can't forget her. . . ."

"Ever," I laughed. "Or when a guy lights your cigarette, you're supposed to lay your hand on his . . ."

"Just barely," Pearly said. "You lay your hand lightly." And we both thought this was riotously funny and lay down on the cool tiles, silly and aching with laugh tears streaming, and also thinking about how Pearly didn't have any life line.

Pearly and I lay on our beds smoking and not annoying anybody for several minutes except with our smoke.

I got out my lilac paper Mama gave me and wrote to her.

Dear Mama,
    We are staying in a VOQ. That means Visiting Officers' Quarters. We've been in classes where the Red Cross explains things we shouldn't do. In Saigon, we're not supposed to walk in groups. They make it seem like Saigon is the most dangerous place to be and we could get near a terrorist. But you never have to worry. They don't let us near firefights. Mary Ann, our Saigon chief, said we're going places so remote we'll

think no girl ever went there before. Most of the soldiers hardly see a base camp, so we get on choppers and take our programs to them.

I thought of Mama's practical hands. Opal was her best friend, but she thought Opal was hocus-pocus. Mama would give more meaning to a girl's suffering irregularity than any lines she might have on the palm of her hand. Ample protein and perseverance was Mama's credo. I picked up my pen. I could handle that. Enormous meals and work. I could do any amount of work. The army gave us play money and dog tags and shots of gamma globulin and malaria pills and rides in buses with barred windows. I felt very sturdy and eager.

Chapter 4

We were all awake. Sunlight shone through the top of our window. We brushed and back-combed and sprayed our hair until you could choke on the hair-spray fumes. Pearly was already gone. A few minutes later I stood by the guard post in front of our hotel trying to cross the street through the stream of pedicabs and girls in *ao dais* peddling by and lines of jeeps. A wall of three-quarter-ton trucks cut me off completely. The street seemed like something you got sucked up in. I stood near the MPs' station in the throng of peddlers and pedestrians, trucks, pedicabs, jeeps, seven, eight, nine abreast.

A girl's pink silk *ao dai* fluttered past, with the plodding truck caravan as backdrop. The girl's delicate legs pedaled steadily and moved her more quickly than the trucks grinding past.

"Goddamn, will you look at that!" a voice said, cutting through the street noise. I glanced up to see a dozen GIs hanging out the back of a truck, wide-

eyed and looking at me. I couldn't cross because there
wasn't any lull in the traffic. I could hardly go back.
They goggled. "Goddamn, look at them round eyes."

"What are you doing in country?"

Back home, I'd have ignored them. You just keep
going and don't look in anybody's eyes. Now, all I
could see were eyes. What that truck did was stop
cold. It blocked three rows of traffic. The men jumped
out of the truck and walked me like I was the queen
of Spain across the street so I could get my ample
protein.

"Where you from?" they asked.

I told them Texas, and there was a huge roar of
I guessed Texas boys or at any rate boys who wanted
at that moment to claim Texas.

It was a creative job we came to do. It was just
really hard to get across what we were doing. "You
don't sing, you don't dance. You play games?" this
guy said who we met in the Enlisted Club that night.
He shrugged as if he were resigned to the weird.
"Well," he said, "bring 'em to my fire base any time."

What we came to do made sense to us in training.

Mary Ann Dunne said, "A lot of you girls want
to be teachers. Be careful not to go at your programs
as if you were making lesson plans, and later, when
you program, don't make it look as though you've
turned a gun emplacement into a classroom. Some of
you want to be social workers. Some of you are art-
ists. Some of you are naturals at the kind of mix of
storyteller/social worker/entertainer that is your job.
You will develop a timing that gives your program
energy. You get to be good at it when you realize you
are the leader, you throw out the ideas and questions,

and the men are carrying the program. That is what you are here for, to bring the World out to those fire bases."

America was the World, Mary Ann Dunne said. "You bring them news about the World in your programs. Program ideas are everywhere."

The headlines for 1969 flashed across my mind. MAN WALKS ON MOON. RACE RIOTS IN CALIFORNIA. CROSBY, STILLS, AND NASH RELEASE "SUITE: JUDY BLUE EYES." That made sense to me. Our programs were to take a guy off a fire base for a while in his head and prove he has a life he is going back to.

"The Red Cross girls are called doughnut dollies. You'll hear that a lot," Mary Ann said, smiling. "It's historic."

"She says that as if it was one of the benefits of the job," Pearly said afterward. "Anybody calls me dollie, I'll flatten 'em."

I wasn't thinking much about that. I was thinking about programming. I asked Pearly, "Are you scared of getting up and programming in front of fifty guys?"

"Shit yeah, of course I am."

Except in terms of appearances, Mary Ann Dunne never once talked about sex. But when it came to doing our job, the issue jumped out and took over sometimes. It wasn't Mary Ann's fault. The army couldn't protect you when you're in so deep and beyond the sweet wholesomeness they brought us for.

The next day we got our assignments. We'd leave from Tan Son Nhut. Mary Ann had gotten each girl on the manifest of a supply chopper, a command-and-control chopper, a Caribou, or whatever was flying into a division's headquarters.

We didn't travel by road. That was almost always iron law except in a base camp. We did not accept rides by ground transport, Mary Ann said. We did not hitch.

The general came. He hailed us, and when he called us "doughnut dollies," it was in such a sad and gentle way, I thought he was sorrowful about his own daughters and missing their growing up. He said our presence would be a "tangible expression of compassion, support, and pride" to cheer sad hearts. He made me proud to be there.

Pearly and I stacked our trays in the MACV cafeteria. I had eaten a lot of protein, and felt wholesome like a child who had done what her mama said. Pearly ate almost nothing because she lived on Fritos and now black licorice. Lines on palms were hocuspocus, mumbo jumbo. Ma ma ma ma said so.

"You look thin," I said.

"What do you mean, thin?"

"Just thin. Take one of these." I pulled my B-complex vitamins out of my pocket. I'd meant to take them. "Mama says they make your blood rich, especially when you're on vacation or at camp and you can't count on what you'll be eating."

"Well, we sure can't," Pearly said, and she took a vitamin pill like we both believed in Mama.

We walked grimly, solemnly back to hear Mary Ann the mahogany bureau scatter our class members from Saigon north to the DMZ.

Mary Ann said they were closing the unit at Dong Tam and possibly some others. "That means you are needed, and you will cover greater territory. You girls going to Qui Nhon will pick up the Seventy-third

Airborne forward run. We have asked some girls to extend to see us through the year. We want you to be prepared for the hard work facing you." She grinned slightly as if to soften the truth. She had dimples. She had been a child, I thought.

We fidgeted, being weary of sitting in a circle, in a single room of an American military headquarters compound in a Southeast Asia that was still mostly rumor and headlines. But we listened to every word.

Mary Ann began calling out the unit names, followed by the names of girls in this new class who would go there. She started in I Corps with Phu Bai, Chu Lai, and Da Nang. II Corps, An Khe, Qui Nhon. Pearly Boudreau—Qui Nhon. Tuy Hoa, Cam Ranh, Phan Rang. III Corps, Phuoc Vinh, Bien Hoa, Cu Chi. Diana Seymour—Cu Chi. Long Binh. IV Corps: Nobody new was going to IV Corps because the 9th was taking home its colors. Cu Chi, a supervisor had said, would pick up Dong Tam/Tan An in the Delta where the IV Corps runs had been.

I would never have actually told Pearly that I found her less snotty than the other girls did. But I had always thought we'd go together. I was miserable that we weren't.

We waited together at Tan Sun Nhut. Pearly was waiting for a Caribou going to Qui Nhon and me for a chopper flying in to Cu Chi.

Pearly ripped off the cardboard end flap from the carton of cigarettes in her bag and printed her Qui Nhon address. I put the piece of cardboard in my pocket.

"Keep in touch," said Pearly. "I always wanted to learn to talk Texan." She whiled the time gawking at people who gawked at her and asking me how to say this and that in Texan. Then she'd parrot my drawl.

"Stay right here," a guy with a clipboard said to me. "It's coming in."

"I'll be here," I said. We were sitting on sandbags by the flight line. Our class had already scattered. Some had left in pairs for I Corps. The girls assigned to Bien Hoa could travel by road and had left in a jeep. We probably wouldn't see each other again unless we got to be program directors or unit directors and returned to Saigon for meetings.

Rotors pounded the air, and one more chopper landed, adding itself to the dozen others on the tarmac.

"Diana," Pearly said, "your chopper doesn't have any doors."

Pearly and I inspected the machine.

"Sure enough," I said. "And I wonder how you get in it"—I spread the cloth of my blue uniform—"in a dress."

Pearly shook her head. She didn't know any more about choppers than I did. We could see the pilot in the cockpit.

"My God, it's a warrant officer," I said.

"Do you know him?"

"I know he's wearing a Nomex flying suit in sage green, and it doesn't burn. That's a bit of WOC information I picked up from going to school by Mineral Wells."

The guy with the clipboard was waving frantically. The chopper was roaring. The guy wanted me to hurry up and get in. Pearly ran with me toward it, carrying one of my bags.

We looked in at the pilot, who was well disguised in all his gear. "I don't know if I know him," I yelled to Pearly over the roar of the rotors. "I might have danced with him." I looked at him as best I could through all his gear. It was as if the helmet were a costume. He was just one of the guys at a Fort Wolters dance, and pretty soon he would pull off his helmet and we'd laugh and stop these pretensions.

I ran and tossed my bag in the chopper I already knew they called a LOH. All GIs were beginning to look familiar. There were so many soldiers. I was pretty sure I didn't know the pilot.

He looked stern. Or maybe it was all the gear he had to wear. I attempted to get in the chopper. The front of it was a glass bubble. I stepped up into the cockpit and saw there was only the one seat beside the pilot. In front of my seat was what looked like a gearshift. The only way to sit was to straddle it. I attempted to do this without showing the pilot one of the eight pairs of panties Mama bought and checked off the list. He wasn't even the boy from Georgia who had seen the ones she got me last year anyway. Pearly, who I happened to catch a look at while I was fighting the gearshift, was bent over in hysterics from watching me.

I sat down and simply unhooked my dress and slip from the gear. Pearly by now was wiping tears away, and when the chopper lifted, I wanted to reach down and pull her aboard like somebody whose life depended on catching a train. Pull her right in. But all we could do was wave wildly and yell things nobody could hear, not even the kid a foot from me who was just a WOC a few months ago.

Chapter 5

Maureen met my chopper at Cu Chi. She rushed me from the landing pad, which was a huge yellow-and-red flash of lightning painted on the tarmac. TROPIC LIGHTNING, a sign said, HOME OF THE 25TH INFANTRY.

She rushed me through a network of ramps between low wooden buildings. The ramps kept us above the red dirt, which was soggy even though the sun was shining hot. I tried to catch what Maureen was saying, but it was hard because she talked faster than any living person and I had to rush to keep up with her footsteps on the ramps.

"We just finished a base run," she said. "We haven't been able to get out. There's a lot of activity."

"What do you mean, activity?"

"Charlie," she said.

There was another girl with us. I was aware of

her footsteps trying to keep up with mine trying to keep up with Maureen's.

"Who's Charlie?"

"You know, VC."

"Oh," I said.

Somebody yanked my hair, and I turned around, nearly dropping the plaid suitcase Mama gave me for high school graduation. It was the other girl, a Vietnamese girl.

"Oh, that's Hoa," Maureen said about the girl. "Our *mamasan*."

"*Mamasan?*" I said. "She isn't any bigger than kids I baby-sit."

"Hooch girl. Whatever," Maureen said.

"You are too beautiful," Hoa whispered to me.

"What?" I said. No one had ever said that to me. I was confused.

"Beau-ti-ful," she said again slowly, as if the word *beautiful* were fiercely hard to pronounce. She touched my hair again. It had come all apart on the chopper ride. "I never saw," she said.

"There aren't any blond Vietnamese," Maureen explained.

Hoa had black hair tied in a silky ponytail with a purple ribbon. The tip of the ribbon hung neatly to the small of her back. She wore black trousers and a waist-length shirt like the *mamasans* selling soap. The shirt would have fit me when I was ten, before I started to develop, as Mama referred to what happened to my chest. But even her ten-year-old-girl clothes hung loosely. She looked like I could make a ring of my fingers around her waist.

"You are too beautiful too," I said, but she shook her head.

Maureen said, "There's enough work here for a six-girl unit, and we're about to have a three-girl unit. Claire's resigning. Saigon is going to be furious."

"Who's Claire?"

"The unit director. She broke her contract to marry a pilot. I don't know who's going to be the new UD. Probably me," she said, glancing around. There were tiny beads of worry and perspiration on her nose and cheeks. "Now I'm the program director," she said. "Josie should be program director, but she won't. Colonel Stone calls me to say what runs are open. He tells us where Charlie is and where we can't get out to."

"When can I go?" I caught up with Maureen. "Is there a run this afternoon?"

She said, "Slow down. You'll burn out. Take your salt pills and your malaria pills. I need you. I need another girl."

"Mary Ann will send more girls," I said because she looked too tired to be twenty-one, which she had told me she was. She could just start going legally to clubs.

We crossed a road and came to our hooch. "That's our bunker," Maureen said, pointing at a sandbagged room dug into the ground with concertina wire in coils over the top. Outside the bunker was a garden table and chairs in the shade of a yellow umbrella. "From Sears and Roebuck," Maureen said.

Maureen showed me my room, and it had streams of blue beads hanging from the doorframe for my door. "It's so cozy," I said. "Y'all make it so homey. I'm not even homesick."

The beads were different shades of blue. And shades of blue did make me think of Mama talking.

Sometimes when I teased, Mama said, "Shades of your father." When I thought about Daddy, I thought of him in that Army Air Corps photo I kept, where he was standing at attention in the horseshoe of men all wearing baggy khakis. In Vietnam they wore baggy OD green.

I looked in an oval mirror above the dresser that was going to be mine for the next twelve months. I touched my face. I would write Mama and ask her to go down to the Post Office Drug and see if they had some more of that Pond's beauty cream that Pearly smelled like. I felt my red cheeks and neck. I was as splotched as Mama's tomatoes. I saw Hoa's face looking at mine in the mirror.

"Hi," I said. I didn't want to be rude, but I needed to talk to Maureen.

Hoa said, "Please teach to me English."

"Sure enough," I said. "Wait just a minute. Maureen," I called, "what do I do on a run? Tell me everything." I walked down the hall of the hooch, peering between all the girls' beads until I came to the back door. It led to a back gate, and I saw our hooch and patio and bunker were surrounded by barbed wire and oil drums filled with sand. We lived in a compound. Someone had painted HAPPY HOOCH and a yellow moon on our back door.

"Maureen!" I called. I felt so alone. I walked out the door with the yellow moon. "Maureen." I stood by the barbed-wire gate and watched the sun burn through a cloud. I heard a typewriter, and followed the sound to our office next door. She had probably told me that's where it was. Or she was preoccupied.

The office door was painted with a sign that read, HAPPY BIRTHDAY, HO CHI MINH.

"Oh, that's old," Maureen said, looking up from the typewriter and seeing me studying the door. "His birthday was in May."

I nodded. I could see his hollow face and white beard. Maureen didn't have any humor. Claire must have done it. "I can't wait to go on a run," I said. "What's it like? Just tell me, so I can picture it."

"It's like standing in a hot sauna with all your clothes on and asking toss-up questions."

"What's a toss-up question?"

Maureen looked at what she was typing. "When was the last time the Boston Red Sox won the World Series?"

"I don't know," I said.

"That's a toss-up question."

I laughed. "Once I asked my mother what it was like to have a baby because I wanted to picture that too. I like to picture everything." Maureen went back to her typing. She didn't want to know the answer, but I told her anyway. "She said it's like having cramps, only a hundred times worse."

"Runs aren't like cramps," she said.

We were not having a sensible conversation. Maureen smiled a lot, but she was not joyful. Pearly never smiled, but she was ebullient beside Maureen.

"I know runs aren't like cramps." I pretended she was Pearly. "Runs are when you haul your program bag through every jungle between here and the Cambodian border. Any group of men you find, you divide them into teams and ask toss-up questions?"

"We only go as far as Tay Ninh City," Maureen said. She had no imagination.

I looked around the office. There was a worktable and paints and other art supplies to create our programs. There were bins of poster board in rainbow colors, brushes, felt tips, a square, and a compass. I felt like we were bringing color and order.

"When can I go on a run?" I said.

"All right, tomorrow," she said. "You can have Second Brigade."

"Can I see the program I'm going to do?"

Maureen gave me a program format that was the typed script we would follow. The program was called "Rock." It had questions like the rock trivia we listened to on KLIF from Houston. I knew we would present the program four or five times tomorrow at two or three different fire bases. Mary Ann Dunne said we would go and talk to the soldiers in from patrols. She said guys would talk to us. They could say things to girls they couldn't say to guys. She said we were there for their mental health.

Once we went to a nursing home to see my great-grandfather. Above his bed was a sign that said, HELLO, TODAY IS MONDAY. The nurse said it was reality-awareness therapy. I thought the army wanted us there for reality therapy to remind people there was a World to go back to. I didn't mind that they called us doughnut dollies. Pearly said it sounded like we were tarts, but I think we were there to do something so noble nobody would mistake us for tarts.

"There's one thing you have to know about going out on forward runs to LZs," Maureen said.

"What's an LZ?"

"Landing Zone. Whatever you do, don't drink a Coke or anything before you go to an LZ or a fire base. There's nothing worse than trying to find a bathroom in the boonies."

That's what I knew about runs.

* * *

It had been cool on the short chopper ride, but now the heat set back in, and my hair hung in damp strings around my face. I turned on a fan on my bureau to let the air dry my strings of hair. It was such a relief. I shut my eyes. I heard rotors beating overhead and a radio playing "Sgt. Pepper's Lonely Hearts Club Band." I only caught fragments of it between the roar of machines and men's voices. I got up to go see where the music was coming from.

Hoa was standing on the road outside our compound with a band of GIs and with a load of our laundry in her arms. She must have been bringing it back from the clothesline down the road from our compound.

"GI *dien cai dau*," she said to them.

"No *dinky*," one GI said. "We give you *beaucoup* p. Easy money. Come inside."

"I no love you," Hoa said. And the GIs broke through the heat with a barrage of laughs.

"*Je t'aime*," one guy said, "*Beaucoup*," he said, tapping his heart.

"GI number ten," she said. "All you."

"A thousand p," he said.

She said, "Never happen. You show me."

The GI took out a brand-new wallet from his hip pocket and let her see all the brown Vietnamese paper money he carried.

"GI too rich," Hoa said.

"Hoa too poor. Come on."

"No, no, no, no, no," she said. "I work for round eyes. I have good job."

"So you get us round eye," they said, laughing.

I watched them touch her as she bent to gather underwear that slipped out of her arms. They touched her waist. They touched her ribbon. They slipped their hands over her breasts.

"Hoa," I called. I was afraid for her, and ran out in the road. She did not look at me like a person pleased to be saved. They all stopped and looked at me as though they were playing a game and me being there changed the rules.

"A new doughnut dollie," the GI said. "Where you from?"

I told them they had to leave Hoa alone. She gathered up all the slipping laundry and went into our hooch. She wore a peasant's sun hat hanging down on a length of woven strap.

I followed her, leaving the GIs in the road, and I went in my room and started to unpack all the things Mama had so carefully picked for me. I sat on the floor surrounded by my new war clothes and wrote to her.

"We study now." It was Hoa staring through the blue beads at my door.

"Y'all come on in," I said. "You better watch who you hang around with. I won't always be there to save you."

She shrugged.

"Do your parents know you come here? I bet you're too young."

"I am eighteen."

"I bet you're not," I said. "I'm nineteen."

Hoa's eyes widened. She moved around dusting with a GI T-shirt. "My parents are no longer on this earth," she said. Her face was so pretty and unemotional she could have meant they had just moved from one village to another.

"How do you know English so well?" I asked.

It pleased Hoa to hear that. She said, "I learn

French from the nuns where I live and English from GIs."

She moved silently around my room and looked at everything Mama had packed. I had a picture in a stand-up frame of Mama and Opal with their arms around each other's waists at the door of the post office. Hoa took that, looked at it closely, dusted it, and set it on my dresser.

"I go to America," she said.

"You are?" I said. "When?"

"As soon as find my husband," she said.

"Don't tell me you're married," I said.

"No," Hoa said impatiently. "It is in the stars. I will know him when I see him. I have not seen him yet. And the nuns scream to me not to come, but I have to find GI."

"Your husband will be a GI?"

"Sure," she said.

I listened to the way Vietnamese made American slang formal. I imagined Hoa practicing with her girl friends. "I am well. Are you?" "Sure."

"You have husband?" asked Hoa.

"No."

"So you are Co Diana. Co is not-married girl."

I nodded. "You are Co Hoa."

Hoa glanced up at me. She had put most of my clothes in the bureau drawers. She held one of the uniform crosses that I pinned on my collar and said, "The nuns wear crosses on leather around their necks."

"Where did you say your mother and father were?"

Hoa shrugged. "My father dead. And my mother die of grief."

"What happened to her?"

"Bad things always are happening all the time,"

she said. "They had not that many days for live on earth. You know? My mother my father were given small portion."

I watched her and considered the idea that you got just so many allotted days. Hoa had touched nearly everything in my room.

Then she pulled a folded paper from her pocket and said could we do English? She had written a kind of essay. "Read it," she said. "Fix it." She wanted me to fix her grammar. She had written about a crane who flies over the paddies until the helicopters come and chase it. I really felt for the crane. She sat beside me and made me explain all the verbs and how to make them match. She offered me a piece of bubble gum.

When I was finished, she said, "You cannot to save me." She meant from GIs. "You teach me."

I found out later she met with GIs every day. They brought her things from the PX, and I thought, Now there is a tart.

Hoa stepped out of my room as silently as she had come. But I could still feel her presence. My room smelled like bubble gum. GIs must give her bubble gum. I felt bad when she talked about her mother and father. But I didn't like hearing a girl talk so matter-of-factly about her parents being dead. My father had died so long ago I didn't have any first-hand memories, but I still wasn't matter-of-fact about that.

I found out later that when Hoa stepped out of my room so silently, she had taken a pair of my earrings with her. She broke my heart. I thought she thought I was beautiful. I thought she liked me.

Chapter 6

Maureen banged on my wall at six in the morning because Josie, our third girl, and I were going to Stallion.

It was so hot, the men wore nothing but fatigue trousers and dog tags and boonie hats to shade their sweaty eyelids and upper lips. Josie and I held, more often dragged, the prop bag for our Rock program between us. It was too heavy for that heat. Josie said maybe we should have taken out the game board. Josie was an old girl. She was senior and, of the two of us, the boss. She'd been in country two months.

When she programmed, she accentuated her mistakes by saying, "Oh, dear," inflection on the "Oh!" "Oh! dear." Men sighed when she said, "Oh, dear." She was the ultimate kid sister.

But it was too hot that day on Stallion. People could barely keep walking around. The entire fire base seemed to be suffering malaise in the heat. I followed

Josie, and we passed bunkers where guys watched as if we were a fabrication of the sun rays.

The fire base was dull brown, everything in sight. It was steamy and quiet except for music from a Sony at a gun emplacement. A heavy, echoing bass guitar seemed to come out of the earth.

Josie found a lieutenant in the command post. He was typing. They typed out here. I could hear our chopper's rotors as it took off again. It would not come back until the afternoon. Josie had arranged it with the pilot. She had stood on tiptoe and yelled in his ear over the roar and wind while I battled my skirt down and caught it between my knees. It was barely ten, and I felt faint.

"Lieutenant Gibbs," Josie said. "This is Diana. She just came in country."

Lieutenant Gibbs offered us Cokes, which I didn't take because I was in mortal fear of needing a toilet. He sprayed water from an ice chest across my arm while fishing out cans, and that felt good.

"Where do we go?" Josie said.

"Gun Three, isn't it? Hey, Bell," he called.

"Sergeant Bell's the top sergeant," Josie told me. Josie talked like she was born there.

I thought I should tell someone I didn't feel well. I would soon.

Sergeant Bell came in. He was the age my father should have been. He had a hard belly. Maybe he did sit-ups in the red dust. His skin had ridges of grit.

"Start down at Bravo Company," Lieutenant Gibbs told Bell. "Then escort them up to the guns."

Bell shook his head. "No way," he said.

"Do them good," the lieutenant said. He nodded at us. "Bravo saw some action," he said.

Josie looked at Bell. She knew the difference in rank, and the lieutenant was our contact. "Okay," she said to the lieutenant, who was checking a clipboard.

"They got a chopper at 1400." Lieutenant Gibbs went back to his typewriter. "Just get them back here by then."

Sergeant Bell didn't answer. He walked outside. Josie gathered up the corner of her half of the bag in her fist and nodded at me to get mine. We followed him through the fire base, where sandbags and planks for paths and men's faces were covered with the same dull dust. I was wearing my new blue dress. We had taken our dresses to a tailor in Washington, and mine fit just right.

We followed Sergeant Bell between gun emplacements and bunkers. Josie smiled a lot at the men and called out hello. It was a long fire base, and it seemed like we were walking the length of it.

"Anybody short?" Josie called out, and we stopped to hand out short-timers' calendars to guys on the gun. We had three types. We had 180-day calendars for the not-short-but-halfway-there. "Sam here's a two-digit midget. Let's see one of them," a guy said about his friend. I gave out a 99-day calendar. Then we had a 10-day for the—as a guy said— almost-out-of-there.

"What the shit. You grimmy," one guy said to his buddy. "You can't take one of them."

"What's a grimmy?" I asked him.

"New guy," he said. "More than two digits." I was a grimmy. I gave the other grimmy a calendar anyway. The calendars were all versions of Snoopy, and when we walked past more bunkers where the soldiers slept, I saw the nonsense sheets of paper tacked on bunker walls. The numbered sections of Snoopy's paws and belly and muzzle were colored in with grease pencil, ink, paint, and what looked like lipstick. I wondered how they got ahold of any lipstick. The fragments of art were all over the fire base.

We passed dull wooden bins of flak vests and steel pots, mountains of ammo, and everywhere the thick smell of canvas and gunpowder.

Sergeant Bell stopped at a tent. We could see the barbed-wire perimeter at a distance. "Bravo Company," he said. It was a big tent.

Men lay on cots in rows protected by canvas from the sky's light. Even so, many of them covered their eyes as if daylight were horrible.

"They're not here for long," he said.

Some of them lay coiled on their side, knees pulled up. They slept like Opal's babies except they didn't have their thumbs in their mouths.

Bravo Company. "Why aren't they here long?" I asked the sergeant.

He shrugged. "Moving them out. Somewhere south."

Josie said, "I don't know about this."

I didn't know what I was looking at. Nobody looked bloody. But I wondered if it was some kind of field hospital. It didn't look like a hospital so much. There weren't any medics or IVs on poles, nothing. No one talked. Rows of cots and men in coils and the only sound was Janis Joplin screaming from a radio followed back to back by a public-service announcement concerning foot rot. Even that was muffled, as if the radio were at the bottom of one of the ammo boxes.

"They been targets for Charlie," Sergeant Bell said.

"Are these the wounded?" I asked.

He said, "These are the guys who got away without a scratch."

Some of the men became aware of us. Nobody talked. Sergeant Bell slid down to the ground and sweated quietly with his boonie hat over his eyes.

Josie said, "Well, come on," and I followed her. I walked in Josie's exact footsteps and did what Josie did.

"Hi," she said to one soldier. She talked to him. She asked where he was from, but he only looked at her. I nodded at people. Some guys tried to talk, but most of them were too dazed.

"Are you real?" a soldier asked as I passed him. I stopped and looked at him. That was the first time anybody asked me that, but I would hear it almost daily during the months I was there. "Yeah," I said. I wished I had something to give him. I could have given him a Snoopy. He wouldn't have cared what I gave him. But I had a ring in my pocket. It was too hot to wear a ring, and I kept it there. I had picked it up in Saigon. It was a tiger's-eye stone, and you could see the tiger's slit of an eye. It was in my pocket, and I put it in the soldier's hand maybe to prove we were both real.

I followed Josie down the long center aisle, being polite. "We're not going to program, are we?" I whispered.

"Not here," Josie said. We were still lugging the program bag.

A jeep pulled up. The mess sergeant had mixed up a jerry can of Kool-Aid. Josie and I walked up and down the rows passing out paper cups of grape drink as if it were a Texas church communion.

Sergeant Bell was still looking comatose, but he arose, in slow motion, after we had stopped at every cot. "Where's the guy name of O'Maley?" he asked somebody who might be an NCO. No one wore rank.

"O'Maley?" he said. "There."

His "there" indicated several dozen men.

"O'Maley." The NCO raised his voice slightly, and I saw one soldier take his arm off his eyes and give the guy the finger. It was the one who asked if I was real. He looked like the others, in nothing but fatigue trousers, bare arms, bare chest, barefoot, barefaced, bare-eyed.

"Distinguished himself today," Bell said.

O'Maley moved his arm back over his eyes.

I went back to passing out grape Kool-Aid even though a lot of guys couldn't swallow it and didn't look as though they would be able to swallow anymore.

Gun 3 was a 155 howitzer. It was a twelve-man mounted gun that could fire thirty-five kilometers. Each of the twelve men told me that. They cleaned it, oiled it, babied it, fired it when the grunts called in for artillery. At MACV, they said we might program at guns, at tanks, etc. They didn't say what to do if you felt sick.

Men in the battery hung over the green sandbag walls and waited while we opened the prop bag.

"Where you from?" one of the guys asked.

"Ohio," Josie said.

"Oh, yeah? Blossom's from Ohio. You two know each other?"

Blossom. I looked at him. The guy's name was Blossom, and he was covered in grease streaks. They talked so innocently, as if they believed the doughnut dollies were a direct link to home.

We had "Rock," and we stood there with our

props. Josie twisted her nonregulation bangle bracelets. "Hi," she said, "I'm Josie. I'm from the state
that's round on the ends and high in the middle."

"Ohio," Blossom bellowed. "Where even the bad
times are good."

"I'm Diana," I said. "I'm from Texas." The men
probably knew where I was from by the way I said
my name, not hurrying the sound of it.

"Diana's new," Josie told them. "Three days."

The whole battery broke up. "Three days!" They
groaned in communal and abject pity. "Nothing but
an FNG. Three f . . ." Somebody knocked over the
talker. Some kind of group ethic made them polish
their language around the doughnut dollies.

Sergeant Bell was sunk back down on the ground
against the ammo boxes. "That's it, boys," he said,
"stretch your vocabulary. Three sunny days in Cu
Chi by the VC . . ."

We took out our acetated boards, which the men
would use to play a game of art charades, and guys
would set to cheering and goading each other on. Josie told them about the concert at Woodstock. No
one there had heard about Woodstock. Then we did
a quick flash-card game with a lyric. It was an ice-
breaker, Josie had explained, because everybody starts
singing the songs.

I thought I was going to have to lean against the
gun. I felt sick in the heat. The blood must have
drained from my face. I was afraid I was going to
faint.

"How do you like it here?" a boy said.

"I wrote my mama it's hotter than Texas," I answered.

"You bet," he said. "Hang around when we fire."

"Don't pay any attention to him. He shows off for the dollies."

"No, I won't," I said.

"Oh, dear," Josie said. She fumbled with the cards. The guys leaned back against the gun and curve of sandbags.

"Okay," she said, "what's this from?"

We went through five songs. The men boomed out the names, the band, the year.

"I have to go to," I whispered.

Josie was holding up a line from "Tears on My Pillow." "We just started," she said.

"No, I mean, I need to."

Josie glanced at me. I knew she would roll her eyes if I said I thought I needed a toilet. I thought I was bleeding even though it wasn't time for my period. I didn't want to bother Josie. It was somehow my fault, and I would handle this myself. I looked around me and saw dull brown under layers of dust. It was eleven in the morning, and there was no way off the fire base.

I walked away from the program. I couldn't stand there and will that sensation to stop and will the blood to disappear and will myself invisible. I had to cover myself. I thought I could use my slip. I walked, looking for a place to stop. There were men everywhere watching me, and I tried to be polite. Some of them were Bravo Company who had come back to life. They stared at me with eyes that looked huge and wild, but I thought that must be my imagination because I was ashamed. Mama didn't even think a girl should file her nails in public, and I was doing this. Opal said girls used to hide away when they bled because they were bad luck. But I kept smiling at soldiers and looking in bunkers in hopes I'd find one empty.

Finally I ducked into a bunker to catch my breath and to stop being polite. It was dark after being in the full heat and light, and I stood and pressed my fingerprints into the bags of sand behind me. I could still hear the pounding of the bass guitar and the Beatles echoing harmony from under the ground. I couldn't catch my breath. I would have done anything then to escape. Why didn't Mama and Opal stop me from coming over here?

I wanted to be back with Mama and Opal—all of us together—with paper umbrellas in our hair. I squeezed my eyes shut to get myself off Fire Base Stallion.

In the dull, walled-in light, I peeled my half-slip away from my sweating thighs and stepped out of it. It was an old, thin slip. I used to rinse it out at night in the dorm sink and let it dry on the towel rack near our map of RVN.

When I rolled it, it didn't make much of a pad. I pulled up my new dress. If the dress was bloody as well, there was nothing I could do. I was sweating so much, I wasn't sure what was sweat and what was blood. I pushed the pad inside my panties.

"What the shit," a voice growled from the dim corner.

I dropped the skirt of my dress and backed up hard into the sandbags.

"I said what the shit is going on?"

I had heard that voice. I stood, my arms stiff behind me and my fingers digging into the wall.

O'Maley stumbled out of the corner where there was a cot I could see now. He had his rifle. He held it in both hands in the ready pose.

"Get out," I said.

He had come very close. He stared, and I didn't feel like a new doughnut dolly to be cajoled. His eyes were dark and fierce. I stared at his warrior eyes. Now he wore a shirt, but he was barefoot. He had been sleeping.

"Christ," he said, lowering the rifle.

Maybe he hadn't seen anything. Maybe there wasn't any telltale stain, I prayed as his eyes passed down over my body, down my bare legs. "Get out," I said again more softly. "Would you please get out."

But he kept staring at me. He could hurt me, I remember thinking. He pulled off his undershirt. The only time I was free from his stare was when the shirt passed over his eyes. He tossed it at me and walked out into the glaring light. I watched him outlined by the doorway.

He looked like every other GI in Nam. He was the same as thousands of others except that I had given him my tiger's-eye and he had given me his shirt and nobody else knew. I held the shirt. It was damp with his sweat. I squatted, laid it across my lap, and rolled it into a tight pad, which I used as I had to. My hands shook. We were both excruciatingly real.

The chopper came early. There was activity, the lieutenant said. Sergeant Bell hustled us over to the landing pad where the Huey came.

"Got here your two Delta Deltas," he shouted. Josie said the pilot called them that on his radio. Delta Deltas were an ash-and-trash mission. She said you'd rather not know what else they said on their radios. She said some of them have been in country a long time, and they got crazy. Meaning three months, I guessed, because Josie had been in country two. Anybody with more was aged.

"Once a gunner gave me his headset," Josie said. "The pilot freaked out when he heard me answer." Josie's voice was muffled when the rotors cut through the air.

I sat by the gunner going home. The door gunner's seat was just that, he sat in the open door, to the rear of the cabin, facing the jungle. There was room for two. My eyes followed the length of the machine gun he held. There was such a roar I lost my sense of hearing, I had only sight. I thought of how Jesse talked about being a wide-open target. He sat in a wide-open door with nowhere to go. I was fascinated by the gun, and then I saw the soldier. He hadn't put on another shirt. O'Maley. He stood and watched us pull off from the ground.

We rose over Stallion. There wasn't anything but the wind between me and the long expanse of guns and bunkers. The wind brought goose bumps out all over my skin, and in the chill of our flight and above the lush canopy of trees, I looked down. I touched my face and felt heat welts across my cheek mixed with the goose bumps. The gunner kept his hand on his machine gun, ready. I watched the gunner train his gun and the patterns of the rice fields and the rivers just under the trees, and I watched for a crane. Stallion was a patch in the distance.

Chapter 7

Now I knew what a run was. Stallion was a third of a run. We should have programmed once more there and gone on to two other 2nd Brigade fire bases, but everything depended on Charlie. Claire left, so Josie, Maureen, and I took all the runs we could manage and that Colonel Stone said were secure.

We were supposed to get one day a week in base camp to do a hospital run and work on our own programs. I was doing a program on photography. It seemed like every grunt in country had a camera. Every grunt wanted to take your picture with his puppy or his monkey or his armored personnel carrier, so I've been researching photography and coming up with some powerful toss-up questions for reality therapy in the boonies.

I went to the PX to buy a camera for myself, and the guy working there said, "Treat your camera like you'd treat a baby." So I jumped in our chopper in the morning with this camera cradled against my belly. It went everywhere with me. I also took a picture of the MP who guards our hooch from sunset to sunrise and one of Hoa in my earrings. I remembered everything so clearly about Stallion that I've got a motion picture in my head of that.

After a few weeks of being on runs nearly every day, I got a base-camp day. In the morning I went to the Special Services library, where I was finding famous photographs for my program. Then me and my camera went to 12th Evac.

Maureen told me about 12th Evac. It was short for 12th Evacuation Hospital. Dust-off choppers medivaced wounded soldiers and brought them there. It was fully equipped, but if soldiers were badly wounded, they were evacuated to Japan or back to the World. They never stayed long at 12th Evac. They were shipped out or they died. If a soldier didn't die and didn't even threaten to, he was returned to his unit.

Twelfth Evac was several wards, each in a Quonset hut, and in each hut were rows of beds. When a girl had the hospital run, she went to the post-op ward, walked around, talked to the men, wrote letters for them if they wanted. Sometimes we took them in wheelchairs, or if they could walk, we took them out, rolling their IVs along so they could have a change of scenery or for sing-alongs in the chapel.

Today I walked into the ward. A duty nurse in fatigues sat at a desk by the door. She didn't look up when I came in. Curtains were drawn around four or five of the beds. Some of the wounded soldiers walked around in bathrobes too big for them with the sashes limp around their hips.

"I met a doughnut dolly," one patient said softly. "You ever been out to Meade?" I shook my head and moved nearer to his bed because he talked so softly. He had to lie flat on his back. There was a bag collecting his urine and bottles of bright red blood ready to fill him, and I wondered how anyone could lose that much blood.

I was in a clean new uniform and looking very scrubbed and American and not so tired as the nurses in fatigues. I'd been in school learning about poetry and how to nurture the body, but the boy only wanted to hold my hand, and he shut his eyes. I didn't know what to do. I watched the blood drip from the bottle, and I watched the boy's white eyelashes.

When I looked up, I saw O'Maley.

He was sitting on a bed, his legs crossed, at the far end of a row of beds. He was listening closely to an officer bent over talking to him. He had a bandage around his forehead, and he shook his head almost sympathetically as the officer talked. The officer . . . I had not been able to get the ranks straight yet . . . stood back. "Tough luck, O'Maley," he said.

O'Maley saluted him. The officer walked down the row of beds.

O'Maley continued to look thoughtful. He had enormous feet. They had given him paper slippers. I almost ran out. I'd thought of him every day. He'd said such a few words, but I remembered his voice and every word he had spoken. It was a deep, gravelly voice, and even if I hadn't seen him, I would have known him from his voice. Still, I would have left, but the boy had my hand. I looked at the nurse, who had begun passing out medications.

"Are you asleep?" I whispered to the boy.

He was sound asleep, and I tried to pull my hand away, but he really had me.

I looked back at O'Maley. He saw me. There

were about a dozen beds between us, but I could see his eyes were different from the warrior eyes he had had in the bunker. I still couldn't gently move my hand away from that of the boy who was from Meade. I'd have written a letter for him. If I couldn't leave, I wanted to do something for him so I could stop watching the blood and feeling O'Maley's eyes. I told that to the nurse when she brought the medication. I said, "What can I do for him?"

She looked at the soldier, and instead of giving him his shot, she felt for his pulse on his neck where it beats so strong. "You already did it," she said. She took his hand from around mine. She sort of shoved me away and pulled the curtain, and I stood looking at the curtain. It happened too fast. The boy had just been talking to me. Then he fell asleep for a minute. I wanted to open the curtains again. I stood there waiting, knowing the boy had died but expecting the nurse to open the curtain again and we would start over.

I stepped back from the curtain. The nurse was matter-of-fact. She finished the medications, and then someone brought in the supper trays and I was still looking at the curtain. Then I looked at O'Maley.

He held up a banana. He was offering me the banana that they had put on his supper tray. I walked down the aisle between the beds to tell him that the boy had just died.

"Didn't know him," O'Maley said. He ate some of his gravy and potatoes.

I said, "He was holding my hand."

"Maybe now you won't go around holding guys' hands."

I thought he had misunderstood. I said, "My mama used to tell a story about her grandmother who died one noontime serving the chicken potpie. She died with the serving spoon in her hand. That boy died with my hand in his hand. He held so hard that I thought I was giving him strength, and I wasn't. He was dying."

O'Maley nodded. "It's worse when you know 'em," he said. Then he went back to eating his potato. I almost pounded his face with my fist because that boy died when I was giving him my strength, but O'Maley's head was already messed up. "He died," I said. I held up my hand the dead boy had held like a dog holds up an injured paw. O'Maley bent down and kissed it. I would have prayed, but I didn't know any right prayers. It felt like a reverence, that kiss. We honored him. After a while they came and took the dead boy. I stood for a long time and watched O'Maley eat.

"What's your other name," I asked him, "besides O'Maley?"

"Big Foot."

I didn't question that. Nothing was normal here.

"You must be my good-luck charm," Big Foot said.

He had a kind of lingering teenage acne. He had the kind of face a kid at home would scrub with Clearasil and put stuff on the bad parts to hide them. People didn't do that in Vietnam. Makeup sweated off in ten seconds. In Vietnam, people went around with oily skin. His forehead was wrapped in gauze.

"Where'd you come from?" he said.

"Texas," I said.

"You're good luck. You're a rabbit's foot." He shook his head, perplexed. "You know what that captain said to me?"

"No."

"He said they don't have my size boots. My boots rotted. A' course my feet rotted, and the army doesn't mind about that. But my *boots* rotted."

I didn't understand.

"There's a reg," Big Foot said. "They can't send me back without boots."

I looked at his paper slippers and then at his eyes, which were very blue.

"I'm marooned," he said.

"That is tough luck," I said.

"For a pair of size-fifteen boots," he said.

"Well, they probably can dig up another pair."

"I'm too short," he said.

"How short?"

"Under three hundred."

"How much?"

"Two ninety-seven."

"That's not short."

But Big Foot was euphoric. He got up almost as if he were going to sweep me into his baggy bathrobe with him. He started talking. He pulled up a chair, and I said I had to get back, but I sat in the chair, and he told me every detail of his patrol. He had an IV, and he wheeled it around as he talked. He told me, and then he told a nurse and all the dumb-ass grunts, as he called them, and he swung the IV around. He was on a roll.

I listened for two hours, and I forgot about all the things Maureen told me to do. The nurse came and cleaned out his scalp and wrapped him up neatly, and he wasn't bleeding anymore. And all the while, Big Foot told the story about leeches and the VC they flushed out of the paddy with a grenade, and the mine on the footbridge, and the explosion that didn't get Big Foot and didn't get his friend, Mackie. But he said they looked at each other. He described Mackie's eyes. And he described every kill. After a while the dumb-ass grunts wandered away because they had heard it all.

I sat in my clean Red Cross uniform with the gold cross and the "ARC" in gold letters pinned correctly on my collar and my spine straight and listened to it all, watching Big Foot's steel eyes.

When I left, I noticed Big Foot was wearing my tiger's-eye on a chain around his neck. It had slipped out of his baggy bathrobe as he talked, and it hung against his breastbone.

Big Foot stayed in the hospital for three days, and then they couldn't keep him in his bed. He didn't have any combat boots, so they couldn't send him back into combat. I soon found out that Big Foot could outwheel-and-deal anybody in my hometown. He got ahold of a big truck so he'd have transportation, and by the time he was out of the hospital, he had his eye out for empty sheds for amours for him and me. It took up a lot of his time while he was waiting for new boots, and I was a continual disappointment to him after he had mapped Cu Chi out in a manner more thorough, I believe, than Charlie. I mentioned to him about our leader's talk on compromising appearances and how I wanted to finish my tour. Girls got sent home for breaks in moral codes. That's what Mary Ann threatened. And Big Foot went on mapping the base camp and coming back and saying he knew of places that were "veritable forts" and impregnable. I said I expected I was too.

Big Foot visited me in the unit's office with HAPPY BIRTHDAY, HO CHI MINH on the door. He came in his fatigue pants and flip-flops. He painted over HAPPY BIRTHDAY, HO CHI MINH and wrote CHARLEY CHARLEY

on our door. Once I flew with a colonel in the command-and-control chopper, or C&C, or Charley
Charley. The people who wielded power. I tried to
figure out how we girls who spent our time painting
props and devising calendars and leading games would
be Charley Charley to Big Foot. But I couldn't.

We kept it light then between us. We didn't know
what we were doing. We never talked about Stallion
until the next Friday when Maureen didn't make me
go with the unit to a social obligation—we had one
almost every night. But on Friday night Big Foot and
I had a date. It was a date in that he picked me up,
even if it was in his three-quarter-ton truck. I wore a
dress, not my uniform but a dotted-swiss sundress
Mama sewed. Big Foot wore fatigues, but he tucked
them in, which made them seem quite formal. He
looked really thin with the fatigue shirt tucked in and
wearing a belt with a lot of extra shoved through the
loops. He had a way of saying something deadpan
and then letting the barest grin ease across his face.
He moved slow, talked slow, grinned slow. He said
he got into the habit of moving slow because he grew
six inches in one year and every goddamn doorway
was out to get him.

If I focused on Big Foot's face, it was something
like a date. We went to a Vietnamese-run café where
we sat at a bamboo table and ate Kobe steak and mealy
french fries we washed down with bottles of warm
Coke. There was not another girl there, not a Western girl. Only Vietnamese girls who wanted to touch
my hair and my sundress and sing to each other about
me. The Vietnamese did not talk, they sang in single
syllables. Everywhere I went, I was stared at by GIs
and singing Vietnamese like I was a freak, so I kept

my eyes on Big Foot that night, and when he looked at me, he let the grin come.

"Christ," he said.

"It's like living in a goldfish bowl over here," I said.

"Aren't you ever alone?"

"Never," I said.

"How do you stand it?"

I said, "I stand it on account of my being so dedicated."

He leaned over and said in the same tone, "God, I find you attractive."

I said, "I'm not going to any fort."

He said, "What if it had air-conditioning?"

"Okay, well, maybe," I kidded, wiping the sweat off my neck. We had never even held hands. There were always two hundred other GIs around.

I said, "Remember that day on Stallion?"

"Yeah."

"The day I came."

"I remember," he said. "We just got in. Don't let them send you down to units just in. You can't do any good there."

"I helped you."

"I can't believe my luck," he said.

And we almost got lost in a gaze, but the *mamasans* were making a ruckus in the kitchen, and it occurred to me that they could bring in all the steak they wanted and milk and California oranges, but we never could quite color the place America.

"What's it like on Stallion for you?"

"Oh, well, we live with the ARVN, the Vietnamese regulars, when they're in, and their women and their dogs. The *mamasans* are always squatting at their fires and cooking fishy-smelling grub. That's the first thing you smell in the morning. They cooks dogs too."

"Their dogs?" I said.

"Yeah, they do. I don't want to talk about Stallion. This is the first night I get to see you. What do you girls do every night?"

"The whole unit has to go to hail-and-farewells and songfests like the one in the hospital. Last night we had a stand down. There were about seventy-five men. Stand downs are all-unit events, but there's only three of us now."

Big Foot shook his head. "What do you do at a stand down?"

"Well, mostly we talk about home. We wear our civilian dresses and get all done up because Maureen tells us not to get slack. We ought to wear makeup and be girls, but sometimes the guys are drunk. We usually don't stay long."

"Drunk is one of the nicer things we are."

"So anyway we eat with them. I've never had so much steak in my life. Last night one guy said he was short and whooped and threw up on Josie's pink thongs, so a lieutenant came and asked if we'd like to sit inside—I think he meant with the officers—but I didn't go. Somebody put on a Blood, Sweat and Tears tape. Josie was talking about playing Password on the Saigon River with the River Rats, but they said cut out the lifer talk. They wanted to hear about what it was like in Ohio the day she left, over and over and over."

I couldn't write to Mama about the stand down. She couldn't picture it. It wouldn't make any sense. Big Foot could sort of picture it, and I told him everything. He watched me with eyes you could swim in, so to say.

"There was a guy in a Hawaiian shirt who kept saluting and saying he'd see us at general's mess. Maureen said he was a FAC pilot, a kind you watch out for. So then I went back to my room. I have rows of beads for a door, and it's the only place I'm alone. I hung up my dress. It is so unbearably hot. I thought I should start wearing my hair in two braids and nothing on my face. No matter what Maureen says."

Big Foot said, "Could I dance with you?"

"Where, here?" I laughed. The Vietnamese played music. They played zithers or something.

He said, "What are you doing here?"

It was half-accusation, and I tensed up. I didn't think I should have to defend myself. His eyes were huge and blue and questioning.

He said, "No, really, why'd you come?"

I said, "I didn't want to just get married and have it all be over. I wanted to see things. I wanted to help dumb-ass grunts like you."

He said, "I wanted to dance with you because I wanted to feel if you are as fragile as you look. You strike me as delicate, there's something fragile and innocent about you."

I said, "You strike me as a pop psychologist."

"And sensuous," he said.

I blushed. Because I felt that way when I looked into his eyes. I felt like it wasn't me who was sensuous. It was me looking at him.

He said, "I just wondered why you were here," and we got up to pay the Vietnamese girl. I did not feel the fragility he talked about. Maybe fertility. I thought I may have been too fertile to keep on looking into his eyes, just looking at his eyes may have done it. I was strong. I was smart. I walked with solid footsteps across the wood floor. I was not fragile, and I did not like him saying that. I wanted facts. I wanted to picture everything. Nothing would trick me.

Big Foot and I got in the three-quarter-ton. I was strong, but there were things I didn't know. "When you go out on a patrol, what do you do?"

"Lately we've been using extreme caution."

"What's that mean?"

"Means we don't do a hell of a lot to draw fire. It's the mines and booby traps that get you. It's a game of chance. I'm a fuckin' lucky s.o.b. to be out of it, but my buddies are in a lot of shit. I could be doing something to save Mackie's hide."

On the way back to my hooch I pictured mines. I pictured how they worked and what they did to humans.

In the morning Big Foot came into the office before I left on my run. He had a slip of paper. "Requisition unavailable," he read.

"Still no boots?" I asked.

"No boots."

"You poor s.o.b."

Hoa followed him adoringly. She didn't understand anything he said. His English wasn't like the French nuns' English and other GIs' English since he was from Boston. But Hoa was captivated. He gave her things to take home to the orphanage. He gave her licorice and yellow plastic bottles of Joy soap. One day I saw her digging outside the compound where she hung laundry to dry. The soil was already loosened, and soon she came to a bag. Inside the bag she very carefully placed a bottle of Joy. She re-covered it with dirt, unclipped the clothespins, and came back with the laundry. I had seen the Vietnamese girls get frisked at the gate. I thought Hoa was probably waiting for some safe day to smuggle things out.

The next day I saw Big Foot coming back from luncheon—as he called it—at headquarters company, chewing a toothpick. It was raining. His flip-flops squished into the mud on the way to the office. Along behind him came Hoa with the laundry, her eyes glued on his tracks and going to huge lengths to miss stepping in one. I watched them from the window. Hoa wore a yellow *ao dai* that day, like the city girls. She was a tiny goldfinch.

"Tell me more about Boston," she said to Big Foot.

He yawned. He usually took a nap after lunch.

"Boston is Fenway," she said, coaxing him, carefully saying the words that were strange to her. I imagined a refrain he might have taught her called "What Boston Is." But he didn't want to play, so after a while Hoa turned and tiptoed again around Big Foot's tracks on her way to the hooch.

I was in my bedroom when Hoa came, passing out the clean laundry. Passersby liked to write notes on our underwear. Today my pants said, "Hi!" and "No Sham Job." Hoa put them on my bed. Maybe she thought that was what people did in America. American girls always wore pants with messages. I thought about saying something about her crush on Big Foot. But I remembered the time I was a junior camper with a crush on a counselor. Somehow the counselors found out and killed it with solicitude. They made the counselor eat with me. So I only said to Hoa, "Why'd you walk funny?"

"Who walk?"

"You. Around footsteps in the mud."

"So I don't have baby."

"What baby?"

"Big Foot baby."

"Hoa," I shrieked, probably like the farewells of the French nuns as Hoa got on her bicycle every morning. "Haven't you got any sense? Don't let him near you. You're a little girl."

Hoa shook her head calmly. "He does not get near me. We have Vietnamese story where a girl steps in giant footprints in the field and she have baby."

"No," I said. "From footprints?"

Hoa nodded.

"That's not true," I said.

"You go then. You step in them."

I didn't see any reason to step in them. Why provoke bad luck? "I'm not going to step in them," I said.

"You see?" Hoa said. "Why take chances?" And we left it at that, each having found a vulnerability to superstition in the other.

Chapter 8

"**D**iana," Maureen said, coming into the office, flustered. "We're getting a new girl. Saigon just called. We're getting up to a four-girl unit again. But Josie's waiting for me at Brigade. I have to run. Would you meet her?"

"Sure," I said, and went back to typing a program format.

"You're going to forget," Maureen said, running around the office in a frenzy to remember things.

"I'm not going to forget. Just tell me what time."

"Noon," she said. "Show her around, please. Maybe you could take her to an officers' mess for lunch. I'll meet with her when I get back."

I wondered how people could speak the absolute obvious, and it never clicked that they were.

"Second Brigade is tonight. Call and tell them we have a new girl. Maybe you want to take her to the PX. And don't hitch. Tell her nobody hitches in this unit. There was an incident with girls hitching in Cam Ranh."

"Okay, I promise. I promise. We won't hitch. I promise."

So they finally sent a replacement for Claire who got married. The replacement came to Cu Chi in III Corps, RVN, and landed on the general's Tropic Lightning pad outside headquarters. I hoped the replacement would have no neuroses and didn't tell people what they already knew. I hoped she was a down-to-earth, normal, hardworking girl. I hoped she liked monsoons. Maybe a farm girl from Iowa who had experienced drought. I wanted a girl who laughed.

I saw the girl's hair before any of the rest of her. It was familiar hair. It wasn't Iowa hair, and it wasn't laugh-out-loud hair. It was ironwood-black masses of curly Pearly hair, and I almost lurched forward to grab her when the chopper touched the yellow tarmac.

Pearly Boudreau jumped to the ground and dropped her bags.

She looked the same except she cut her hair. Her curls were shorter and not boinging off her forehead. She had what Mama called an Italian boy haircut, and it showed up her long, slim neck and sharp nose. The best thing about her, I thought as I watched her jump out of the chopper, was Pearly's odd mix of vulnerability and brashness. I should precede her, to explain her, I was the only one who saw the soft part. She made Cu Chi whole to me.

The pilot saluted her. She pulled a boonie hat on low to shade her eyes and held on to it until she got out of the wind from the rotors. She had about a dozen unit crests hanging off the hat. She stood there watching me, unsmiling, from underneath her boonie hat with the dangling crests.

"Hey, Pearly," I said.

"Hey yourself."

Pearly started off in the wrong direction, dragging her bags. I caught up with her and put my arms around the girl, which nearly knocked her down. "It's you!" I squealed.

"Yup," said Pearly.

We looked at each other. Neither one of us looked that new anymore. Barely two months, and we were a duller blue. I tousled Pearly's hair. "You have boy's hair now. And an armband." She wore a black armband on her left arm. I remembered Pearly said she hoed zucchinis in New Hampshire with one on her arm to say her country did not stand for her. Now she wore one and a boonie hat hung with twelve U.S. Army unit crests.

"So your UD finked out?" Pearly said.

"She was real sick," I said.

"I heard she was getting married."

"That's what I mean."

I carried her suitcases. I led Pearly through the base.

"I'm program director," I said. "I think."

"How'd you manage that?" she said.

"Well, not officially. We didn't have any ceremonies."

We giggled. "There's only been three of us. You'll see when you meet the girls."

It was two o'clock and time for the afternoon rain, and precisely then when we were walking on the wooden ramps between the close buildings, it started to pour.

We came to the office before we came to the

hooch. Since it was raining, I led Pearly up the office stairs and dropped her bags on the floor. We stood dripping, and Pearly wiped her face with her sleeve.

"Nice," said Pearly, looking around the office. "Don't you eat? You're skinnier than ever."

"It's too hot. Let's go sit in the rain."

We did. I clicked on the Beatles *Abbey Road* tape on the tape deck. Then we sat on the steps with our heads back and our eyes shut. The rain was persistent and warm. "Let's pretend we're in the Waldorf Astoria whirlpool."

"Okay," I said. "And when we get out, somebody will come and paint our toenails pink."

We stretched out our legs. I got what I wanted. Pearly was weathered, had her mental health, and liked monsoons. She was a midwestern farm girl from New Hampshire. Her life line was a worry, but I would protect her. I would never put her in any dangerous places. I would protect her from I didn't know what.

"God, it feels good to have you here." We had not opened our eyes. We were still at the Waldorf.

Pearly said, "I'm pretending I'm home. Things are made of wood here like home, but there's nothing green here. Except guys in OD."

"That doesn't count as green," I said. The rain felt lush. "Pearly," I said, "if you wanted to be with somebody over here, it'd be real hard to do it."

"I know," she said. "Would you rub my small of my back?"

"Your small of your back?"

"Yeah."

"Have you noticed," I said, pressing my thumbs into the arch of Pearly's back, "there isn't anything

you do alone? Everything you do, somebody probably was watching. Even if you were doing it for only
a little while."

"Sounds pretty bad," Pearly said.

We heard troops approaching.

"Do we have to get out?" Pearly said.

"Yeah, honey, we've got work to do."

We went inside and wiped the rain off our faces
with our sleeves and laughed. I wanted to tell Pearly
how much I loved her. She was funny, wise, outrageous. If I told her she was funny, wise, outrageous,
she would look at me, bored, and tell me a story about
her mother who made potato dumplings and spooned
them down her anorexic sister. "Stupid girl," she
would say about her sister. Pearly had no ego. She
had her own Pearly world. I loved her. I didn't tell
her. You couldn't tell that to a girl.

She told me stories about Qui Nhon, where she'd
been. She said, "You know, if anything happens to
me in this pit, just say the good things about me. Say
good things, okay?"

"Sure."

When Big Foot lumbered in, my stomach hurt
from laughing. "Pearly, meet Big Foot," I said. I raised
my eyes past his OD fatigues to his face.

I shoved strands of wet hair off my cheek. He
smiled and watched Pearly stand up. "Holy shit," he
said. "Are skirts going up in the World?"

Pearly liked him. Maybe it was the flip-flops he
wore with his fatigues. She saw the patch on his sleeve
and asked if he'd get her one.

"You'll have lots of chances," I told her. "We get
to Stallion when we can."

"Whose crest?" Pearly said.

"Fire Brigade," Big Foot said. "Men tempered like fine steel."

"They couldn't find any combat boots to fit him," I explained. "So they won't let him go back to the jungle. There's a reg," I said. Having Pearly there and telling this story from scratch let me see how a part of Big Foot would just as soon be there with his buddies. With Mackie. He could breathe deep here, but a part of him wanted to be tempered like fine steel.

Pearly was in her room when I got back to the hooch. I found her curled on her bed with her sweaty cheek against a wadded white pillow. She wore only a bra and a half-slip, and they weren't like new either, like our dresses.

"I liked you better with hair," I said.

Pearly groaned. "My neck needed air. I need air all over. Big Foot's got it bad for you. I wondered if you knew that."

"He thinks I'm a rabbit's foot. Everybody's superstitious here. He'd like to put me in his pocket." I had everything to prove. I played games. I knew Big Foot liked me.

Pearly merely raised her long, arched eyebrows, because she saw through me. She said, "He has outstanding lips."

"Outstanding lips!" I laughed. "You lifer."

I sat cross-legged on the floor under the beads at Pearly's door. Pearly had long fingers, and she smoked a lot. She lit her cigarettes with a butane lighter she said they gave her when she left Qui Nhon. It had the LOG Command crest.

I told her Big Foot's story. "I saw him on my first run, the day after we left Saigon. And then he got some shrapnel in his forehead and he was in at

Twelfth Evac. When I went, he began to talk, and he didn't want to shut up. He told me a lot of stuff I didn't want to hear, but he had to talk about it. So I listened. And then I kind of warmed to it. I wanted to hear more. I stopped squirming and listened. I just let it come into me like this thick air comes into you and slows your breathing. I wanted to hear the ugliest, ghastliest details so I could think, Okay, now I know. I pretended I was picking up a body bag so I'd know. I wanted everything to play across my mind so I couldn't get taken by surprise, because I already knew ways people died. Like I read an article once about people falling off a bridge in their car and how they escaped or suffocated. I wanted to hear the worst. Now I feel kind of jaded with it. Big Foot was such a good accomplice. Maybe because a boy had just died. A boy on the ward."

Pearly had been listening closely. "Do you ever get scared?" she asked.

"You mean like in a chopper?"

"No, just in general. Just being here." Pearly looked at me. Her face was no less quiet and composed. She said, "I guess you don't."

"I am afraid for other people."

"Sometimes I'm in the war," Pearly said. "Not just cheering on the side."

A picture of Pearly with an M-16 flashed before me. The eyes were grotesque. "What do you mean?" I wanted her to take that picture away.

"I'm just saying that if you look at things, the war is all that's real. Let's face it. What good are we? I want a gun. We might as well do some good. It's insane. Recreation girls. The kind of recreation you do in the bushes. One each: recreation slash boom boom girl."

I knew that's what GIs called Vietnamese girls who came from their villages to offer themselves for money. I told Pearly that was bullshit.

"It's not," she said, and narrowed her eyes on me.

"All right, what happened?"

"I was just walking down the road to the PX."

I could see Pearly just walking down the road. Pearly had a relaxed sort of easy gait. "You weren't walking alone?" I said.

"Goddamn, can't a person walk down the road? Can't a person walk to the PX and get her supply of M&Ms?"

"You have to use common sense. You can't walk around alone. You can't slink down the road."

"I don't slink."

"All right, what happened?"

"This jerk offered me money."

"What?"

"Money. For sex. He said, Why else would a girl come over here?"

"Oh my God."

Pearly looked at me. "You're such a baby," she said.

"I am not."

"Did that happen to you?"

"I don't slink," I said.

"Go to hell," she said. From Pearly that was affection.

"You too," I said.

"I'll slink to hell in a miniskirt. The army can't tell me what to wear and how to walk. I'm not in the goddamn army. Weren't they hot to call us recreation girls." She lit a cigarette and blew small, disgusted O's into the heat.

"I'm trying to imagine what I'd do if somebody did that to me," I said.

Pearly shook her head. "Never happen. You'd never catch on. You're hopeless. They'd have to keep explaining, and then they'd end up falling in love."

"Go to hell yourself, Pearly."

"Yes'm."

"You know, you could use discretion."

That made her hoot. Earth-girl Pearly who never shaved her legs. I said that partly because she was laughing at me, but Pearly had no ego, and she'd do whatever she wanted.

"Opal says women are glue and they hold people together—you think we don't do that?"

Pearly sat up and crossed her legs and let the fan dry the sweat on her belly, and she didn't answer. She got out her Pond's and smeared cream on her parched, tanned face. She followed her cheekbones and made a circle of white cream around her eyes. "Sometimes I think it's harder for them to have us hanging around here."

"I think we can make it better. I think of us kind of like social workers. Guys talk about things to us."

"Yeah, they do," she agreed.

"And I think I was jealous. That boys go far away and do things that are dangerous and violent, and girls teach."

"You came for the violence?"

"No. I don't know why."

I went out to the patio. I paced and wiped sweat off my neck. I remembered a letter from Mama that was still unopened in my pocket. I sat in the red dirt on the steps to the bunker and ripped it open.

Dear Diana,

How are you, honey? Wish you were here to help decide who was coming and who was going for Thanksgiving.

I try real hard not to think about you. Got people counting on me for one thing and another so what good's it going to do for me to worry about you in helicopters? How the Red Cross could let you do that I don't know. Maybe they know something I don't which is more than likely. But when I watch the news anymore Manfred says I come near to indenting the arms of my sewing chair. Saw Dennis Dorset the other night at Wyatt's Cafeteria. Going on and on about his Glenna. You remember her. Glenna was doing this. Glenna was doing that. Glenna was in a dance recital. Glenna was taking voice. I let him go on and on and when he was wound down, I got up with my tray and told him my Diana was in Vietnam. I left him with his mouth wide open.

Write to us now, Diana. Everybody asks for you at the post office.

Your Mama who loves you

Chapter 9

It was Sunday. The Cu Chi Unit was gathered under the yellow garden umbrella for brunch and to decide what to do. Pearly brought us up to four girls. We'd have been short a UD if Saigon hadn't called and officially named Maureen UD. But now we were short a PD. We only had an acting PD. Saigon had named Josie because she'd been there so long. But Josie demurred. Saigon said we should work it out, which is what we were trying to do.

Josie had picked up a coffee cake at the Brigade kitchen. We ate coffee cake with our fingers and drank cold milk, and I listened for Big Foot to come along in combat boots, which I prayed I would not hear. I wanted the sound of flip-flops. Maureen had a milk mustache while she lectured us. Josie said she wanted her name taken off the ballot. "You won't catch me with stars in my eyes," she said.

I thought Maureen must be feeling the weight of responsibility.

"Okay," Maureen said. "Josie's out."

I got restless and began pacing up and down our corrugated-metal garden wall flicking cigarette ashes in the dirt. It was hot, and I wore a scarf rolled like a headband to keep my wispy hair off my face.

"On another point," said Maureen, looking at all of us. "Wear makeup. And stop talking GI talk. Act like a girl. Not like you're in their platoon. Okay, who'll take minutes and send thank-you notes?"

Josie shrugged and got that job.

"That makes you PD, then," said Maureen, looking at me.

"I hope my mama will be proud," I said.

A chopper flew over. It slowed and hovered over our yellow umbrella with the gunner hanging out and waving. I stopped pacing and held the umbrella pole down in the wind. We didn't want to wave. It was Sunday. It was our day off, and we shouldn't have to. But to make the chopper go away, we gave in. The chopper continued to hover. It shook our glasses and spilled our milk on the table. When it was gone, Pearly was still looking after it, and I thought she knew the pilot.

"We need a social director," said Maureen, looking at Pearly.

Pearly lit a cigarette. "I don't do social," she said. Maureen smiled her smile to say things would never quite be the same after that rebuff. She went on to read the social commitments herself.

"Tuesday night, Second Brigade dinner. Everybody goes," she said. "Wednesday, Twelfth Evac songfest, Thursday, dust-off is having a party. Tonight, general's mess," she said. "Attendance is required."

"It's a sit-down halfway decent meal with a soup course," Josie said to Pearly. "You just go and talk to the officers and get a good dinner."

Pearly didn't want to go.

The day stretched on, and I was getting worried about Big Foot. I thought he would show up and he would show me the requisition the army couldn't fill and would never be able to fill. There was a stash of C's in our kitchen. Guys gave us their canned peaches and chocolates and other prizes. Pearly and I ate C's for lunch, and I waited to hear. He had gone back to his unit. I was very afraid.

When dinnertime came, I told Pearly, "You have to come to this with me. I can't go without you."

"I don't want to eat with a bunch of dirty old men," she said.

"They're not, mostly. Why don't you get dressed, Pearly."

"I don't want to."

"No, just this once."

"Who can eat? It's too hot."

"I can. It's better than C's. All you eat is C's."

"All right," Pearly said.

"You'll come?"

"Sure. If I can wear my bathrobe."

"You're going to wear your bathrobe?"

It was red corduroy, and it had a collar that showed her collarbones. Pearly put it on and said, "I could doll it up with jewelry." I went to get my jewelry box and found some pop beads with a slightly pinkish tinge and put them around Pearly's neck. I stepped back to look, popped off a few beads so that the necklace hung just to Pearly's collarbone. With the extra beads, I made a bracelet for Pearly's left wrist. She put on teardrop earrings and dusted her cheeks with blush and narrowed her eyes on herself in the mirror.

Maureen called from the gate, ready for a showdown, but Pearly put on her white sandals and went with us to general's mess. We had an entire four-girl unit. We paraded through the base on wooden planks to keep our sandals above the dirt in our sundresses and bathrobe. I wore my dotted-swiss dress, wishing I were wearing it for Big Foot.

General's mess was the ritual Sunday night gathering of the general with his field-grade officers and some lower-level company grade too. They welcomed us. If any of the officers suspected Pearly was wearing her bathrobe, they were too polite to ask how come. I was assigned again to sit at the head table, along with Pearly. The officers talked about body count and gave the girls at the head table flowers.

We sat at round tables, and in the center was an enormous lazy Susan laden with food. I was seated by the general, who had a button by his plate to control the lazy Susan's spinning. Before we ate, the general made a speech that I think was something like a pep talk to his officers, commending them for the week's body count and missions accomplished. He talked about a company on Stallion who were heroes, men who had shown they were proven under fire and rightly belonged with the Fire Brigade. He said they had counterattacked viciously to smash the offensive, and the enemy had staggered back from the line of contact. Then he rang a bell, and we began to eat, and I thought this was not the way Big Foot would tell it if he had been there. I looked at the men eating and drinking and thought of the boys lying in a fetal coil with a tarp protecting them from the sun. I felt very confused.

Now and then I watched Pearly. She was cool. But she made small talk with them.

I knew the colonel on the other side of me slightly. It was his command-and-control chopper that I'd gotten a ride in once. He reminded me a little of Manfred. He was short and fit, with a chiseled, driven face. I was surprised at the end of the meal when he took a small package from his pocket wrapped in tissue paper and gave it to me. "Something to thank you for the sacrifice you are making by being over here. I know you don't smoke."

"I do," I said. I unwrapped it and found a butane lighter with the yellow-and-red Tropic Lightning emblem. "Oh, how sweet," I said.

"A memento," he said.

I took out a cigarette from my pocket to try it. The colonel held the lighter. I wondered if Pearly saw this and thought of the two of us on the bathroom floor at the Metropole Q giggling. We had just come in country. We had never flown in a chopper. We giggled about how to charm a boy. You touched a boy's hand as he lit your cigarette. I thought the colonel didn't need to be charmed. I held the cigarette in my mouth with my chin jutting and let the colonel bring the flame to it. "How sweet," I said again, taking the lighter. "Thank you."

The officers talked about their kids and their R&Rs. I liked the lighter and thought these men were decent enough people. They were like anybody hanging around the Post Office Drug, talking about their lives.

* * *

"Evening," our MP, Barrett, said when we came home. He was shy. He always said, "Evening" with huge force, as if it came out of his belly or his groin. But he never said another word. He patrolled our gate, carrying his rifle.

"Where are you going?" Pearly asked me because I was hanging around by the umbrella.

"I don't know. I might go to the office for a while."

Pearly let me go. She didn't make me sit and listen to her lambaste the officers.

I wanted to go for a walk, but I didn't get to just walk around the camp at ten at night looking for a grunt. I talked to Barrett from Mobile for a while. It embarrassed him horribly. So I told him I had to go finish some things in the office. He let me out the gate, maybe because it was too painful to keep trying to talk to me. He shouldn't have let me out.

I turned the office light on and left the door open for the small breeze. Outside was black. It was a little too still. I wanted to see Big Foot, and I had no way to find him. The night was so dark. What if we were overrun, and I was here away from the bunker and away from everybody? The MP should not have let me come. The world was so dark.

I rubbed off last week's runs on the acetate schedule board with a cloth and cigarette ash and assigned the runs for the next week. I planned the runs as if every place from Crook to the Cambodian border were secure.

I went to the worktable for a match to light a cigarette. I remembered the butane lighter in my pocket and used that instead, and I sat at the worktable. I could smell the butane on my fingers while I waited for sounds, but I was distracted by seeing a paper in the box where I got my mail. It hadn't been there that morning. Sunday brought mail like any day, but I hadn't gotten any that day. I picked it up.

The writing was an unfamiliar thin blue scrawl. The address was only "Delta Delta," one of our nicer nicknames. I ripped it open. Inside was one line in red. It said, "Be my lady."

I put the paper on the worktable and stared at it. It was army paper. "Be my lady." I knew the line. It was a line from a song I knew well because I played the tape over and over, and I heard it on fire bases. It was a Crosby, Stills, and Nash line from "Suite: Judy Blue Eyes." I heard it coming from a radio on the beach in Galveston.

The red letters looked like an awful stain, and I turned the paper facedown.

I went back to the schedule board. I tried to think about who I should assign to Brigade, who to Tay Ninh. But the red letters stained the run board. It was just a note from some grunt, but there was something malicious in the scrawl. I glanced at the door, but I made myself finish the schedule. I made myself press letters in black grease pencil across the acetate board.

The wooden step at the door creaked, and I dropped the pencil. Nobody came in. The MP was twenty yards away. I only had to scream. I looked at the window and the door, making a split-second decision between them for how I'd get out. But then out of the black, Big Foot leaned into the office light. That's when I was aware of my heart. It had stopped, and Big Foot got my heart beating again. I went to the door.

"Big Foot, Goddam you, you scared me," I said, kneeling down to where he was at ease on the floor.

I touched his dark hair and the circle of his ears. I whispered, "You scared me to death."

I was glad I was wearing my newish sandals that weren't too badly worn from scuffing through dust. I had saved one pair for good, not knowing what "good" would be. Big Foot was "good."

"Where've you been all day?" I was still whispering. I turned off the office light and sat beside him.

"Reading," he said.

"Reading?" I felt like I was talking to a child. "What were you reading?"

"I was reading about this guy Zorba who went to war and did awful things, but he says he was all that was real. He says, 'When I die, the whole Zorbatic world will die with me.'"

"Where were you?" I said.

"In my truck," he said. He put his head in my lap. "I was pretending I was home in Dad's truck. I could even pretend I was parked down this country road in the pines and I could smell pine sap. I swear. What have you been doing?"

"I had to take Pearly to general's mess. She went as a housewife. She got dressed up in a bathrobe and pop beads."

He kissed me. It was a gentle, slow kiss, ever so slow.

He looked at me. No jokes. No nothing. I couldn't begin to read his face.

"I hear stories about things that happen in country," I said. We were living in slow motion in the dark, and I had to touch Big Foot's chest; I held on to his fatigues to keep myself from floating up. I listened to the night while he held me and kept me from floating up. It was still, and I began to cry with no idea why. Only that I was scared this was the best it would be.

I heard our gate open and shy Barrett call, "Diana," because he wanted all his chickens in.

"Just a minute, Barrett. I'm coming."

We heard him turn and the sound of his boots on the road.

"Big Foot," I said, "did you write me a note?"

"If you're getting notes, they're not from me," he said. "Just a minute. Don't go."

"I'll see you tomorrow."

"No," he said.

And then I heard the sound of his boots as he was standing. Not flip-flops. He was wearing boots. I leaned down to touch them in the dark to know for sure.

"Oh, God, Big Foot."

"Don't mean nothing," he said. "I'm too damn short. Don't mean shit. Write to me."

"I'm never going to write to you. This hurts too bad."

"I don't care what you write. Write me what doughnut dollies do at general's mess. Then write me a bunch of garbage about love. You know, how you love me."

I said, "I'm never going to write you."

ARC Unit
Cu Chi

Dear Big Foot,
    Here's your letter. This is the last one. We are too busy trying to bring holidays to all you grunts.

I'll write you about general's mess. After this, I'm too busy.

Maureen says there's one thing we have to do and that's go to general's mess on Sunday nights. Pearly went with us again. The general gave a speech to start off the evening, a rundown on the state of the war, the body count, and about the outstanding bravery out on Trojan. He said Bravo Company held off two ground attacks, with backup from artillery, and you all are heroes. He said it was a remarkable effort.

He just talked about body count for Charlie. That must mean you are okay? He runs down the enemy body count for other units. Then he says tonight he is especially delighted to welcome us lovely ladies. Then we eat. The general has a button by his plate and he moves the food around on an electric lazy Susan. I'm not *even* kidding. That's how he passed around the beef burgundy.

He was a nice enough guy. He offered us his trailer to take hot showers and sit in air-conditioning.

You told me over and over about the patrol you were on with Mackie. I wonder what's happening out there.

Yours truly,
Diana

Trojan

Dear Diana,
Once in a while they send mail forward which is about the only humane thing I can think of the army does. I got a letter from my sister in Connecticut. She tells me all the times her kids are sick and I hear from Mom and Dad but they're

pretty busy. I'm not positive any of them are real anymore. You're getting to be the most real person in the world.

You want to know what we're doing. We've been building bunkers around the perimeter to hold on to this place, and in the night sappers try to break through. We machine-gun them down when they're sliding under the wire and the flares go off and we can see more of them running out of the woodline like ants and we start shooting them down before they get to the wire. We got 400 the past two nights counting air strikes. We follow the blood trails back to the woodline. Eight of ours took it in the sweeps. The lieutenant made us keep sweeping till he said the chances were we'd all take it. So we went back and watched Spookies come and hose it all down. When it's over we feel our bones to see if we're alive. There's your heroes. There's your general's re-markable effort.

I don't know what we're doing here. I think we're just out here for Charlie to shoot at. It's got nothing to do with lazy Susans and beef bur-gundy. We have the ARVN camp where the women fry up this fishy-smelling junk and dogs. Everytime they hear a chopper they sprawl on the ground. I'm sorry. You're the only one I have to write this to.

                                                        Big Foot

Chapter 10

The night before Christmas, Pearly stayed out all night. I covered for her, but I yelled at her like her mama should have when she came home. I went into her room dragging her Santa suit and mine. Colonel Stone had gotten us a chopper all day, and we were going to distribute Christmas gift bags—the Red Cross called them ditty bags—to every GI we could get to before dark.

"You're a fool," I said. "You're going to get hurt. This is no place for stuff like that. Besides, they'll catch you and send you home. And then I won't have you either. Who were you with?"

"Larry," she said. He was one of the guys who flew us around on 2nd Brigade runs.

"Well, don't do it again."

She said, "I don't love him," as if that made staying out all night just fine. "You're a fool to love anybody here."

"So why'd you take such a risk?"

She looked at me. "I'm just telling you I don't believe in true love. It was one of those cases of needing affection like you talked about. We didn't let anything else happen. I only slept with him. The only problem is that we fell asleep, and in the morning he was still holding me." She looked away. "And that was very nice, but it was not true love."

Pearly's face was as white as her name. I looked at her slim neck as she turned away from me. She was all angles and bones since she cut her hair off. She looked so tough except for the little bit of space she had between her front teeth, and now it was the little bit of space that stood out. She wasn't tough at all. She was as delicate as anybody.

"There's something about you," Pearly said, taking off her yesterday's uniform. "You know what you do? You paint with a fine brush." She took my hair and pulled it all back so she exposed all of my face. "I paint with a fat, broad brush, meaning I do something and then I chip away and peel away on what I did because I didn't mean half of it. I can be impulsive."

I laughed. "Impulsive. Pearly, just don't do it again." I dropped the suit on the bed beside her. It made her skin look even whiter. We were going to Stallion. We were going everywhere and Stallion too. I wasn't thinking much about Pearly except now she looked so white. But Pearly wanted to talk. I let her talk as long as she would start putting her arms and her legs into her Santa suit.

"But you," Pearly said. "You use fine strokes. You add touches, stroke by stroke, and every stroke is thought-out. I think you're building something."

She pushed my hair back again to make sure I was listening. "You're the reason I'm still here."

"You'd go home?" I had my suit nearly on.

"Diana, I can't figure your mind. How it could never occur to you to go home."

"It did. After my first run."

"No, I mean it's an effort every day for me to stay. You are so full of some kind of a sense of duty that takes you above all this shit that the war is about. With you it has more to do with souls than countries. How do you keep from getting cynical? My friends at home tear up everything. Oh, Christ, my headaches."

"You shouldn't stay out all night."

"Don't yell at me. I'm a soul."

"I know. Do you want some jelly-grass juice?"

That was a drink Hoa brought us. It had the consistency of pollywogs.

"If you gave it to me, I'd drink it. I want to go to bed," she said, lying down fully dressed in red fur.

"You can't. We have a chopper at six. It's Christmas." I gave her two aspirin and some canned pineapple juice. I brought the juice in a Dixie cup decorated with holly berries. We heard Maureen and Josie ringing Christmas bells down the hallway and into the latrine.

"Are we going to Stallion?" Pearly said.

"I told you yes."

"Well, then, let's go," she said.

We were on the chopper. I was shaking, the wind chilled me so much. It was Christmas. We were all together, all of us girls with our bags of Christmas gifts. I crouched in the wind with my Nikon pressed against my fur.

Pearly said, "I'm not going to let anything happen to you." Sometimes we switched roles, and she took care of me.

We landed at one fire base after another. I ate thirteen Christmas dinners. We served in the mess tents. God, is it hot in a mess tent in red fur.

We went to Stallion. It was our seventh stop. I stood dazzled by the lights the mess sergeant had strung around the mess tent. It rained, and the men came in across the wooden upraised floor, and I studied every face expecting his would be Big Foot's and trying to remember if this boy's face was Big Foot's. I put circles of mashed potatoes on soldiers' plates and made a well for the gravy that Josie served. I kept on putting down the potato server to snap a picture of a GI in nothing but dog tags and OD pants with his Christmas dinner.

It was so hot, but we didn't have our uniforms on under our Santa suits, so we had to keep them on. Maureen fainted. She was serving the turkey, and she asked if the person wanted white or dark, and then she fell over on the guy. At first we thought she'd been hit by a sniper, but there wasn't any blood. After we took off her fur, she got her color back. We gave her Kool-Aid and watched for snipers. We girls were very close that day. It made us four girls kind of close our circle. We were all thinking it could have been a sniper. Or our chopper could get shot down. But we seemed to be charmed.

I saw Big Foot when Maureen collapsed in the faint. He had been sitting on his steel pot waiting for me to finish serving. He had his rifle across his knee. When Maureen collapsed against the boy, we all thought we heard the b-r-r-r-r of an AK-47. Every-

body hit the ground. Big Foot flew into us to make
sure we were down like bowling pins. Everybody
stayed down, their eyes sharp, until it was clear
Maureen hadn't been shot. It was just a fact that people get picked off when they're not looking for it.

We quit serving for a while and made a circle
with Maureen in the medic's tent. That's when another Huey landed, and here came the division band.
This is a true fact, trumpets, a saxophone, a trom-
bone, an all-brass band. They set up in the circle between the 105 guns. They played Christmas carols
while some other guys broke out the beer and sodas
the general sent along with the band. Pearly said there
was no holding the general back if the body count is
a healthy number.

They played "Silent Night." I had to get a shot
of that, so we all went out and stood with the men.
The trumpets were really loud, and some people kept
their fingers in their ears, which is incredible after
the deafening sound of the artillery they've exploded.
Everybody sang "Silent Night," and then one of the
trumpet players played the verse again solo, sweat
dripping off his whole body. It was beautiful. I hope
Charlie heard. I took a picture of him.

I left the others while he was playing and found
Big Foot nearby. Nobody could talk. The brass was
louder than artillery. We stood near each other. What
could we have said?

But then the chopper came, and we had to leave,
and the division band formed a walkway for us to
pass through on the way to the chopper pad. They
honored us.

After Stallion and six more fire bases, we went
home. We had served meals in thirteen mess tents
and given gifts to hundreds of men. I had pictures

and more pictures. My pockets were bulging with film. We were grimy and sweaty and exhausted, and at our feet was a body bag the pilot was taking back to Graves Registration. I remember what Big Foot said in the hospital about the boy who died holding on to my hand. He said, It's worse when you know them. On the flight back I think we were all thinking, Please let me not know him.

We saw Pearly's Larry back at Cu Chi. Pearly hung back with him and asked me to, and we let Maureen and Josie go on ahead.

"You want a ride?" Larry said. "My Christmas present. A fun ride. I'll show you the sights."

He was talking about in his LOH, one of the small, bubble-shaped choppers. Pearly and I looked at it. "I'll teach you to fly it," Larry threw in. It was a lark. Pearly was nearly bursting, she wanted me to go so bad. I had my camera, and I would make poster-size prints. I was nearly bursting to go too.

"It's illegal," I said.

Pearly was getting in the chopper. I could hear the bell ring on her Santa hat. She held out her hand to pull me up, and it was Christmas. We had worked all day and Big Foot was not there and I imagined a ride like a carnival ride and I was a little girl who wanted one thing nice on Christmas. I took Pearly's hand and she pulled me in.

I don't think she'd have gone without me. Something funny had happened that day. There was something then among us girls that hadn't been there before. We felt it when we were in the circle while Maureen was still swooning, and we could see the arch of the trumpet player's back as he played a carol in the parching sun. We girls were from different worlds. But after that we let each other be what we were. We shrugged at each other's vanities. And if we needed to, we knew we could cling to each other.

Larry had on his flame-resistant Nomex flying suit. He put on his headgear that made him immortal, and the rotors lifted us up.

It was a carnival ride. We flew south over the Ba Bet Bridge that was mined every night, and every day an engineer swam under the metal crossworks to take off the detonating wires. We crossed so much water. There was almost as much water as land. Rivers, canals, swampy jungle, here and there a forest of mangroves. Hoa said it all used to belong to the sea, and her grandfather helped build the canals to drain off the land for more rice. Hoa talked like the rice itself was sacred. The Vietnamese grew it, they had to transplant the rice after it sprouted into the field—by hand—they prayed for it, ate it every meal, gave thanks for it, and they used it as an offering to the spirits of their ancestors. I wondered if my camera could catch that green.

Nui Ba Den kept me oriented. It is a dark, round volcanic mountain, and we could see it to the northwest of Cu Chi when it wasn't foggy. We flew near it and the rubber plantations. We flew just over the tops of the trees so radar couldn't pick us up, and then we'd climb fast to fifteen-hundred feet where small arms couldn't reach, only SAMS. Larry said not to worry about SAMS. I wasn't worried at all. I felt like maybe angels feel, swooping in and out of the canopies of trees. I took off my headphones and gave in to the beauty and the lushness. I shot a picture of a water buffalo with three boys on its back. We were so low I could see their faces and imagined laughing faces, but they were a blur. LOHs are fast, and we skimmed over the trees, and I was shooting pictures like my pictures would be the only pictures of South Vietnam. We swooped over square miles of rice paddies and wild reeds and now and then fields of sugarcane. I felt godlike. Seeing it all. Understanding it all.

But then we did something that pilots do not do. We came down an open area and it turned out to be the wrong open area. I had a flash of a memory, a Ft. Wolters Dance, men shaved nearly bald telling other peoples' war stories about coming down the wrong open area. Charlie can do a lot of things in an open area. A claymore in a tree. Or he can string a wire across the area so thin nobody could see to knock the chopper out of kilter. They told me a helicopter is balanced just so. If you were to touch your finger to its tail at a hover, the pilot can't recover.

Larry and Pearly and I were in a break in the trees. It was like the ultimate moment of understanding when out of nowhere the jungle gives way to open sky.

We were racing. It was a kind of suspension of life, it was a kind of teetering between life and death and Larry knew. Larry had to know. But the green all around was so beautiful and seductive. We would make a swipe through and then climb to safety and we would be heroic.

I was rational. I composed a list of things to do that my mind had come up with after we cut through the trees and Larry came down the open area. And it was so beautiful and I remember thinking I wished I could have had time to write once more to Mama and I wished I could have seen Big Foot one more time. But I let go so I could race. And that's when we flipped.

Charlie didn't have to fire on us or detonate a claymore. He just caught one of our skids on a wire and Larry couldn't recover.

When we flipped I knew I was dead and I don't remember anything except the bolt-hard impact and waiting for the thunder of our explosion.

We crashed on Larry's side, not my and Pearly's side. I went on taking pictures. I got a picture of Larry who hit a wire. That's a picture the UPI wanted. They wanted my roll of film. I told them I didn't *even* work for them, and I was giving them nothing. I don't know why I shot it. It's just that I was conscious after we went down and I was still cradling the camera and so I took a picture of Larry who was staring over his head. He was staring behind himself like a bird can do but a man can't. He was looking behind himself with banjo-wide, awed eyes. That's when I shot the picture. I was ready to shoot a picture of the VC who I knew were coming. I was ready for them to come.

But then I felt this grip of fingernails and then whole hands on my arms, and I saw Pearly clawing to get back to me. She was like a baby clawing into my lap and shrieking, and she laid her cheek on my cheek and shrieked. I knew she wanted me to make it go away. Her eyes were enormous, and I cradled her face against mine and I got blood on her white cheek, so I thought we were cut. I thought she shouldn't shriek so much in case Charlie's ears were near. "Pearly," I coaxed her. I put my fist over her mouth and struggled to get us out the opening. "Pearly, help me. You have to climb." I think she wanted to explode. She shrieked into my ear and clawed me as if she wanted to get inside of me. She could not bear herself. She wanted to be dead.

A Huey came and cast a shadow over us, and then men came to take us out. Pearly kicked at them and ripped their faces.

"What's her name?" the pilot asked.

I told him, "Pearly."

He said, "Be still, Pearly." He kept saying it while she fought him. He said, "Be still, Pearly. Pearly, be still. You're going to make it fine."

She wanted to stay out in the jungle, but they took us back to the unit. Maureen cried, and she called Saigon. She told Mary Ann we were all right, but Pearly wasn't. She thought she killed somebody. Larry was showing off for her, showing what a jock he was. How low, how fast, how there wasn't anybody he couldn't outfly.

Maureen tried to put Pearly's pajamas on her, but she couldn't. Pearly was trying to pull her hair out. I caught her in her room behind her beads slamming her pretty black Italian boy head against the wall, and when she grabbed her hair at the scalp in her fists, I grabbed her. We lay on her bed. Pearly coiled into herself and into my belly and breasts. I could smell her hair that had been sweaty from her Santa Claus hat. "Pearly, be still."

Chapter 11

It was Sunday and already January.

Pearly had moved her stuff to the bunker, and she wouldn't come out. She lived in there with exotic Asian animals that I imagined in my head and worked myself into such a panic over that I spent Saturday night down there too. "I came to protect you from pythons," I whispered in the morning when she discovered me.

"Go away," she said. That's what she mostly said now.

"There's a staff meeting," I said. We always had our staff meeting under the umbrella on Sunday morning.

Pearly didn't answer. She had not taken a run since Christmas, eight days ago. Maureen was letting it ride because Saigon said Pearly and I could take it easy for a while. Our hurts didn't spill much blood or expose our bone, and what blood there was Pearly had drawn with her own fingernails. But Maureen said a while was up. We didn't have enough girls as it was.

We had to appear before somebody doing an investigation. We said we were on a Christmas run.

"I got away with murder," Pearly said. That's when I imagined the pythons and spent the night with her.

There were two letters from Big Foot yesterday. I had them memorized. I lay on the cot in the bunker waiting for Pearly to tell me a story and let Big Foot fill the silence. I could hear his voice distinctly. It was like if you shut your eyes how you can imagine yourself under your own faded, lumpy comforter in your own little lair of a bedroom with dried-out flowers and glittery streamers for wearing at a football game tacked on your closet door and with a picture of Scarlett O'Hara kissing Rhett and a locket. I heard Big Foot's voice as distinctly as I could picture myself being there instead of being under a poncho liner on a cot with the potential pythons and Asian rats.

"They're talking about a stand down for us," Big Foot wrote me. "I'll believe it when I see it. We take mortars day and night here. Hunter-killers are part of the scenery. I'm trying to think of something to say that's not about the war. I think about going some place I've never been. Mackie's always talking about Buddhas. He just came back from Bangkok. He saw a lot of gold Buddhas on thrones. He had a guide and she took him to every Buddha temple in Bangkok. He brought me back a silk shirt. Not really my style. I asked my sister to send me a polo shirt. She said she was glad I had time to relax after work, but she hasn't sent it yet. The silk one makes your skin crawl."

The second letter was short. "We're coming in. Whole Bravo Company. Any chance, Diana. Do you come to all the stand-down bashes? I'll watch for you. I'll be standing by a sandbag wall in flip-flops. That's an order. You will wear shower shoes in rear areas. Otherwise I'd have worn my Oxfords."

"Breakfast," Maureen called.

"Come on up to eat," I said. "They're waiting."

"How did we hit that wire?" Pearly said.

I said, "We couldn't see it. Nobody could know it was there."

"Yes, but how did it happen?"

"It was stretched between the trees."

"Tell me again how it happened. We crashed on the side?"

"On his side."

We had done this more than once. Pearly wanted to get everything straight. I got up and sat on a box beside her.

"Just the thinnest strand of wire," I said.

"We were so low I could smell the elephant grass. The green of the jungle is so bright it's as if somebody painted the color on. I think the colors are brighter here than they are in the World."

I pictured Larry looking invincible in his helmet.

"I can hear their voices," she said. "The guys who rescued us. I can hear them from a huge distance. They kept telling me I was fine. Diana, I don't want to talk to you anymore."

"No, just this once, you keep talking."

Pearly stared at a splotch on the wall. But I didn't let up. I was still into reality. I took Pearly's square jaw in my hands. But Pearly pulled away. I made her sit up, and I brushed knots out of her matted hair.

Her hair was thick, and I gripped next to her

scalp and had to force a brush through it. "Mama used to braid mine when it was wet so she didn't have to listen to me howl when she brushed it."

Pearly didn't howl. She never winced, and I was no more merciful than Mama had ever been, and tears came to Pearly's eyes the same as they had to mine.

"Cut it some more," Pearly said.

"You hardly have any anyway."

"There's some scissors." She pointed to her duffel bag on the ground.

I got the scissors and cut her hair. Black curls lay like a nest of feathers on the bunker floor. That seemed to give her some relief.

I came up to the patio where Maureen and Josie were eating their coffee cake and drinking their milk under the umbrella.

"Did anybody feed Pearly?" Maureen asked.

"She was in the kitchen this morning eating C's," Josie said.

"I think if she's well enough to do that, she can come out. She can be a committee chairman. She can fulfill the unit commitment and go with us to general's mess tonight and all these events they expect us for. Pearly," she called.

"It could be," I said, "that general's mess is why she won't come out."

"I have to call Saigon," Maureen said. "She'll be sorry if I have to do that."

"She's already sorry," I said. "She keeps telling the story over and over like Big Foot told his story on the ward."

"I know she's sorry," Maureen said. "But she can't stay here like this."

Pearly appeared in the bunker door in her red bathrobe.

She was pale and bloated from staying indoors and eating little green cans of starch. I thought about how Maureen told us to wear makeup and act like girls and to "quit acting like you're in their platoon."

Pearly looked about as much like she was in a platoon as Veronica Lake. She didn't have long, straight hair like Veronica Lake, but she had the unflinching eyes. I used to watch the old Veronica Lake movies and imagine being tragic like her. I imagined swooping my hair back in one dramatic, telling gesture. But looking at Pearly now, I saw nobody could really be like Veronica Lake. Veronica Lake could change her clothes and take control of things. Real despair was embarrassing. Pearly was embarrassing to look at. She was getting to be irritating. Her eyes were circled in red from crying. She couldn't even change her clothes.

"We've got work to do," Maureen's pep talk continued. "We don't have room for spaced-out girls." It was true. We had three brigades to program to, the navy on the Saigon River, the men on Ba Bet Bridge and Nui Ba Den. We needed strong girls to do the unit's work.

"Okay," Pearly said, "I'll be social director."

I covered my whole face to stop up my laugh at the idea of Pearly, who cried when she came out of the bunker, as the unit's social director. The others covered their mouths, and no one laughed out loud. Okay. Pearly had offered a compromise.

Maureen took Pearly a sheaf of papers concerning social invitations. Pearly came out as far as the MP's chair, the MP having gone home at sunrise. She began to read through the invitations while we ate coffee cake and drank our milk.

"Sunday night, general's mess," Pearly said. "Attendance is required. Monday night, songfest, Twelfth Evac, seven o'clock, and a cookout at the Scout Dogs, four to seven. Tuesday—stand down, Bravo Company, Second Brigade."

"Isn't that the guys from Stallion?" Josie said.

I nodded.

"Isn't that Big Foot?" Maureen said.

I nodded again.

"Oh dear," Josie said. "Seventy-five drunk and horny grunts."

"I suppose you want to go," Maureen said to me.

"Yeah," I said.

"Well, you can't go unless we all go—not to a stand down—and Tuesday night is Brigade."

"I know that," I said. Maureen was one for protocol. I looked at her neat, composed face. She was a good girl. She didn't want the Cu Chi Unit to shirk formal military obligations. I felt so removed from her.

"I'll call Brigade," she said, "and say we're skipping a week. Let's take Diana to this stand down."

I should have been grateful, but I felt like a child. Too many people had control over me. I would have gone no matter what Maureen did.

Bravo Company. It probably wasn't worth it. But he was coming into Cu Chi. I couldn't not go.

A chopper hovered over us again. Our Sunday mornings had gotten to be a known ritual. When it was gone, we saw that Pearly had ducked inside the bunker.

Pearly couldn't get herself to general's mess. On

Monday night she sat on the bench outside the chapel at Twelfth Evac where the chaplain's assistant led a songfest. Maureen was getting impatient.

At five o'clock on Tuesday night I went into the bunker.

"I need you," I said to Pearly. "I've come to help you get ready."

She sat on the edge of the middle bunk bed with her legs crossed. She wore her Red Cross dress uniform and black heels, which were our going-home clothes.

"Look, honey, if you don't come to the stand down, I can't go. And if you don't go, they're going to send you home, and if you think nobody here understands what happened to you, you can believe nobody at home will."

"I'm social director," Pearly said, implying that made her indispensable.

"Get dressed, Pearly. We have to go."

Pearly got dressed in her black shift that made her look like a barmaid, but less so since she got her Italian boy haircut. There wasn't much to it, just a little cotton from her shoulders to her thighs. I put my arm in Pearly's, who was less demonstrative.

We all rode in a jeep, Josie in the front and us three in the back, which was better than having to ride in a truck and jump out the back like calves. The trip wasn't long, but we were hot and not totally of sound mind. The driver entertained us with a soliloquy on doughnut dollies.

"Five types," he said. "One. Your true nun. You know the type. Two, your asexual. Got a vise grip on the job. Three. Your basic hooker."

"Is this multiple choice?" Josie asked.

"Where was I?" he said.

I said, "Maureen, how do you find these drivers?"

"Number four," he said. "Your ol' pal. You know. One of the guys. She can drink you one to one, and you could read her your Dear Johns."

"How many Dear Johns can a person get?" I said.

"*Beaucoup*," he said. "You wouldn't believe."

"We'd believe," we said, laughing.

"Five," he said. "True love. The kind of girl who could walk around in a tarp and she'd still . . ."

"Tarp girl," we laughed, doubled over. "Who wants to be tarp girl?"

We left him, heartbroken, and understanding well how he could amass Dear Johns.

We pulled into the stand-down area. The site was a field with trash cans of iced beer—all the beer you can swallow in forty-eight hours—homemade grills that were metal drums, split and mounted on sawhorses and filled with coals. Across the coals were dozens of steaks with black lines where the grill cut across the flesh. Potato salad, baked beans in army vats. And the men. Pretty drunk, the drunk enhanced by the day's glare. Men slammed a volleyball over a net. Rec supply had outfitted them.

By the time we Red Cross girls got there, the sun was down and the faint outline of a half-moon shone above the hiss and steam of the grills.

I skimmed across the crowd. Big Foot was tall, but so were a lot of others. He wouldn't stand out. We stood out. I looked at Pearly to see how she was taking things. We stuck together and tried to be what the army sent us over for. Wild animal tamers. We

drank Coke and made small talk. Guys brought us
Cokes and plates of food and stories. Guys just wanted
to come up and talk.

I was talking to a kid from Lufkin when I saw
him. I couldn't really have described him—say, if my
mother had asked, "What's he look like?" I was almost surprised by what he looked like, because that
wasn't the familiar part. He could have been taller,
he could have been darker.

One time after he had been gone a while, I had
asked Pearly what Big Foot looked like, because I
couldn't for the life of me remember. "Kind of your
basic Mick," Pearly had said. "Sexy eyes. Good lips.
Deep, gravelly voice. He looks like a two-timing
womanizer."

"Yeah, right, Pearly," I had said. "I'm glad I
asked."

The familiar part, when I saw him, was something that cut through me. I would say it had to do
with sex. I listened to the guy from Lufkin, but what
I heard was lines from the Bible somehow tucked away
in me. "Let him kiss me with the kisses of his mouth."
That was getting nearer to it. "His fruit is sweet to
my taste." Lines like that. They were in the Bible. I
didn't want to walk away from the boy who was talking, but I couldn't hear him. Big Foot saw me. He
was standing by the sandbag wall, as he said he would
be, not in his Oxfords. He was with a guy who wore
a silk shirt unbuttoned who must be Mackie. Big Foot
had those sorrowful blue eyes. I had forgotten. He
had a joyless face and a voice too deep. Had I thought
he would leave the gravelly voice on Stallion as if that
were his warrior voice and not who Big Foot was?

I knew we couldn't stay long. I went to stand in

the dust between a Sheridan tank by the road and a throng of GIs. Big Foot walked over toward me. He stood with his hands on his hips over his fatigue pockets, looking less formal than the night we had a date and he had smelled like after-shave and told jokes.

Soldiers continued to come and offer me food, drink, smokes, matches, patches, gossip, looks of love, war stories. I listened to the war stories. Big Foot never wrote those in his letters except his answer to mine about general's mess. The music blasted. The men shouted above it louder and louder as the night got darker.

Someone had brought me a steak and a mound of potato. The steak was rare, and it bled when I cut it while I listened to the war.

I thought, Let me just know what it feels like to be touching him. Please, could we kiss. A lovers' kiss. And once I had that, there'd be no end to what I'd want. I would be wanton. I stood chastely holding my paper plate of potato salad, surrounded by men, plotting how I could be wanton. I wanted to ask him if he still had his map of impregnable forts for two people, but he seemed so distant and sad, and I wondered if we made a little baby if we could have been less sad. I would have done that. I had known the boy from Georgia a dozen weekends longer than I knew Big Foot, but we had always kissed with most of our clothes on. It was just that I was from a small Texas town where it was the custom to make a boy wait. Texas seemed unreal and its customs contrived. I remembered one of the songs Hoa sang that she translated. The song said that the laws of nature were the true laws of humans. Hoa was making more sense than Mama. Big Foot and I were of nature. I felt like we fit into something bigger than us.

"Maureen's going to make us leave soon," I told him.

He said, "When do you get R and R?"

"Next month."

"Same same," he said. His face was Greek, I decided. Irish-Greek. He had freckles across his Irish-Greek nose.

"Where are you going?" I asked.

"Mackie keeps talking about Bangkok. I owe it to him to see these goddamn Buddhas."

He had a clipped way of talking and very low, almost gruff. "Goddamn Buddhas," I repeated. Our eyes had not left each other's, as I imagined it was when people said, I take this man, I take this woman.

We could have run. We should have. But there wasn't much of any place to go.

That wasn't the end, though, of Big Foot and Mackie for the night. The top sergeant drove the Delta Deltas home himself in a tank because *Beaucoup* Dear John had in some way gotten incapacitated, the top said.

Back home, Josie invited some of the MPs for a sort of party. They had an ice chest of beer and were having a wonderful time.

Pearly and I pulled up the last lawn chair. We sat in it together and quietly drank. The beer was cold, and the MPs kept passing the cans.

"Shit, shit shit," I muttered. "That's what I waited months for?"

Pearly nodded and wiped beer off her chin.

"I've waited months to see him, and when I do see him, I wish I hadn't because it's so frustrating. The letters are better. You can read them and reread them, and they're kind of schmaltzy, but in letters you say things."

Pearly shook her head. "Stand downs are number ten."

We had drunk several beers between us.

"I hate people," I said. "I hate Big Foot."

"Me too," Pearly said, and tried to get up.

I put my leg across her. "You're not going anywhere," I said.

"I'm going to bed."

"Not down there."

"I don't know."

"When's Tet?" I said.

"I don't know that either," Pearly said.

"The first day of the first lunar month."

We slowly lifted our eyes and saw the sky hugely lit with stars.

"Where's the stupid moon?"

"I don't know," Pearly said.

"Let's go to Tet," I said.

"Where is it?"

"Everyplace. Not here."

"Everyplace."

"Pearly?"

"I'm going to bed," Pearly said.

"I never drank beer before. It's kind of going to my head."

"You never had a beer? How old are you?"

"I don't know, about nineteen."

"God, you're latent."

"I don't think a person can be latent. They can be late."

Pearly looked at me and poured her beer over my head. I shut my eyes while it ran off my hair and down inside my dress.

Beer dripped off my eyelashes. "You're still not sleeping in the bunker," I said.

I poured my beer over Pearly's head and made Pearly look like a pixie. "God, that feels good," she said.

We leaned back, refreshed, and watched the stars. I said, "Hoa told me about Tet. At Tet every sorrow is set aside. We'll go to Hoa's house for Tet."

I must have fallen asleep with my head on Pearly's shoulder. I had gotten Pearly out of the bunker, and I wasn't going to let her back down. I didn't remember falling asleep, but I vaguely remembered Pearly hauling away on my arm to get me to wake up. And as if in a foggy dream, I saw Big Foot and his friend Mackie big as life on top of our bunker. I didn't know the facts till Pearly told me in the morning. She said Big Foot was in a rage. There had been a storming of the bunker. The MPs wouldn't tell us anything. All of a sudden it became something among men. But they said it was a doughnut dolly's fault.

Chapter 12

ARC/Cu Chi

Dear Big Foot,

    You know we are only four girls and everybody is painfully chivalrous to us here. Let's write and I'll never go on the Stallion run and we'll never have to see each other because I'm thinking maybe that's best. We can go on writing like we have been and pretend I'm not at headquarters. Let's pretend I'm back in Texas. I'm sorry they caught you on our bunker, but you were hard to miss. I don't understand at all what you were doing.

                    Your very good friend,
                    Diana

Big Foot answered me from Stallion.

Stallion

Dear Diana,

Not seeing you is not the answer to my problem. I like your braids. I like the way you stand with your hand on your hip and tell the CO to fuck off when he told you to go inside with the officers. I like watching you all right. You need makeup about like a flower needs paint. I liked having you spare me five minutes. Jesus Christ, Diana. I've got more than five months to go. I'm not going to spend it finding new ways to suffer.

After we got good and drunk, long after you Cinderellas went off with the top, Mackie and I found our way to your hooch. It's the only one barricaded like a 5 star's—concertina wire over the top. You are the nation's wealth. But we climbed up and guess what we saw? You and Pearly and that redhead—Josie?—lounging in lawn chairs under an umbrella drinking beer with a dozen MPs at your feet.

The problem is that people aren't supposed to scale the doughnut dollies' barbed wire and sit on their bunker. This joker at your gate with his weapon ready told us so. We think you and Pearly were fuckin' noble to say you knew us and if you hadn't been more soused than us, it might have done some good. You seemed to think the whole thing was a veritable riot. Josie was rolling in the corner. Do you remember any of this? You draped yourself over the gate, pleading you'd let us in when the guard's back was turned. "Sure," he said, "and they climbed up the bunker to perch like doves." Oh, you liked that one. And you and Pearly sang, "Leaving on a Jet Plane" for us till they marched us out of sight. For your peace of mind, Diana, they had pity and just took us home to our lieutenant. He was vulgar but impressed. I can't actually say what he said but like the rest of the goddamn company he remembered the one in the dotted dress, a little too fuckin' genteel to be tramping through III Corps mud. But you probably already know where they took me since you're such chums with the MPs. They dragged Mackie away. They probably hanged him.

Maybe I'll see you on the jet plane,
Big Foot

I wrote him back.

ARC/Cu Chi

Dear Big Foot,
    I think you overreact. I take it you like the way I look. You're saying compared to a few thousand men you'll take me. Don't you see? Everybody loves me in some awful, impersonal way. You were different. I never saw you but you were more my friend than anybody. I mean, sure, I have lots of guys who are friends, dozens, hundreds if you count all of those we program to, but they are my job. They're like brothers, like sad people to cheer up. I don't want to go to bed with them. They drain me. They're like patients.
    Your letter was really screwed up. Of course I remember you on the bunker and Pearly and I

did sing "Leaving on a Jet Plane." But I didn't drape myself on the gate. If nothing else, my mother taught me good posture. Pearly said I may have leaned against it a little. And I didn't tell that officer to fuck off, I told him to go to hell. Generally speaking, I don't say fuck.

As ever,
Diana

P.S. I'm glad you do. You're the only one who does. All the other guys are afraid to corrupt me. You talk to me like a regular person.

Stallion

Dear Diana,

How are you?

Nobody brought out any games this week. I'm having to work myself up so I don't write pure shit. Have you ever sat in a bunker five days and five nights with a guy in a silk shirt playing blackjack? It used to rain and give us a break and now it's just hot without any relief. We wait for news of Charlie. We used to sweat and shiver at the same time and now we just sweat.

Mackie says he's sneaking over to the ARVN camp where they've got some girls. There's a house right outside the perimeter. I told him there's no future in that house. He's going a little crazy out here. I get R&R soon but he just got back. He says it's better not to go 'cause you feel so fuckin' rotten coming back. I've been letting your letter sink in. I read it every hour or so. Come out if you can. I know you'll be busy. If

you come with Maureen you'll do your game
about six times, slop up the food, go around to
every bunker with your calendars. Most of the
guys already have them plastering their wall.
They had a game on the moon flight. It was fine,
man, it was a good break and a laugh. Just stay
away from the platoons fresh in. They can't take
smiling girls. This reads like a veritable sermon.
I bet your mother's letters are more catchy. Exactly when do you get leave next month?

                                              Big Foot
     I can't believe you really stood here where
I'm standing. Did I dream it?

                                            Dong Tam
Dear Big Foot,
     I went south to Tiger's Lair on a dust-off.
There was a nurse—the only other female I'd seen
in a chopper. She was holding up an IV over a
guy on a stretcher. She stood with her fatigue
trousers beating in the wind all the way and when
the chopper was still hovering she was the first
to jump out and then the stretcher carriers jumped
and they ran the soldier to a truck. What good
is any female in this country unless she's got an
IV? She never looked at me. I was wedged in by
the gunner, there were so many wounded. She
never looked at me even though we were the only
females. It was because she knew I didn't have
an IV.

                                               Diana

Stallion

Dear Diana,

I can't think of any answer to what you say.
I guess it's true, except we'd be so goddamn forsaken here without you. My sister's got this little
kid who wrote me. He said he guessed he needed
more life than me because he's younger. He thinks
they send the old ones to Vietnam. Maybe you
do need less life if you're old. Less potatoes, less
blood. I feel very very old except when I think
of you. And when I think of you I think I love
you.

Big Foot

ARC/Cu Chi

Dear Big Foot,

What a nervy kid. You say you love me you
think. I have been offered rides on F-4s. I have
been offered weekends in Singapore, a chance to
begin a musical career with Special Services. I
have been offered a general's trailer with hot
water. And you say you love me you think. I
don't want to love you, Big Foot, no kidding.
You are a pathetic sight, all you skinny grunts.
I like your eyes and how you talk. I hear your
voice sometimes when I'm lying in bed. I feel
like a schoolgirl to feel your eyes on me. This is
going to hurt a lot.

Pearly and I go on as many runs together as
we can. She isn't recovered from the crash.
Sometimes I feel like I'm pulling her back so she's
not just a shadow. But I'm holding on. I'll get

her back. A lot of girls including her think this is no place to get into things like love. But of all the people over here, you are the one I had to meet so I didn't have any choice.

I look the way I do I guess because I have my mother's bone structure. She's the town postmistress. She used to wake me up to tell me to sleep straight. She was very concerned about the development of my spine. My father won a Purple Heart in North Africa in World War II. I used to look through his scrapbook Mama kept about the war and try to find my father's face in all the group photographs. Mama writes me almost every week. Sometimes just a few lines to say the Christmas cactus bloomed. She says don't get attached to any officers over there and every time, I promise her I won't. She says in WW II the doughnut dollies really had doughnuts and they hung around with the officers.

I read a lot of novels. Mama complains wherever I am is a fat novel with my comb inside for a bookmark. I studied nutrition at college but I would rather be studying poets when I go back. That won't get me a job. Maybe I'll sing in a tavern when I go home. I love to sing. I sing Judy Collins songs. What do you want to do when you get out of here? And I like cinnamon toast with cappuccino. Honest to God, Big Foot, why am I writing this garbage? I don't know. I can't see you. Is there any chance you can come in? Maureen lets us come home by nine or ten after all the events we have to go to. We could sit in the lounge and talk about old times.

I'm trying to work out the date I get leave.
Sometime in February.

Love,
Diana

Big Foot did come in with Mackie. They came
in while the base was on a red alert, and we took
some mortar rounds out by the Scout Dog Unit. Big
Foot had come in to see the dentist, but he came in,
in truth, for the minutes he had in our bunker. He
had been there so briefly, that was like a dream too,
and the reality of it existed only in the letters about
it that I could read and reread. Reading and writing
the letters took longer than the time we had.

Stallion

Dear Diana,
        I'd take the drill seven days a week if I'd get
to see you afterward. And they drill, man, they
figure if you're coming all the way in they'd better drill something. It was worth it to touch your
face. More than five months I have been imag-
ining what you felt like. I can't talk to a fuckin'
person out here. The lieutenant thinks I'm
touched. He wants to hurry me off on R&R. He
thinks we picked up some stuff on my dental
check.
        I've got the papers for 11 February, 14 days
and counting—for Bangkok. We could meet in
Saigon. Can you? All I need is enough life for
14 days.
        Your guards are nothing if not diligent.

What's it take to get into that compound without bringing on reinforcements?

Since Cu Chi was taking rounds I was glad you stayed in your bunker, even though the shelling was a good 2 km off. But the alert got us inside. Mackie was going to wail but I said that was going too far considering where the rounds were hitting. That was some game you were playing. The army buys you for us and you buy 3M games for you. Fair enough. *Sinh loi*, man, I mean about breaking your streak. I'm pretty good at trivia games. You didn't think I knew any fauna of Southeast Asia. I lost points on your English poets, deceased, category. But I read everything Kazantzakis wrote, or at least what I could get ahold of at the Special Services library. You already know that. We know a lot about each other.

Mackie doesn't know when he's gone too far sometimes but his category, Bravo Company—Soldiers of Irish descent, deceased—won me the game. We weren't cheating. Those three guys I put were real. I can see you chewing your lip over Kazantzakis characters. I'll forgive Maureen anything for the ten minutes she gave us after the all clear. I've seen you for a total of six and one half hours now. Do you want to go dancing?

Love,
Big Foot

ARC/Cu Chi

Dear Big Foot,
You two looked like escapees from a camp

in your silk shirts, except for the ammo. If you hadn't come slamming in here like two psychos with your weapons hanging off you, they'd have let you in nicely. We have this picky rule that soldiers don't come in armed.

But I'll go with you. I don't know, Big Foot. You did look less like a waif this last time since you were wearing a shirt. It was a really ugly shirt, though. You can tell Mackie. I think Hoa has decided if she can't have you, she'd like to have Mackie. He seems kind of stoical, kind of like a Buddha himself.

I can be at Tan San Nhut on the 11th. I wonder how old you are.

Love,
Diana

And I wrote him again.

Cu Chi

Dear Big Foot,

I told my father . . . did I tell you I talk to my father? The funny thing is he answers me. I told him we were going to Bangkok. He said to tell you he's glad you're a corporal and he says for you to keep your head down.

Hoa keeps stealing my underwear and what comes back off the line has messages. I'm wearing ones now that say, "Hi, Sweetie." Bras at the PX start at 38D. I don't know who they think is living here. I am out of anything pretty. My skin is parched and my dotted swiss decomposed, but I love you.

Diana

Stallion

Dear Diana,

I told Mackie we were going and here is what he said: you got to be shittin' me. There was a spark of life in him.

I didn't tell my father. He says talking to me is like talking to a wall and we haven't talked in years. But I've been thinking about him. He fixes clocks and all my life there's been a bunch of broken Seth Thomases in the parlor chiming midnight all times of the day and night. Dad never heard them. You know how some people get used to sounds and things. But I never did. I used to wake up to the whirring noise that comes before the bonging. For days I've been hearing the fucking whirrr—but no bong. My head's going to bong like the Liberty Bell at Tan San Nhut.

I love you,
Big Foot

So much had happened since Christmas. Death got so close to the whole unit. Real death, and now real life, the kind you could taste. How clear it was none of these men was charmed. I thought of the boy who I gave my strength to while he was slipping away, and I had to wrap my arms around myself to keep the chill back. No matter how much power Big Foot and I willed to that tiger's-eye, Big Foot wasn't charmed. Death happened all around. But not to the girls in the Cu Chi Unit. Pearly and I hit a trip wire and we didn't die, and Maureen could have been hit by a sniper but she wasn't. We were the charmed ones. We walked through fire and were untouched. I thought Opal was right about what females could do, and I never anymore worried about us.

Chapter 13

My mind was whirling. I didn't know how I could live through a day and a night. Today was Sunday. Tomorrow was Bangkok. I could not picture Bangkok. I pictured golden shrines and hearsay from grunts who came back. I pictured walking beside Big Foot in a golden city. I pictured us walking together as if that was our right. We were everyday people. I pictured us someplace nice, like a beach, eating Cracker Jacks. No one served me bloody steak, and no one gave me his skinny, mangy puppy so it wouldn't get cooked.

We were on the patio. I had washed my hair and was letting it dry in the sun. Maureen was sunbathing, stretched on her front and exposing a long bare back. Her purple straps trickled across the cement. Pearly was watching the white clouds, and I wanted to talk to her about sex.

I didn't know anything about sex. When I was

eleven, Mama gave me a pamphlet with a diagram of
the fallopian tubes. That was as close as we ever got
to talking about sex. At school in Texas, if a girl had
slept with a boy, she would be too ashamed to say
she had slept with him. If my friends had, they would
never have told me what happened to their bodies. It
was a weakness in a girl to want somebody that way.
I felt very weak.

"Pearly," I said.

She had lined her eyes in black that morning.
Her eyes were dark and her neck so white, and I
wished we could sit in the rain like we had the day
she came and pretend nonsense things.

"What if I get pregnant?" I said.

She turned her black eyes on me. "Getting pregnant is not the problem," she said. "Getting pregnant
would be a neat trick."

"You mean while they're counting bodies."

"And stringing human ears around their necks,"
she said.

We had seen that. And Pearly had slept with a
boy who was dead. We breathed the same air as the
boy, and we saw his banjo eyes. It made sex more
important. It was life, and I wanted to talk about
it. I was skimming the trees, awed by the green,
and I knew about the wire and I needed to talk about
life.

"What if I wanted to get pregnant? What if I
wanted to step where he stepped and get real fat with
a baby Big Foot."

But I couldn't get Pearly to talk about life. I
wanted to pinch her face between my hands the way
Mama used to do to me to get my attention, but she
still wouldn't. I threw my head back to let the sun

singe my hair and burn its shape on my eyeballs.
That's when I remembered Hoa.

I remembered the bright red packets Hoa left on
our pillows. She said red was for luck. Inside was a
piaster for wealth and a sticky sweet fruit wrapped in
banana leaves. She said that was for health. Tet was
the name of a battle to me. Mama sent me clippings
from *Time* magazine about where Charlie might strike
this year at Tet. But Hoa pedaled over here with the
echo of the nuns screeching after her—you could hear
it because she was so cheeky like Pearly used to be—
and all she could talk about was the feast and the
dragon parade. I looked at the desolate brown and
OD green of Cu Chi Base Camp.

"Pearly," I said. "Come on."

"Don't you dare," Maureen threatened.

We had already gotten our periods in sync, and
now we could read each other's minds.

"Nothing will happen to us, Maureen," I said.

She said, "General's mess at 1800," and there was
the scene of all us girls sharing hair spray and earrings and beads and feeling risqué going out without
nylons because these men were like our uncles and
algebra teachers.

"We're going to a dragon dance," I told Pearly.

Pearly didn't look so much different anymore.
She was her same cynical self. But she stuck by me.
She called me Sanity. If I wanted to go to a stand
down, she'd go; if I wanted to go to a dragon dance,
she'd go. I thought she needed a dragon dance. Hoa
said it was red and yellow and loud, and that sounded
like life.

We walked down the hall. "How we going to get
there?"

"I'll get us a jeep."

She nodded. We had never driven the roads in the countryside. The roads weren't secure. Pearly didn't question me. I was Sanity.

Sanity got us a jeep. The only problem was we got the same jeep driver. He had received several more Dear Johns since the last time we met, and he told us about all of them driving through the country. The road was paved. It was like a modern strip through an ancient land of hand-cultivated fields and water buffalo. In our blue dresses, we were bright targets, riding high in the jeep, bumping through hamlets and past shabby roadside cafés where armed boys drank Cokes from bottles and stared.

Dear John was armed. He had a flak vest and a steel pot beside him on the seat. I picked up the flak vest. It required the strength of both arms to do it. I put it on over my dress and felt the huge weight press into my shoulders and force my body into the jeep's innards. Pearly took off her boonie hat and put on the steel pot. Dear John had drawn peace signs over the helmet's camouflage fabric and written "War Sucks."

I thought of the men we knew there. They showed off their tracks to us as if they were showing off their Chevy convertibles. I remembered one place where it was one guy's birthday. Somebody put a lit match in a C-ration pound cake for him and everybody sang "Happy Birthday." I didn't want anything to happen to us. I wanted to stay with these people.

The countryside was very lush. This was Vietnam's early spring. The country was in bloom with yellow blossoms and fruits that were not familiar, but when I tasted the ones Hoa brought to me, they had familiar tastes. Watermelons were shaped like basket-balls, peaches were bald, and plums were white. But if you shut your eyes to taste them, they tasted like home. We saw another café where a row of banana trees leaned against a small wooden shack. A girl sold tea and cigarettes and 105-mm brass shells shaped into vases. And more armed boys stood under a corrugated metal awning.

We got to the village where a dozen children blocked us and begged for anything, and I snapped pictures of their huge smiles. "Move it!" Dear John yelled. "Move, you little gooks." But then he stopped short and hit the ground because there came a barrage of fire.

"Chrissake, hit the dirt!" he yelled, and Pearly and I shot out of that jeep and dropped to our bellies at its side. There wasn't time to be afraid, except I was aware I had on Dear John's flak vest. I lay wedged between the jeep and John. I could smell a very sweet smell, some kind of flowers in blossom, and the smell of the Fourth of July, and Dear John, who smelled like the fried chicken they had served in the mess tent. I also heard the blast of gunfire. It filled the village street. I gripped Pearly's arm as if to keep her from running off and buried my face in her sleeve, in her black armband.

I felt a hand on my shoulder. Ah, I thought, ah, you will not hurt us. I will protect us. If I had a gun, I would have used it. I thought of the boys drinking Cokes from bottles. I would have to use it on them. If I had one. Oh, shit. I opened my eyes in a fury, but I saw the black eyes of a very small boy. He didn't have a rifle. He had a string of what at first looked like ammunition, but I saw they were red firecrackers. I looked past him through the children. The road was littered up to their ankles with red casings from firecrackers. The barrage of gunfire still filling the air was firecrackers. The boy smiled. He was missing his front tooth and he called me "Diana," pronouncing the syllables slowly and loud. That's how they welcomed us to Hoa's village.

Dear John got up quickly. Pearly sat there cross-legged, staring the little kids down. Then the band of kids led us through the village to Hoa's orphanage. We passed a tall tree in full bloom with red blossoms that looked like the redbud tree in a Texas spring. Men and women and little children stared at us from every doorway. The orphanage was a small house with a thatched roof and with yellow branches that made an arch at the door. A nun opened the door. She wore a white cap with a white cloth that fell to the small of her back. We entered a room with bamboo walls, and on the walls were long panels in red with yellow characters. The children chattered and squealed over the blast of the firecrackers and what sounded like a pig through the back door.

I said carefully a phrase Hoa had taught me: "*Co Hoa o dau?*"

The sister gestured to the children to be quiet and chased after one boy, barraging him with a high-pitched singsong tirade of words that in the end must have meant "Get Hoa." The children wanted me to take their pictures. They asked for "chocola, choc-ola." Some of them were missing an arm, and one girl ran on a crutch and one leg. I looked around the room at the table laden with crockery vases of flowers and spread with food.

On another table was a bowl of bananas and mangoes and the white plums. They burned red candles, and beside them three sticks of incense in a small vase. And everywhere was the perfume of the blossoming branches. On the table were photographs of families and some other photographs were taped to the walls and I understood that the nuns had let the children do this to honor their parents.

A chill went through me. I looked at the table and the children who were helping to prepare the favorite foods of their parents who died. They wore shorts. They had thin brown legs and long brown faces. They had white teeth and dancing eyes. They licked their lips. They were hungry too.

Pearly said, "If red's lucky, they are drowning themselves in luck." She had a fistful of red casings. She looked so beautiful that day. Her black hair and her white cheeks and the red explosions in her hand and the thunder all around us.

Hoa had translated a Vietnamese saying for me. "Human beings cannot stand in the way of heaven's design," she had said. Another time she had said, "What is to be must happen, as day follows after night." The Vietnamese seemed to have endless ways to say that. And she said they blamed all losses on themselves. They had not honored their ancestors enough. They had to pray more and sacrifice to make a better Karma.

"They're honoring the dead," I said to beautiful Pearly. Pearly shined, and I thought I brought her back.

She said, "The dead are going to cover their ears and run."

And we laughed with this image of a bunch of live and dead people carrying on, feasting and gossiping. The Vietnamese talked as much to their ancestors as to their children. They held on to old souls.

We could feel it that day at this party with spirits. The air was so sweet. I was nearly overcome with reds and yellows and the sweet, flowery air.

The cloth on the altar was red, and the flowers were heavy with perfume. They were in this world for now, and they were celebrating. Tet was everybody's birthday.

Hoa flew in. I could tell she never suspected we'd come. She fluttered around, bringing us things and saying, "How happy, how happy." And not knowing we'd ever come, she'd taught the children my name. The little thief loved us. She nodded formally to me and to Pearly, and then they all began a rush of preparation.

"Where's the dragon dance?" I asked.

"No, we eat. We eat and eat," she said. "You are come." She rubbed her frail self as if Tet would make her stout and muscle-bound. We went with her and sat on straw mats and drank strong tea that bubbled and six courses of food. Hoa explained all the dishes and what was in them.

"Try," Hoa said.

We had bowls of soup that we ate holding the bowls near our chins and scooping the soup in our mouths with big spoons. Pearly drank it down.

"Hm, what is it?" she said.

"You call it chrysanthemums.".

"The flower?"

"The top tender stem and leaf of the flower."

We tasted a thin broth with peppers and rice and fish and gingerroot. It was spicy and tangy. We ate what Hoa called water coconuts. She described how the tree grows in the river and the coconuts grow in bunches. She said the children smack the whole bunch on the bank to harvest them and cut them in half for the meat. We ate mung beans in a sweet cake. The mung beans were yellow-orange, the color of pumpkins. And finally there were rice cakes, sweet bananas and rice that were boiled in banana leaves.

Dear John did not like chrysanthemum soup. He explained he'd already had fried chicken. One of the girls was solicitous of him. She had lost her right arm at the elbow and served him sweet cakes, which he wolfed, with her one good arm. Then he started to come on to her, and when Hoa's back was turned to the brewing tea, and while John was sprawled on his mat in a kingly way, Pearly jabbed him in the gut with her knee.

"Haven't you got any manners?" she hissed.

He looked around at her like a surprised slapped child, but he looked back at the gentle girl and told Pearly, "Butt out."

He and the girl moved away, and we could hear them in the corner, him with the single line of French everybody knew and giggled over in junior high. *Voulez-vous coucher avec moi?* and I thought he could have done better. The girl smiled, and Dear John ran his hand down her one arm. The girl wanted money. He touched her black hair and tried to make her eyes dreamy like his, like boys do. But she lowered her eyes, giggling, and said "Five hundred."

"Yeah, sure," he said.

"Now pay me," she said. "Pay me."

When they had left, Hoa said, "Now little sister can have money for buy incense to burn at her ancestor's altar. Now she will have incense for every night. Better to soothe the spirits." Hoa spoke in the same tone she had used to describe chrysanthemum soup.

"Was this village bombed? Is that why so many children are hurt?"

"Free-fire zone," Hoa said. "Not today. Before. They tell us to run for our life. But my parents say this is our home."

"Who told you to run?"

"They have speaker, how to say it?"

"Loudspeaker?"

"Yes, loudspeaker from the helicopter. I was a little girl. To Vietnamese, home is our mother, you know? We love our home as we love our mother. We could not run away."

We walked back toward the jeep. Pearly whistled, and Dear John came out of hiding. Mama had sent me a bag of candy valentines. Pearly and I gave each child a valentine because they followed us, a throng. The children scrutinized the red writing, the "Hug Me" and "Be Mine." They carried the valentines in their palms, watching them as they walked as if something might hatch from them. Hoa said, "Come back tomorrow for the dragon dance." Not tomorrow, I knew.

Maureen was furious. Pearly and I had gotten back to the base by 1800 hours, entirely too early to miss general's mess, so we got Dear John to drop us off at a signal company's headquarters where they were showing a movie. It was a comedy, and we came out holding our sides and transplanted to the World. By the time it was over, we had missed even the coffee and lingering of the mess. But Maureen had called the MPs and was about to call Saigon when we walked into Happy Hooch.

Maureen lit a cigarette and glared at us. She called the MPs back to say we were found. "Never do this to me again," she said. "Never."

"No, never," we said together.

We were charmed.

Chapter 14

couldn't sleep. I got up and did what had become a habit when I couldn't sleep. I wrote to Big Foot, but I didn't plan to send it.

I love your letters. I'm almost afraid to see you. That's not true at all. I want to see you so bad that I'd almost rather keep waiting to see you, because when I see you it will be here and then it will be over. That's what I'm afraid for, when it's over.

They don't have much in the way of pretty things at the PX. I went to look. It's real hard shopping for things like that because guys are always stopping you and saying I know you, you came to Meade or wherever. I'm always bumping into guys like that. But I bought a tape. I got another Crosby, Stills, and Nash. I remember listening to them on the beach at Galveston. And

Pearly listens to Janis Joplin—"I Got Dem Ol'
Kozmic Blues Again, Mama."

We're a pretty close unit. We give Maureen
a rough time, but we'd probably all die for anyone of us.

I got offtrack. I was leading up to something when I was talking about the PX, how
things there start at 38D. I couldn't exactly write
Mama and ask for black lace undies. But I want
you to like me. When I wrote that, I was imag-
ining your hand on me. On my not quite 38Ds.
What I was leading up to was that I'm pretty
much a virgin. So that's how it is. I never wanted
anybody before you.

I thought that was a better letter than the one I
sent. It was less flip. I wasn't flip, but I didn't send
this one. By the time Big Foot read it, I probably
wouldn't be one anymore. He would have figured
everything out, and that would be over too.

Pearly and I had howled over the way to charm
a boy by squirting spray cologne on the letter before
you fold it. Opal had packed a mister of Straw Hat
in my trunk, so I sprayed Straw Hat on the letter. I
folded it and put it in the box with the letters Big
Foot wrote. It smelled like heaven.

At six in the morning the girls were in their baby-
doll pajamas and bustling around the hooch in a bleary-
eyed way. I got up to go to the bathroom and was
entranced with the activity. I sat cross-legged on the
couch in the lounge and watched them.

"You're gonna be late," I sang. They had early
choppers to catch. I had a midmorning chopper

to Tan Son Nhut. Maureen put her hands over my eyes.

"It's okay," Pearly said. "Just make her promise to act surprised."

"All right, who snitched the cake mix?" Josie said. "Somebody opened the box and ate straight cake mix. That's disgusting."

The girls were baking me a chiffon cake. They baked one layer in a skillet because we didn't have any cake pans. Hoa came in. There was a lot of muffled giggling between her and the cooking girls. After a while she brought the laundry to the lounge and watched American cooking with wonder. In the end we ate wedges of the white chiffon cake and drank Lancers in thick army coffee mugs. Pearly made a toast: "To you and what's his name, the guy on the bunker."

"O'Maley," I said.

"O'Maley," she repeated.

I was so happy. Big Foot O'Maley.

Maureen looked at Hoa, who flew to the patio and flew back with a package. "You are not *so* big," Hoa said to me. She made a huge circle to describe how big I was not. "Might be okay." She gave me the package. It was wrapped in crinkly paper, which I tore off, wadded, and threw at Pearly.

Inside was a negligee. Black. With barely a front, but that hardly mattered because all of it—the little bit there was—was translucent. I held my hand inside, and everybody could see how translucent it was, and they all sighed.

"Let's send it to Mary Ann," Pearly said, "to enliven the spirits of the Saigon nuns."

"Where'd you get it?" I asked. I held it and

rubbed the silkiness between my fingers. No one had silkies like that.

Hoa shrugged.

"Not in your village," Pearly said, looking hard at Hoa.

Hoa shrugged again. Maybe one of those places we passed in the village was a brothel, I thought. Maybe it was black market. Hoa wasn't telling.

"Hope it fits," Maureen said.

"It'll fit," I said. I crammed it in my pocket.

When the colonel radioed me, the girls had gone except for Pearly and Hoa. After I talked to him, I told Pearly, "I gave you the Tay Ninh run today."

Pearly nodded.

"You're getting out to Nui Ba Den. There'll be a Chinook at First Brigade after lunch."

Pearly smiled. She had her hands in dishwater. "I knew I'd get there. I was curious about the name when I heard it. It means Black Virgin Mountain. How'd it get that name?" Pearly asked Hoa. "I know you know. You know everything."

"I know this," Hoa said.

"Who is the Black Virgin?"

"None of us," Pearly said.

Hoa shook her head. "She had a betrothed," Hoa said, "and he die in battle. The girl could not bear he would no longer be on earth, so she jump from the mountain to die. They could be in same world. They name the mountain for her so people remember to pray for her soul."

It was still a choice run. Everybody wanted to go to Nui Ba Den. "It's not that anymore," I said. "It's a communications outpost with a rock quarry at the bottom and some soldiers three thousand feet up."

"You mean girls don't jump off anymore?"

"Just stay away from the edge," I said.

"Hoa didn't say she fell off," Pearly said. We had been standing at the sink flicking soap on each other. "Diana, for God's sake, go get dressed."

"You sound like my mother," I said, and put my arms around Pearly's shoulders. She was slightly too reserved to hug back, but she accepted one decently. She smelled like Pond's Beauty Cream. Her hair tickled my cheek until Pearly raised her soapy hands and removed my arms from around her neck.

"Where's the television?" Pearly asked.

I looked at the table where the TV usually was. "It's gone," she said. "So's Claire's tape deck."

The previous UD had left her tape deck when she left.

"Somebody borrow them?" Pearly said.

But Maureen came back. She said a gold bracelet was missing from her room.

"Who's been out?" I asked.

"Nobody. It's just six-thirty."

We checked the front door. It was still locked. But the back door had been jimmied. We went to talk to Barrett.

"Never heard a thing," he said.

"But you were there?"

Barrett looked like he was going to cry. He'd probably fallen asleep. We decided we didn't care that much about an old Philco and that maybe Maureen should clean her room and see if the bracelet was around. The MPs sent reinforcements, four more boys to write a report. Maureen told Saigon. They got a new lock and fired Barrett. We got a boy from Lafayette with whom we tried to keep a strictly business relationship.

* * *

That morning after my shower, I was alone in the hooch for an hour. I wrote Big Foot again. I loved letters because I always had the chance to make it right and righter. I would always remember that hour I spent in the hooch. It was full of dreams in a room sweet and foggy with cologne.

Chapter 15

It was here, and then it was over. Seven days
and they were over. It was still February. I felt soft.
I felt so soft and tender that if I could see Big Foot,
I would need to touch him as badly as if I were blind,
touch his rough cheek, trace his collarbone, slide my
thumb in the space between his fingers. I would rock
him.

Stallion

Dear Diana,
   It's dry as a bitch. I wish it would rain and
it'd make some sense that my insides feel packed
with mud. I laid out by the tower in the dirt
waiting for it to rain because I remembered you
came out of nowhere once after it rained. But
the guys dragged me in the bunker and I know
I can't handle it in here.

Coming in this bunker is like somebody slammed me in a trap. I've been holding this pen on this wrinkled paper ever since. We're getting out soon, back to Trojan.

Diana, I can't write. Maybe we should let this go. When I got dropped on the pad and saw the sandbagged wire and the mamasans still squatting and clucking, I was gutted. All right, I love you but it hurts so goddamn much. I have 114 days to go. 114 days of this shit and flashes of you at the window brushing your hair.

How are you? Are you okay? I never spent seven nights with a girl before. I never spent any nights with a girl. They were probably the best I ever spent.

I can't take it here. Mackie always says, Clean your gun, man. So I'm cleaning it and cleaning it and cleaning it. It's wearing away. Mackie always says before R&R you're a warrior, and after, you're a killer. Tonight I x'd 114 and if I kill, tomorrow I'll × 113.

Big Foot

Cu Chi was unchanged. Everybody counted days. Soldiers wrote "Fuck You, Vietnam" on corrugated metal walls when they caught their last plane out. They wrote it around the base on the cement, on the walls, on hangars.

When I got back to Cu Chi, I didn't feel the same. I had bought a wig. It was long, straight, and black. I wore it to general's mess. I brought Thai bracelets for each of the girls, and I wore a ring with

a gold stone. Big Foot had bought it for me, and I
wore it on my left hand.

The sense of counting was stronger. Letters were
my sustenance. A letter in my box when I got in
from a run kept me out of Pearly's bunker. I loved
them and kept them in my pockets.

Cu Chi/ARC Unit

Dear Big Foot,

I'm okay. I was thinking we forgot to go
dancing. I don't think it was seven days. And I
don't remember any Buddhas to tell Mama about.
I haven't written home since the night we were
both writing postcards. I should have written to
your mother. Something like, your son is a veritable prince, as he tells me. It gratifies me to
know him, not to mention to sleep with him
where we are here by the Gulf of Siam. You
gave him beautiful eyes. You can't be all bad.
He bought me a topaz and once he took me to
the zoo where people stopped and stared at us
and said, "Ah, God, that bliss like theirs would
flush our day." I hope your mama likes Thomas
Hardy so she'll get it if I wrote it.

I woke up this morning crying. This ache
doesn't lift even in sleep. I'd been crying sound
asleep. What are you doing? I need to know. I
pretend we're still together. You're just by the
door having a smoke and I think I'll go and then
I think, no, I'll keep my eyes closed a few more
minutes.

Diana

Stallion

Dear Diana,
     I'm on the run. Don't stop trying. Keep on
writing. Write about our hometowns. Are you
coming out on Thursday?

Big Foot

Pearly and I went back to Meade, the fire-sup-
port base where we had gone during Tet. But this
time things were starting to catch up with Pearly. I
knew she didn't sleep, and her exhaustion started to
show. We were with some guys who were showing
off their track like it was a Chevrolet. They gave us
a tour, showed us where they had to sleep and eat.
Pearly sat down on an ammo box.
     "Are you all right?" I asked.
     "I think I'm gonna faint."
     A guy with blond-white hair told her to drop
her head down between her legs.
     She did. It was cooler in the track than under
the sun. I put my hand on Pearly's neck. It was
sweaty. A guy with dimples passed Pearly his canteen. She unscrewed the top, which was connected
by a chain, and let the chain and the canteen drag the
metal floor. I poured a palmful to splash on Pearly's
neck. There were calendar girls on the ceiling. Round,
healthy girls. I felt more like a soldier than a calendar
girl.
     "She's been working too hard," I told them.
     The men sat hunched over their knees, their dog
tags dangling. One soldier in the corner held a puppy.

Pearly raised her head and drank from the canteen. Her face was ashen.

The boy with the dimples introduced himself as Chet. Chet had a baby boy himself. "Just got word from the Red Cross this morning," he said. They opened green C-ration cans of cookies to pass around while Pearly's color turned more fleshlike.

Chet said his son was probably bald, because he had been. The blond boy said he was from Nacogdoches, Texas, which was not two hundred miles from my hometown. We had eaten thick burgers in a basket at the same diner. Pearly drank some more water, and we opened C's with peanut butter and spread it on saltines with a jackknife.

"Give me the P38," said the boy from Nacogdoches, and he opened some peaches. It was one of the nicest meals I had had in country.

"Named the baby Hank," Chet said.

I grinned at him. The boy's family was a regular country-western jamboree. Pearly slurped some peach juice.

"We'll get the hell out of this place if we stay lucky," the boy from Nacogdoches said. "Only one goddamn thing can get you. That's a fuckin' mine. They can make a mine to blow up a man or blow up a tank. Don't need Charlie to set it off. They got one that knows just how heavy a M-113 is, and the weight of us chugging over it triggers it. Sort a' damned either way, if you're a lousy grunt walking. Or in a 113 rolling. They figured it just right. Got twenty kilograms of TNT. Nobody lives through that. Blows out a crater seven feet wide."

"Every time we go out," Chet said, "we sit the same place. 'Cause the last trip was the lucky trip.

Like kissing the dice," he said, and shook some imaginary dice in his hand. I almost thought I heard them click.

"Luck of the goddamn draw."

The puppy kept getting caught up in the quiet kid's dog tags. It was a ginger-colored puppy. She licked peanut butter off the boy's fingers and fell asleep against his tight, tanned belly.

We stayed over an hour, chain-smoking and looking at a transistor TV, critiquing the jokes and the outfits, like Friday night in the World with your friends.

I wanted to tell Big Foot about that puppy, but I didn't.

Cu Chi/ARC Unit

Dear Big Foot,

They took Stallion off the run. Now they say you're getting too much activity. You didn't tell me that. Just tell me the truth, O'Maley. Even if you are invincible, immortal, and all that. What are you doing?

I'll tell you what I'm doing. Maureen got this real lifer idea for us to do a radio show on AFVN. Pearly and I do it. Pearly doesn't sleep much and she stays up planning these shows. Deadpan Pearly and me, Scarlett. Picture me in green velvet. Pearly embroidered flowers on her uniform belts. Flowers on the belt and the black armband. That's just so you can see us if you tune us in. We take requests and send songs out to soldiers, do public service announcements, stuff like that. Our theme song is "Leaving on a Jet Plane." Do you think you can get us a show in Boston? I wonder if Mama would mind if I moved to Boston. Probably not. She'd probably think that was better than Cu Chi. Pearly says she's going to grow up and be a contractor because in the army she learned to scrounge and boss people around. What do you want to do in the World?

Pearly and I took a run to Meade today. We're getting tired. Everybody seemed tired on Meade. We didn't program. We sat in APCs and listened to stories about Charlie. But it was very lazy and it was what it must be like to be old and recollecting. Pass around the smokes. Shoot the bull. Nobody's got anywhere to go, nobody wants to be anywhere else, at least for that hour. People might as well be where they are, if there's somebody there to talk to. I take every forward run I can manage.

I love you,
Diana

Stallion

Dear Diana,

When we were in the hotel, you told me about Opal. I started to believe in her too. Christ, I'd believe in anything. But I started to believe in her because I believe in you so goddamn much. I'm still wearing the tiger's-eye you gave me on a chain around my neck. It's kind of a knot there and it's letting my head go off to better places than this body can go. My head's off in . . . I don't know. Where do you feel like living? I feel like living in the World with you. You can pick the particular place. I'll go to Boston. Or you like Galveston a lot. I could work on an oil rig. Tell me some more about Galveston. I want to imagine us there.

I've been trying to write a song about the night express we took from Bangkok. I think of us on that train a lot. Something about how we had that whole car to ourselves and any one of sixteen seats and the way you smiled. I could call it "Sixteen Seats" but I keep thinking of your smile. You are very sexy. Sometimes you make me speechless. No one ever did that.

I used to be a Romeo, but it doesn't much matter what I was in high school. I had girls. I almost married one, but she moved to Water-bury in the nick of time. I changed my mind. I want to write about you and the sixteen seats.

For Diana on the Night Express
or
O'Maley Gets Faithful

Diana smiled.
Diana smiled.
Diana smiled.

I'll tell our kids, God, she knocked me over with her smile on that night train in

Thailand. Do you want kids? Will you still
smile?

Big Foot

Cu Chi/ARC Unit

Dear Big Foot,

Sometimes I am so afraid I want to run and
there is nowhere to go. I could scream, I could
shriek, but Pearly calls me Sanity. The unit is
balanced just barely so I can't scream. We might
all go shooting off like sickos. They need me on
the radio with the colonel to write the schedule.
But I need you. Sometimes I can't catch my
breath. You're right there somewhere and when
it's dark I think you might come. Remember when
you and Mackie tried to get in the compound
from the bunker roof? So I listen for you. I
dreamed we camped on the sand at Galveston.
We were eating at the diner and you got that sly
grin you get, like when you buffaloed the guy
for my ring. I traced your lips with my finger.
We didn't have to count the days.

Big Foot, there's a place at the seawall, it's
a stone staircase across from where I used to work.
And I never could leave the beach or leave my
job at the diner unless I'd touched the stone at
that staircase. There was a worn place, a groove
in the stone like something the rain could make
over eons and I always put my fingers in the
groove. I had to do it so I could go on. I was
thinking that if the world ended and I happened
to be alive and you happened to be alive that

that staircase could be a place to meet, in that case.

It's March. Think about June. And we'll be home forty-nine days after you.

Diana

Stallion

Dear Sanity,

I'm still wearing the tiger's-eye, still like a pit. Did you know you were related to the moon? I know that because I looked up your name in a name book. It's called *What to Name Your Baby Girl*. This guy's wife sent it along with an umbilical clamp and a tiny wristband. He showed them to everybody out here. But you're some kind of moon goddess. I could of told them. Some light to beat the crawling horrors the hell out of our heads.

Anyway, I'll pack the moon power with me when we go out.

There's a place called the Heights at home where there are small apartments. It's up behind the First National where Mom shops. I used to hate to look up the hill at them. I bet they each had two rooms and a john. There were always pregnant girls pushing kids in strollers up the hill or down the hill or over the dock weed to a puny swing set that bumped 'cause it wasn't anchored. At night these guys pushed the strollers over the weeds. And I used to think, God, what a fuckin' excuse for living. Now I'd like to push our kid over the weeds and see you leaning against one of those doors with a hand on your hip. Don't

worry. It's pretty busy. Don't worry if you don't
hear for a while.

                                           Big Foot
P.S. In that case, that's where I'll meet you.

The next day I found another envelope in my
box. I was relieved and could count one more day
done. But then I saw the handwriting, and it wasn't
his. It was another one of those "Be my lady" notes.
I would talk to Pearly, and we would go tell the MPs.
They would fix this.

Chapter 16

Pearly was not to be found until after suppertime, when I found her back in the office making props with absolute concentration.

I tried to talk to her, but I couldn't get any more out of her than a glazed-over stare. I said, "I don't know why I talk to you, Pearly." Pearly didn't look up. I didn't think about her tiredness or the dizzy spells she had because she never bothered to take the salt tablets. I wanted to shake her and get her attention.

I took her arm to physically get her attention. Look at me. But Pearly wouldn't talk.

"I'm going to Vung Tau," Pearly said after a while.

"What?"

"Vung Tau. V-u-n-g T-a-u."

"With who?"

"Mike."

I stared at her. "Mike who? Do you know how

many Mikes there are? Did you pick any Mike?"

"Mike," Pearly said again. "The Mike who flies Cobras. I don't know his last name."

"Why?"

"I have to get out of here."

"So you're gonna go someplace where you'll be the only round eye on the beach. So what are you going to do when word gets back to Saigon?"

Pearly put down the Magic Marker she had been writing with. "Remember that real mellow day we went to Meade?" she said. "We were so exhausted we were numb. We talked the whole afternoon to those guys in the APC."

"Yeah," I said. "And one had a baby named Hank."

Pearly didn't say any more. Maybe we were both thinking about how it had been a good day in a string of sweaty, mosquito-ridden days of nonstop forward runs.

"All right, what about them?" I said impatiently.

"I had the hospital run today," Pearly said. "One of them made it."

"What do you mean?"

"They set off one of those mines. One guy made it. I couldn't tell you which one it was. He recognized me. There was hardly anything left. The nurse told me they were so good they could save almost anybody. They are so practiced and the choppers get them in so fast."

"What do you mean, there wasn't anything left?"

Pearly was putting her stuff away. I watched her long, elegant fingers. I watched her graceful moves and not her eyes.

"He wanted me to think of a way to put it in a

letter home," Pearly said. "He lost his legs, and one of his arms, and what was left was covered with a hundred pellet wounds that the surgeons had to cut the dead skin off of. I couldn't tell if it was Chet or the one with the dog or who. But all the others are dead. Don't send me there anymore, Diana. I'm not going. I'm never going on a ward again."

I didn't lift my eyes from the order Pearly was making of our calligraphy pens and paper and rulers and paint.

"So, yeah, I'm getting out of here for a while," Pearly said. "Saigon's begging girls to extend. What are they gonna do, fire me?" She lit a cigarette and leaned against the worktable. "You're incredible," she said. I looked up at her, and I wished she would stop talking. Her eyes were red from the smoke. She still had her long, unshaved legs. Pearly hadn't worn makeup in a long time. So it wasn't the lack of makeup that made even her face dull. When she talked, she only used her lips. "You're incredibly good," Pearly said. "It makes me sick."

"Pearly, please stop."

"Yes, you are. Good good good, and nobody can do anything about it. Not even you. You'd have written that letter."

"No, I wouldn't have."

"Yes, you would!" Pearly yelled. "You talk about what we're doing here. You say we're doing therapy. You know what men think?"

"No, they don't," I said. I screamed through the rest of what Pearly said, which seemed only to highlight it.

"This place is too sick for people to act human. And you can't see how bad it is. Why can't you see? You still talk to guys like you're in that diner in Gal-

veston, like it's one long flirt and you gotta check the
mirror to see if you're still cute. You're still worried
about what Saigon will think, and you talk to every
goddamn GI as if you were personally responsible for
his soul. I feel sorry for anybody so goddamned . . ."

But she stomped down the wooden steps, not
finishing, and kicked up dust in the road in her holey
blue tennis shoes. "I would not have written that letter!" I screamed at her in her fog of dust, even though
I knew I would have. "I would not have!"

I slammed the door of the office as if I'd slammed
the door of the tank, and closed myself in with those
men eating peaches and celebrating Pearly coming back
to the color of flesh and the coming of the baby named
Hank. And their puppy who was dead like them. And
I saw the scrawl, "Be my lady," from the unknown
soldier. I wanted to be everybody's lady, in the sense
that I would give them each one of my handker-
chiefs. I would be Lady Marian.

I didn't like myself. I would have gone home that
day because of Pearly. And I didn't go home that day
because of Pearly. I hid in the office. Maybe I could
sweat my vanity out of me while I cried for those
boys we watched *Laugh-In* with. After I cried a long
time, there was still me, Sanity, who made the
unit run.

Pearly came back from Vung Tau. It rained, and
we programmed in mud. I had a mud fight with the
soldiers on Crook, and that went into my record.
Pearly told me I probably would not have a lifelong
career with the ARC.

On our office day Pearly invited me to go with
her to learn to repel. She had made friends with a
ranger. "What is it?" I said. "It's a way to jump from

a chopper," Pearly said. "See, you wear a harness, which is connected to a rope, and you hold the rope tight to the small of your back. Then you lean back, past being parallel to the ground, and drop your feet."

"You have no end of ways of seeing if your number's going to come up," I said, but I went because we were charmed.

We didn't jump out of a chopper. We jumped from a forty-foot practice tower in the rain. The ranger was very kind and didn't let go until we were sure of ourselves. Afterward we were panting, and sweaty under our ponchos. I figured that was Pearly's way of apologizing.

I started helping out at the hospital. I stopped in at suppertime, which didn't matter because these men on the post-op ward did not eat. They were not boys with families and good senses of humor. They were unconscious with tubes. I went to ward off surprise. It had been several days since the last letter from Big Foot. I kept writing. It was like phone calls home on the MARS Line, where you had to do all the talking, and then the other person did all the talking. Roger over. Or maybe it was more like talking to somebody unconscious and you had to wait even longer for a response. Anyway, I had to do all the talking and then wait. Over. Over. Do you read me? Over.

I went to the post-op ward to see horrific things. Once I brought the nurses a puppy that some artillerymen begged me to take home. The nurses had seen so much that was horrific, they stared at the puppy as though they'd never seen one. It was too soft and too adorable. The nurses worked sixteen hours a day. There was a plaque on the wall of the ward

with Twelfth Evac's motto. It read, SKILLED AND RES-
OLUTE.

I helped men walk if they were lucky enough to
be able to. It helped them clear their lungs. I emptied
bedpans. The nurses got used to my coming. The
men were medivaced out after only a short time. There
were new men almost every night. They leaned heavily
on me, and they moved up and down between the
rows of beds in the smells of rubbing alcohol and ac-
rid skin in a world of green walls and scrub gowns.
They all wore blood on their clothes. I watched the
nurse giving injections.

There were others like the boy from the APC.
Who could I tell about these soldiers? I began to pick
my correspondent. Not Big Foot. Big Foot didn't need
to know about these boys. Not Mama. What good
would it do Mama to know? I wanted to protect my
mother from knowing. There were things too horrific
for her to have to know. Mama should open the post
office, cook suppers in our knotty-pine kitchen, and
feel the hot breeze come through the window. I helped
a boy sip water with a straw and thought Mama never
had to know. She had Manfred, and together they
could decide what to believe about the boys who went
to Canada.

Manfred had a use. Working in the ward was the
first time I thought of people as having uses. When I
got home, Manfred would still do all the talking. It
wouldn't matter to Manfred that I had been here, that
I had seen firsthand. That wouldn't hinder Manfred.
He was secure in his beliefs, and he would protect
Mama provided Mama let him.

Pearly came. We sat in the dark on a bench outside the doors to the ward where I had sat with Big

Foot. A kid in a bathrobe sat on a bench across from us. He'd had an infection, he said, but unfortunately he would be better soon. We heard the chaplain's assistant's guitar. We heard him singing "Hey Jude" from a few wards down. Some voices trailed along with his, but the chaplain's assistant had a nice alto voice, and it was his voice that outlined the night.

"What kind of practice did you have to come over here and fight guerrillas?" I asked the kid in the bathrobe. "Did you have any more than me? Why's it all boys in there?"

The soldier didn't know.

Pearly said she thought it had something to do with Erector Sets. Guys build things. Then they shoot them down. I thought of Big Foot's hands doing that. I knew too much. I knew the smell of the jungle. I knew his body that was in the jungle tonight. I knew the curve in the small of his back and the pressure of his hand on my body.

We listened to the clear, simple voice of the chaplain's assistant.

"Shut up and leave me alone, I hate your guts."

"What?" I said.

Pearly said, "That's what Hoa says. I taught her. She says it all the time now."

Pearly and I tried to pretend we were back at the Waldorf Astoria. I still hadn't been there, but after all the times I'd pretended with Pearly, it was as if we now had a joint memory of being there, most likely in furs and bright red lipstick, like women in the old movies.

"Do you want to be called a girl or a woman?" I said.

"I wanna be a lady," Pearly said like Mae West. "What are we now?"

"Lady-girls," I said. I flung one end of my fur stole over my shoulder.

"Lady-girls who have been to Cambodia," Pearly said.

Tomorrow we were supposed to hand out Cokes iced down in a garbage can to GIs at the border. We whipped out our personalized butane torches to light each other's cigarettes and the soldier's cigarette. Pearly was being her old self that night.

"I miss Claire," Pearly sighed.

I laughed and startled the boy. "We never even met her. We never saw her face."

"I know," Pearly said. "But I use her old wash-cloths."

"I heard she didn't marry the guy," I said.

"Girls wouldn't get involved with anybody over here if they had any sense."

"Lady-girls."

We went home and went to bed exhausted and cleansed and full of each other's speech that night. It felt like we had passed on a part of ourselves to the other for the night's dream. We went to our own rooms behind our bead doors, me across from the bathroom and Pearly nearest the back door. I think I dreamed Pearly's voice. I wasn't sure what Pearly was talking about, but I slept wrapped in her droll, staccato speech, and I bet Pearly slept in my drawl.

Chapter 17

In April, when Nixon was bombing Cambodia, I scheduled runs like always, but the colonel often canceled them on account of the activity to the west.

One morning very early when I was on the walkie-talkie phone in the office with headquarters, Hoa came in.

"Come," she said.

"Where?" I said.

"Now."

The colonel told me we weren't getting out that day, and I hung up. I had been listening to the radio. I was thinking I would have to do the radio show Saturday night. The man on AF Radio Vietnam was reporting on news from the States. Without many details he reported that national guardsmen killed four students at Kent State University. There had been an antiwar rally, he said, as if it might have been a spaghetti supper. I tried to picture four students shot on my campus, maybe near the stone benches where you could go and reflect with Saint Francis. Four students shot and killed. I vaguely wondered what the body count would be that day in RVN.

I didn't want to go with Hoa. I felt so weak I didn't know if my legs would walk. My eyes ached because I didn't sleep. I looked at the statistical report I should be writing. Being so tired left me dreamy, and I went in a dream state with Hoa. Outside it was foggy. The afternoon would bring a heavy monsoon rain. Hoa nudged me. "Come on," she whispered. I left the radio booming Vietnam rock.

Big Foot stood in the dirt road. He was a mirage. I knew that. Big Foot stood in every dirt road. It was like when I lay in bed and imagined him at the door and I could keep him there as long as I kept my eyes shut. In this mirage Big Foot was wild in the eyes like a tiger, and they softened as I watched. He dropped his ammo and his steel pot in the dirt. Hoa went up and said, "How is Boston?," and I saw his eyes shift for a second to Hoa and back to me. It was Big Foot. At least I had imagined him more fully than I had before. Being around Hoa made me cautious of my thoughts, and precise. To Hoa, spirits were as important to feed as her little sisters and brothers. Around Hoa, I felt more a part of a complex world that I didn't understand. It wasn't comfort. It was more like a reason for being born and dying. There was a bigger pattern.

It was a spirit world all worked into the everyday world as finely as the crocheted patterns Mama worked. She turned cotton thread into intricate designs that then became a bedspread to warm you. And here was a spirit or a man or both. So I said to him too, "How is Boston?," and I touched his ribs to see if I could feel the bone. He was so skinny. And then I felt his hand on me.

"Are you real?" I said. He had asked me that once.

He was real. He pressed me to his chest, and I felt every bone. I felt his rough face. I felt his pulse, and we stood there somewhere between worlds until after a while I heard Pearly's voice. Mackie was there too, in the fog.

They had a plan. They had a truck, and they said they were going to take me and Pearly and Hoa on an in-country R&R. They had a conference with Hoa.

"Do we have a run?" Pearly asked.

"We can't get out on a forward run," I said. I kept my eyes on Big Foot so that he wouldn't vanish.

Mackie was lugging a pack. We followed him down the road to the jeep they appropriated. Pearly and I walked closely. Our soft shoes made muffled sounds in the dust. Our dresses had been scrubbed so often they were pale and threadbare. I was also thin. Probably too thin. I wished Big Foot couldn't see me just like this. I put on my poncho because it was misting and I was chilled. The cold plastic stuck to my skin.

I looked at the weapon Big Foot was carrying. It was bigger than his M-16.

"What's that?" I asked.

"Weapon," he said.

"I know it's a weapon. It's not yours."

"Traded off," he said.

"What was the matter with yours?"

"This one's better for blowing mines."

"Will there be mines?"

"Maybe," he said.

I wasn't worried. Pearly and I were charmed, and so was Big Foot, with us.

We came to the jeep. They got in, and Big Foot said some magic words at the gate that got us off the post and made it possible for Hoa to sneak out anything she might have in the bag she carried.

Mackie played host. He arranged all the gear and tapped his fingers in a frenetic, off-the-beat way on his radio. When he wasn't looking, Hoa felt the fabric of his Thai silk shirt.

We drove across roads built over dikes. On either side of the road rice paddies stretched so the ends were out of sight. They were flooded by the rains. I could see shoots of the rice plants springing up through the water. The road itself would have been washed away if it hadn't been on upraised land.

We passed a roadside shack and café where two men sat at a makeshift table and chickens pecked the red dirt.

When we reached a stone structure on a hillside, Hoa told Big Foot to stop. This is where we were going. It was the temple I'd seen once before. There were shacks nearby where girls came and went. Maybe some of them found a GI, and they lived in San Diego or Scotts Bluff. I hoped so, if that's what they wanted.

We looked at the temple. We were higher up than the base camp. Below, we could see patches of fog, but where we were, the sun was trying to shine. We walked around the temple. It was made of stone, laid at right angles. Inside was a stone altar, and a monk in an orange sarong prayed at the altar. The monk had shaved his head. He didn't look any older than we were.

I didn't want to disturb him. Big Foot spread

out a poncho liner on the grass in front, and we sat to watch the fog lift and spread as the wind blew. The wind also blew the scent of the monk's incense that he burned while he prayed. But Hoa was coaxing us to come inside. She gave us each a stick of incense she brought in her bag. Before we could go in, the monk came to us. He bowed to us and spoke in Vietnamese, touching the side of his robes where there would have been a pocket if he were wearing Western clothes.

Big Foot dug in his pocket and gave him the few piasters he had. The monk took them and said, *"Diem quet."* He held his hand to his mouth as if he were smoking, but he didn't want a cigarette, he wanted a light. I gave him my 25th Infantry Bic. That made him happy. He moved from candle to candle inside the small temple, lighting each, so that the inside was alight and so beautiful that it drew us all in. Hoa put rice cakes on a brass dish and touched the sticks of incense to one of the candles. These three sticks she set in a hole in the stone. There was a Buddha inside with a Christian halo over his head.

Hoa came to sit between us lady-girls. Our eyes darted from candle to candle, and Hoa told about a wooden statue who came to life to tell people who slept at the temple to be strong, that they would have the strength to face all the sorrows that would befall them.

"We come here to bring food for the spirits of our ancestors," Hoa said. "We come here to talk to them. My mother tell me I have strength to face my sorrows. She come to my bed at night. We talk and talk."

Then Hoa said, "I bring you something."

"What?" I said.

Hoa opened her basket and brought out a turtle. It was very small. "Look, a baby turtle," I said.

"We need a knife," Hoa said.

"We're not going to eat it?" I said.

Hoa shook her head. She took the knife Big Foot handed her. "To free another," she said, "to make them safe, carve the name here." She held the knife as if to carve a letter on the turtle's shell. "This turtle was captured," she said. "He would be sold in the market. If we set him free at temple, we free the person whose name he wears."

"Just by carving that person's name?"

"Sure," Hoa said. She gave me the knife.

I held the knife and looked at Big Foot. Then I sat beside Hoa. I put the turtle on my thigh across my worn blue uniform. The shell was not as hard as rock. It took the letters I carved in very easily. I carved Big Foot across the geometric shapes of the baby turtle's shell. I walked several yards from the temple and let the turtle free in the red dirt.

"Hey, Big Foot," I said.

"Hey, Diana," he said.

"What'd you pack?"

He started hauling stuff out. He hauled out everything from Elsie's milk to breakfast biscuits the cook just made that morning. The army also shipped in fruit so people didn't get scurvy. They liked their fruit from California. Big Foot had California oranges and imported bananas. No peaches. I put a biscuit and a banana on the plate with the rice cakes. It looked very pretty inside.

The monk must have thought it was worth having us all hanging around that morning because we had brought light.

"You have fifty-six days," I said to Big Foot, and then I had to cut off the things to say. I watched the monk and wiped Vietnamese dirt off my face and grit out of my mouth. I lay in the dirt and let the smells seep into my heart. They were smells that would mean Vietnam. The smell of the pungent incense came over me like a small puff of someone's breath.

Big Foot came nearer, but we didn't touch. I was on fire.

"My dad's got this thing about not being a burden to the family when he dies," Big Foot said. "He doesn't want anybody to have to mow his plot, you know, put out the carnations on Veterans' Day. So he says he doesn't want a plot or a stone. There's enough of them littering up the roadsides. Just throw his ashes off the Upper Deck."

"What's the Upper Deck?" I said, wiping the dirt off my face and sitting up.

"An overpass into Boston. He thinks that beats being in one of those cemeteries that go on for a solid half a mile. But I don't think the cemeteries are for anybody already dead. They're for the other people. If I die, I want a tombstone someplace. I don't know where. Maybe a portable one and my mom can lug it around."

"Good," I said. "Then nobody'll have to mow."

We went back outside. The fog had broken and left a gray sky. This was an in-country R&R, so we messed around making comments about the scenery. We pretended to be hoity-toity gentlefolk on holiday, and I shot photos of everybody posed against banana trees and stiffly beside the orange-robed monk.

Mackie waltzed with Hoa. It was the kind of waltz kids learned in sixth-grade social clubs, a box step in three-four time. Hoa was entranced. I shot a picture

of her. She had pulled her hair back and wound it in
a ribbon. Her blouse was bright pink. She looked like
a city girl. Then Big Foot danced with me, and Pearly
shot a picture of us. My hair was down, since no one
cared if it touched my collar. I had raised my skirt
over a bent knee to ham it up. Big Foot seemed especially towering, and I had leaned back to look at
his best feature. Pearly was probably right. He was
looking at me with blue laughing eyes, and I was surprised, when I saw the picture later, that I was
laughing back, after everything we knew. But I was.
I thought how deceiving a picture could be. It caught
our faces that second when Pearly pushed the shutter
button without showing any of the fear we had, only
us smiling. I thought of a picture of Mama and Daddy
when they looked in love—so obviously in love—and
now I thought of what Opal said about Mama having
paid her dues. That picture could not catch the fears
and disappointment that were likely in Mama's head.

It was that day that Hoa made her selection from
among the entire American Army. She picked Mackie
to be her husband. He was an old-looking, shuffling
eighteen-year-old Buddhalike boy in his Thai silk shirt,
unbuttoned. When Hoa told Mackie she had picked
him, he hesitated a little. She explained to him further so that he would completely understand, "Nothing in the stars can be changed or altered."

"Heavy," Mackie said.

Hoa picked him out of ancient tradition, custom-
ized to an American Army post. She followed him
puppylike.

Then we ate all the food Big Foot and Mackie
scrounged. We made sandwiches on hoagie buns with
cold meat and ate LRPs too, which were a variety of
freeze-dried meals from chicken cacciatore to beef

Stroganoff, and all you had to add was water. "This is a miracle that they can do this," Pearly said. I ate more than I had eaten in the two weeks before. We had a dozen open pouches of LRPs in front of us. Hoa tried her best to eat them too.

That's when the monsoon rains came, and we sprawled inside the temple, full and flushed and oddly put back together again. We were too full to go any-where, and we all lay down to sleep while the monk watched his candles slowly burn.

"I have never been so tired in my life," I said to Big Foot. I closed my eyes, and we slept lightly touching. We were trying to spare ourselves the pain we already knew would come when we had to let go. I focused on the feel of his breath on my cheek.

When I woke up, I saw the others were still asleep. I woke up slowly. The rain was still heavy. But it was late afternoon, I thought. Big Foot struck a match, and I smelled the smoke as he lit a cigarette. "I didn't mean to wake you up," I whispered.

"You didn't," he said.

"This has been like a dream in a dream."

He didn't answer. I looked at him. He was look-ing at me.

"Are we real?"

"Do you know what contingent reality is?" he said.

"No."

"I'll tell you."

He came to me, and when I felt him, we were both absolutely real and reprieved for another day.

Chapter 18

Dear Diana,

I dream about seeing you back in the World if we ever get out of this place. We are discovering mountains of rice. If anybody was fighting a war to win it might mean something. The lieutenant says coming up here to Cambodia is nothing but buying time. One guy says the war is over but nobody told us.

Mackie and I picked up a new radio, so we're gonna try to catch your show on Sunday. Charlie listens too.

So now we're saving Cambodia from the commies. If we don't stop them here, pretty soon they'll be on the Upper Deck.

Mackie says tell Hoa he loves her truly, only he's too young.

I'm figuring out how to go someplace like

Harvard on the GI Bill. I want to go to Harvard
Law School. Right now I'll settle for a six-pack
and real food and dreams of you.

Big Foot

Cu Chi

To Big Foot,
   I wear my topaz on my left hand and think
about if I was wearing a wedding band. It is very
big and it spins on my finger. I went to the PX
in it. I felt like I was dressed in something flam-
ing red when I turned the ring around and
everybody should have looked and said, Wow,
there goes a married lady-girl.
   Opal always called me an old soul. I think
you must be too. I think that's how we got together.
   I did the radio show with Pearly again. She
looks at the microphone with these huge, lumi-
nous eyes. I wonder if you can see them when
you hear her talk. Well, since I got Pearly Boudreau—say Boo! with a puff—Boo!—drow—out
of the bunker she has been mouthy to me. It was
better when you were here.

Diana

I didn't hear. I imagined meeting Big Foot at the
temple. "Sure." I would get fired or shot at, or I could
touch him the way I had touched him. "Sure." The
idea made me lie in bed trancelike, with impossible,
minutely detailed plans. I thought whatever we did

we would be blessed by God, Buddha, Confucius, and all the wandering spirits who might be eating the bananas.

Hoa brought me an envelope.

"What's this?" I said.

"I worry you be gone one day I come."

I opened the envelope. Inside was a card. It was white, and on it Hoa had painted a plum blossom and bright green leaves. Inside, in small black strokes, she had written, "I be small sister, you be old sister."

I knew that was strong talk for a Vietnamese, to call someone "sister." It was real affection. I thought of Hoa's hamlet where so many people had died.

I still didn't hear from Big Foot. I wrote, not knowing if he got my letters.

Cu Chi

Dear Big Foot,

I'm full of Hoa's stories. Hoa has a story for me every morning because she knows I'm waiting for them. She tells me stories about all these people who love each other but they don't have happy-every-after endings like Mama told me and I bet your Mama told you. Nobody kisses a frog who turns into a prince and they love each other forever and ever. In Hoa's stories people steel themselves and learn to endure. Love is still magic but it's more for how it makes you know things. Like she said, "the garments his love has given you."

Hoa watches what we do and is curious about American girls. More than curious. She listens closely and uses our words. Her English is twice as good since Pearly and I came. I wonder what she will do when we go and leave her with all the craters we put in her country.

I'm waiting for a letter. I don't think I can wait another day.

I woke up in a sweat in my room behind my bead door. I'd fallen asleep with my pen in my hand. I heard the door close to the lounge and I was rigid awake. I was lying on my back and felt my heart pound against my rib cage. My body was terrified before my mind knew why. I lifted my head so that the pillow couldn't block a shadow of sound. I heard the click-click of the door latch. I studied the sound to know if the person had gone out or come in. Sometimes Maureen got up. Maureen was a worrier. Sometimes she got up in the night. But it didn't feel like Maureen. It felt like something from outside the unit.

I touch her hair. Never before do I touch such hair that curls against my finger. It make the American girls, their eyes, to make rain. Mine too and all my brothers and sisters when I tell them. I tell the girls I need to get bananas. They bring good fortune for the spirit. But they don't understand. And I worry for cats. They are very bad luck. I know about these things.

The person had gone into the lounge. There was nothing more to steal. He had already stolen everything. I thought of ways that I could get to the guard. The person in our hooch must have slipped past the guard, but the guard had to be there. He would be

right there by the gate with his M-16 across his knee.
I imagined myself with my own weapon and the skill
to fire it. The door opened. There were footsteps. It
was too late to find the guard. I lay frozen across the
sheet listening to the footfalls as he moved down our
hall. They stopped, then waited, then started.

*One thing about the Americans. They have no culture.
They do not know things about the Buddha and feeding our
ancestors, how important. How important to grow our rice.
I want to learn all American because my father and my
mother tell me to learn so I have money for incense and
better to take care of ancestors and to feed their spirits. And
never to forget to honor them. Americans have so much.
Only they have no religion.*

*The baby turtle I get at market to set free Big Foot.
On his shell we carve his name the boy she love. When set
free the turtle in the temple, the GI free too. One can be set
free by setting free another.*

I thought of the story Hoa told about how many
days you got in your life, and when I heard the clink
of the beads in my doorway, I was a grunt in the
paddies where I'd seen children taking their baths.
Big Foot had heard the clink of the beads over and
over and over. It held time, to be terrified. I was a
cartoon girl with hair electrified. Big Foot would have
a weapon. He would be watching for trip wires in
the grass, wire across the banyon trees. In that same
second when I heard the beads, I knew anything was
better than to lie still. It felt like exposing my throat.
I willed my legs and my arms to draw up, and I
grabbed the thing left on my bedside table.

* * *

When my friend die I be sad and not know so well to help because my friend have no religion. Men do terrible things in my country. Vietnamese against Vietnamese in my own village. American against American. That does not surprise. Boy against girl all the time, all the time. I burn incense for my friend, and when I dream, she come to me and tell me stories. She know things now.

I stood in my cotton pajamas screaming murder and outrage at the shadow in my room and sprayed sickening-sweet perfume into his face.

I screamed. My consciousness was a black scream. My scream was myself and my life. I screamed for help from the other girls over and over. I aimed for his eyes and nose and mouth to burn him and make him gasp to breathe but he had caught my hand and slammed me against the metal frame of the bed. He had a knife. He smelled like he slept in monsoon mud and he smelled like something I had never smelled before but I knew it from the way Big Foot talked about it. It was what death smelled like and his clothes were wet with mud or maybe blood. I didn't know. I knew he had pulled the knife across my arm. He cut through me. I thought he would cut my arm off. He opened up my arm like I was a peach. "Pearly!" I screamed. My blood made a pool on my poncho liner. The burn in me was ferocious and I screamed.

Big Foot, his eyes they will make rain to see American girl die. I feel sad for Big Foot who I love too much. Before he leave, I go to his room many time. I sweep floor. I pull his sheets tight on his bed. He give me Joy soap because he say I am Joy. I cannot. Vietnamese girls giggle. We tease

GIs and they give us everything. The American girl want nothing. Their father did not die. They are not hungry. I have soft GI shirt for rag to clean his room and I stay and do not talk and he like me well, but his heart I think has one door.

Now I have a new friend called Mackie.

I dream to hear my mother. She come when I have a lot of cramp, when I bleed and I am bad luck and make the sweet wine sour, my mother come to me. Her shadow come to kneel beside me and stop the hurt.

My terror made me ferocious. What would he do, go from room to room if he got past me? I fought and bit his face. I bit his neck. I clawed him and I had the eyes of a tiger that I'd seen Big Foot with. I fought him away. I put that in my stock of facts about the war. One night someone broke in. I lived it as if I were retelling it. I needed to tell Pearly. I had to go find her. She was so close. "Pearly!" All the while I was screaming.

They found me there still screaming in my room sick with sweet air and the bottle emptied. All the lights were on in the hooch. Maureen was sitting with me. I lay coiled on my poncho liner and let Maureen stroke my forehead. Maureen sobbed horribly, and I felt bad. "It's all right," I said, but then I hadn't said anything out loud, I couldn't talk.

Maureen had brush curlers dangling from her hair. They were supposed to make her hair flip up. It would flip up through breakfast, and then would hang limp in the humidity. I touched Maureen's hair and looked at all the blood that ran down my own tanned arm. There were things I should ask. But I was so tired. I liked the feel of Maureen's slow, rhythmical strokes on my forehead and in my hair and didn't try to stop her crying. I was alive. I hadn't lived enough days. Maureen wasn't doing anything about my arm. Pearly would drag me off to Twelfth Evac when she came. I let my eyes shut. But then I heard boots in the hall. I cried out and grabbed onto Maureen. "Don't let him . . ." I didn't know if I was crying or whispering or talking at all.

"He's gone," Maureen said.

"Who is here?"

And then I remembered what I thought while I fought at him. I was keeping him from getting past me. I was keeping him from going from my room to another room. Where was Pearly? There was more than one person in the hall. There were five or six or all the army. They thundered past my door in their combat boots.

"MPs," Maureen said. She shook her head, and I knew something more was going on. Nobody asked me about my arm or what happened to me. "Where are they going?" I asked.

Maureen didn't answer. Josie came in wearing her uniform and no shoes. Josie wanted to be with us too, and sat at the head of the bed so that the bed vibrated with Josie's shaking.

"Shhh," Maureen crooned like a mother. She stopped stroking my forehead and put her arms around my bloody shoulders. "He stabbed her," Maureen said.

GI stab my friend Pearly. First cut her throat so she does not scream. He stab her many many time.

I listened with the same concentration I had devoted to the sound of the clicking of the door. I looked at Maureen and waited for the next words. She would say where she was stabbed and what the medic had said. They would have called the medics. Maybe some of the boots were the medics' boots. Maureen began whispering again and I worked very hard to cut off the sounds in my head so I could pay attention but I couldn't hear anymore.

Josie and Maureen held me there on the bed. "They're taking her now. And we have to talk to some people. What we need to do is get dressed like Josie did. It's just us three. We've got to stay together. You get dressed," she said. "Then I'll get dressed. And we won't let each other out of our sight." I felt the pressure of Maureen's hands on my shoulders while she talked.

It didn't make sense. The nurses could save anybody. I lifted my arms and let Maureen drop my dress over my head. I stood and let them button it. No one could find the belt. My arm burned insanely bad, and I thought they should do something to hold the flesh together. Josie saw that and wrapped the pillowcase around my arm, but I had already gotten my dress bloody. Maureen put on one of my dresses. It looked silly because it hung to her calves. We were in the hall when Hoa came. Hoa stood, fawnlike, in her peach-colored *ao dai* softly draping her hips. She carried her rice bowl to have her breakfast. She shook her head solemnly.

Maureen stood in the hall looking dowdy at twenty-one in her calf-length uniform and curlers. She talked to the people who came. People kept walking down our corridor. Their eyes moved right and left looking from room to room because they had never been inside the doughnut dollies' hooch before. Maureen talked to people in a quivering voice, and sometimes you couldn't hear her.

"This isn't going to look good," an officer was saying by the back door. "Civilian female stabbed sixteen times by a friendly."

"Don't they have a guard here?" someone asked him.

"Dimshit missed the fuckin' thing."

They asked me questions.

I don't remember my answers. I said I wanted to talk to Pearly.

Someone said, "That's the dead girl."

I remembered the knife across my arm.

"Who cut me?" I said. I saw "Be my lady," on a scrap of AFVN stationery.

"Sick bastard," somebody said. "Somebody on barbs," he said. "They're getting hold of some mean stuff."

I said, "A GI? I love GIs. I'd have done anything for him." The soldiers looked at me. I said, "Why did he cut me?"

They didn't answer.

I said, "I'd have done anything. I could have helped him. I could have listened to him and helped him." I heard a horrible animal noise, I couldn't stop the animal cry coming out of my throat.

"Killed too many fuckin' gooks," someone said. "He cracked."

Pearly knew about that. We were very funny. She always knew. We were our own trip wires, recreation girls. We came to the jungle with the brass band, the Philippine singing girls, the cold beer, the mail. Only we stayed around. We made friends. We were their ladies. Lady-girls. In between atrocities.

I see Pearly clearly. I see her long neck and black cropped hair. She is cut too. She is cut sixteen times.

I see us both in her bed. I see us both clearly. She is dark, and I am blond. We both have skin like peaches, and we are cut.

I needed to talk to her, and I started down the hall.

"He's a crazy," a soldier said, stopping me. "We got him. He's not coming back."

My head was absolutely clear, and I had to tell Pearly I understood, but they stopped me, and my body was ripped with sobs. A medic came. I screamed for Pearly and fought while he began to draw his needle through the flesh of my arm.

"Me," I told them. "It was supposed to be me."

The sergeant shrugged. He was a wizened old man. "No supposed-to-be about it over here." I looked at his gruff, grizzled face.

"It was supposed to be me," I said again.

The sergeant's eyes mocked. The kid had been *dinky dau*—crazy, he said. War did awful things to people. He said the body count had been high that night on both sides.

We go to pray beside my friend when she die. Better if we hire the monk to come to sing. He make sure her spirit rest. A monk could sing all the good things. I put her clean dress under the blanket. She wear on journey to God's house.

I leaned against the wall beside a lei Pearly wore home from a dust-off party.

Hoa brought her tiny hands together and bowed to the form on the bed. I knew vaguely that the soldiers were going to put her in a body bag, and they would not take the bananas that Hoa urgently wanted. Hoa could do things the army could not. Hoa was only sixteen. I watched her small, practiced hands fold a clean blue uniform. She packed the pop beads Pearly wore for general's mess.

People wanted to come into the room behind the blue beads. Hoa told them, "Not yet." She left and returned with a stick of incense and said singsong words. I stayed against the wall while Hoa went about a routine she knew well and had done often. Beside the bed were two books. I took the books.

I felt cheated. Pearly mortally cheated me. I woke up in time. Why didn't Pearly wake up? I had heard a sound before the latch of the door. Like a gurgling. It would have been the blood gurgling in her throat.

I felt the wizened sergeant's mocking eyes and listened to the rhythm of Hoa's songs. Hoa sang in single, harsh, guttural syllables she worked in the back of her throat. I absorbed them with the lines and circles of Pearly's body. I climbed into her lap the way she had climbed into mine when the chopper crashed. I put my face beside hers, which was gored. She was mutilated. I held her until two boys came and took her, and then I held her pillow.

"We pray for safe trip for her spirit," Hoa said.

I waited for the singsong voice to pray.

Apple tree, pear tree, plum tree pie,
How many children before I die?

"Bad luck. Bad Karma," Hoa said. "That is what war is."

Chapter 19

I had never worried about inside. I had always worried about outside. I had never worried about a GI. When I saw their boyishness around me, they sickened me. My mind could not grasp, enemy. Now there was no distinction. There was my unit and there was everything else. I didn't have any fear now. I was fearless. What else could they do to me? I went to the doctor Pearly went to and got some Dexedrine. That was easy enough. I got some Dexedrine so I wouldn't dream. I stayed up all night and looked at Pearly's books. I looked at the print of Kafka and Conrad and the rough-cut edges of the pages. I went on a run. That was easy too. Everything was very easy. I stopped writing. When Big Foot wrote, I put the letter in Pearly's dresser drawer. I didn't read it, and I didn't read any of the others that came after it. I found out the friendly who killed Pearly was from Bellevue, Nebraska. He could have been any GI. He could have been Big Foot. There was no distinction.

I didn't write to Mama. What could she do to me? I stayed with Maureen and Josie. We didn't work in pairs now. We worked in threes. Sometimes we still got dressed in the same room.

Mary Ann came up from Saigon. She had made me and Pearly quit repelling off the headquarters tower. She came on a Friday when we should have been doing a dry run of next week's program. We might have done it anyway, but Mary Ann wanted to console. We sat under the umbrella and watched her laboriously pick her words.

"Would you like to go home?" she asked.

None of us had considered doing that, even though we had been in country ten-and-a-half, twelve, and thirteen months, respectively. Maureen had extended. Josie was very short. But she sat in the webbed garden chair as if she would never leave it. We could not imagine sitting at our own kitchen tables. That was more unbearable.

Mary Ann said she'd send somebody TDY, then, to fill in on the run schedule. But the unit had already knotted up, and nobody else could help.

I had forty days to go. Big Foot would have seventeen. If he killed tonight, he would have sixteen. Who could I kill?

I plotted the night in my mind over and over. I discussed it with Pearly out loud. I traded places with Pearly. I shortened Maureen's skirt, put shoes on Josie. The sergeant became Hoa's wizard to consult about when to bury Pearly. The moon had even been full that Sunday night, and it hadn't done any good. The wizard sergeant put handcuffs on me. The wizard sergeant put handcuffs on Pearly because she had let a pilot—Larry—be heroic for her. I reworked and reworked it. I created a new little pocket of reality with the reworked words, and I still couldn't breathe in the night.

I stayed close to Hoa. Hoa moved like a bird through her housekeeping duties. She brought me rice and made me chew it.

I held viciously tight to Pearly. It was such a stupid mistake. If the boy had just noticed the Italian boy hair. I watched Hoa. I talked to Pearly in my head. She was squatting in the shower washing her Italian boy hair, instead of Hoa who was squatting washing our dresses.

"We're here to remind the soldiers that they are human and come from families."

Pearly wouldn't straighten the curve of her back— my small of my back—and look up. But I was only a little girl in a blue dress who had lured a boy out of his humanness so that he had come with a knife.

"The war lured the boy," Pearly said.

I looked at Hoa. People do awful things, Vietnamese against Vietnamese, man against woman, all the time all the time. GI against GI. I heard Maureen say, Don't go around talking like you're in their platoon. Don't go looking like it either. Wear makeup. But people had forgotten they came from families and have to go back and be some girl's boyfriend.

Who lured the boy?

I wished Pearly would uncoil and stand tall and I would reach up and rub her wet hair with a towel. Hoa stood up, and I followed her to the door. She walked down the road outside our compound to hang our dresses on the line.

"Hey, girl." It was the guys who had hounded her on other days. "Come on and spare us some time. Hey, girl, be nice."

Be nice, be nice.

"Shut-up-and-leave-me-alone-I-hate-your-guts."

They offered her 300 p, 325. I watched from the door. Three hundred and fifty p for incense, maybe scented like sandalwood with that much money, for her ancestors' altar. I walked out, and when the men saw me, Hoa slipped between them and left. I stood in the road and was vaguely aware of the mud and the rain. I remembered what Mama called yellowing, what happens to old people's sight, everything they see is distorted and discolored and way far away, and that's how I saw my feet in the mud and those men.

There were two of them. One of them had oily skin and an oily walk—maybe an athlete—and oily talk. "Look at this babe," he said to his buddy about me. "I'm short, doll. Send me off good. How much, sweetheart? You name it."

I couldn't move my feet out of the mud. His hand grazed my hair, and I couldn't move.

I went with the GI down into Pearly's bunker, and we left his buddy in the rain. Even while I was in the bunker, I could see his buddy more clearly. I could see the rain dropping off the buddy's rifle. All I remember in the bunker was the smell of the athlete's sweat. I saw his lips and his mustache stretched in a spasm. His stink was on me all over, but I didn't feel it. I wanted the pain to cut me like a knife, but I couldn't feel it.

I heard Hoa yelling. She said, "You fuck any Goddamn GI . . ." and so on, the same threat Pearly always gave her. She got me out of the bunker. Vietnam was a goldfish bowl. I was lying flat on the bottom of the bowl with my gold sides in a spasm. It was so hard to keep breathing.

Hoa took me to Pearly's room and gathered Big Foot's letters in my lap.

"Now we open," Hoa said.

"No."

"Now you write."

"Not anymore."

She said a Buddhist prayer for Big Foot. I didn't have any prayers or feelings.

I counted Big Foot's days out of habit. I was distanced from him, but he was in my sleep, he was with me when I woke up, he ate with me, he slept with me, he talked to me. I told him, Leave me alone. I hate your guts. And I counted his days.

Josie, Maureen, and I kept on working the runs. We went out in threes. We went to the wards, we went to the bridges and the tracks and the howitzers. I stayed up at night researching questions for our programs. So many facts were packed in my head. We wore makeup and talked to the men about the World. We did a program about the people who had walked on the Moon, a place that was as real to me as New Jersey or the boulevard through Galveston.

Big Foot had 359 days in country. I thought he was in country. I wouldn't know if he wasn't. If he got hit, the army wouldn't have sent me anything, no telegram or a friendly visit, because we weren't related. His father who fixed clocks would get it. I didn't want to know anyway. Maureen and Josie and I worked packed days in threes, and I didn't look at faces.

If Big Foot was here, he had four days to go, and then I would have been free too, because I could be left alone with Pearly in my sleeping and my sleeplessness. They got me both ways. But I knew he was coming. I knew he would come through like everybody else who wrote "Fuck You, Vietnam" on the tarmac and the walls in farewell. I steeled myself to his eyes.

On his 363rd day I tripped over him and his ammo on the office stairs. I stopped still and leaned against the office door. He looked up at me, and he would have seen I was wearing Pearly's boonie hat and Pearly's black band. I wished he weren't there. There was nothing to say.

He didn't look at me directly. His eyes were not focused. They reminded me of the eyes I saw on Stallion that first time I saw him on a cot in the sun.

His eyes shifted and seemed to take in my face in quadrants, as if he couldn't bear to look at me whole. He drew me down to him, and then he rested his palm squarely on my neck and crushed my hair. I couldn't look at his eyes.

"Is Mackie already gone?" I asked.

"Yeah, he's gone. He got medivaced out."

I didn't want to hear.

"They got him out fast."

I remembered the smooth curve in the small of Big Foot's back. "He's a lucky bastard," Big Foot said.

Big Foot didn't go away. He broke down. He sobbed beside me, and I didn't touch him. I didn't rock him. I didn't cry. I wanted to tell him a GI murdered Pearly, and then I'd tell him about me and the oily man in the bunker. I wanted to crush him, but he was already crushed. I felt the weight of his hands on my shoulders and listened to him cry.

I could taste salty tears. I thought they were Big Foot's. Somehow he'd gotten me to taste his tears in my mouth. But they were my own, and without a sound tears washed over my face and mixed in my mouth with my spit.

"You quit writing," he said.

"There was nothing to write."

I hated the fact I was crying. It seemed to let down everyone who was dead, that I should get such cheap relief, but it was relief. I was getting my first gasps of hard breaths. For the first time in months I thought about home hard enough to see it and smell it. I remembered Stewart's Beach and the sound of the waves and the way it folded me in its arms.

"Why didn't you write?"

"Because of Pearly."

"Because Pearly was killed?"

"I hate the army."

"I'm not the army."

He didn't understand.

"It wasn't your fault. It was an act of war. It was a freak."

I couldn't talk to him. I couldn't explain to him that I knew why Pearly was killed. She was a sacrifice. One of us had to die. Nobody got out of Vietnam without paying. If you came over as a cute college girl with nice skin and neat values, you wouldn't go home as one. This was war. Nobody got off.

He said, "You got me through. You kept me sane."

Big Foot loved the cute college girl with nice skin.

I was so tired. Big Foot made me taste his tears and mine, and now he made me feel his exhaustion and mine. He dropped his arms over my shoulders, I put mine around his waist. "You nearly killed me," he whispered.

I said, "I expect there was plenty to die of."

I couldn't look at his eyes. I told him I was fear-less.

We went in the hooch where he felt my collar-bone and my hipbones as if to see if I had built up hide and was less frail, but I couldn't look at his eyes.

He told me about Mackie while I rubbed Viet-nam red dirt off his back.

He said, "Mackie bought it in a graveyard."

"You said he was medivaced out."

"He was. The doc gave him the thumbs-up." Big Foot shook his head. "We were in a gook graveyard. The place was charred, and the only thing upright was the gravestones. And on every stone was the same name. Before the fight I asked Mackie, 'What do you make of that? Every goddamn stone's got the same name.' He said, 'That's not a name.' It was Vietnam-ese for 'hero.' "

I thought that's what Pearly's stone should say too.

I was sitting on my heels on the whiny metal-frame bed rubbing the red dirt off his back, and I nearly exploded with the realness and closeness of Pearly. Pearly in her red robe. Pearly Pearly Pearly everywhere. I breathed deeply and let the pain flush through my heart and my lungs as I listened to him talk. I thought of Hoa and how she handled sorrow. She expected it. It was life.

Hoa had given me a letter for Mackie. She had wanted me to write Big Foot so I'd put her letter in mine and Mackie would get it. I opened my letter box to show it to Big Foot, and I read it to him. She wrote, "I miss you every day. Can I see you by write until I can come to your America?" She had folded the paper so that it was a present, the way you had to unfold and unfold to get to the words. It was a page from a composition book folded, and when you lifted the corners, it was like lifting the wings of a bird.

"You told me about a staircase to the sea," Big Foot said. "When you get home, I'm going to look for you there."

I didn't answer. It was the place we were going to meet if the world ended. The idea had made us strong. I imagined us there. I would have done anything for him, but I could only put part of me there. I still couldn't look into his eyes.

"When's your DEROS?" he asked, looking at me, and I looked at him, and when I did, I saw my old self. To look at him was to look at my old self, and that was a killing thing. I saw my old self in his eyes. He had said, Without you we would have been forsaken. I was glad I could do that. I did not want anybody to feel forsaken. But I couldn't save the boy when I held his hand and gave him all my strength. I couldn't save Pearly. There was nothing I could do except not forsake them.

Big Foot had to outprocess, and I walked him to our gate. He said, "What's it like in Galveston now?"

"The leaves on Texas trees will be their deepest, heaviest green."

I kissed the palms of his hands.

I loved you Big Foot Veritable Prince.

Someday we might meet at the seawall, when I have clothed my old self, and the woman you hold in your eyes is a reflection I can bear.

There were five girls in the Cu Chi Unit if you count Hoa, and Hoa is always there in the telling. Of the five of us, three are in the World, me in Texas, Josie in Ohio, Maureen in New Jersey. I never saw Josie or Maureen again, but Pearly—I can hear you talk. I can see your eyes. You are my conscience. And Hoa is my light.